SPLIT by WAR

A Guernsey Family copes, 1940–45

Lynette Enevoldsen

Copyright © 2024 Lynette Enevoldsen

All rights reserved under Canadian, International and pan-American Copyright Conventions. No part of this book may be reproduced in any form or by any electronic or mechanical means, including information storage and retrieval systems, now known or hereafter invented, without permission in writing, except by a reviewer, who may quote brief passages in a review permitted under copyright law.

Title: Split by War, a Guernsey family copes 1940-45/ Lynette Enevoldsen

Book Cover Design by 100 Covers
Formatted by Christine Choquet

ISBN, paperback   978-1-7383915-0-9

Although this publication is designed to provide accurate information in regard to the subject matter covered, the publisher and the author assume no responsibility for errors, inaccuracies, omissions, or any other inconsistencies herein.

Photos in this book belong to the author's family, except for two whose sources are unknown, as indicated.

Maps by Lynette Enevoldsen

This book is dedicated to my parents, Arthur and "Frances" Enevoldsen, and to my sister Janice. Their steady, supporting presence has always been there from my childhood onwards; and to Annie, who did her best to make things better.

It is also dedicated to all of us who were torn apart for those five long years;

and to those who are being torn apart by war now.

Fermain Bay from *Woodlands*

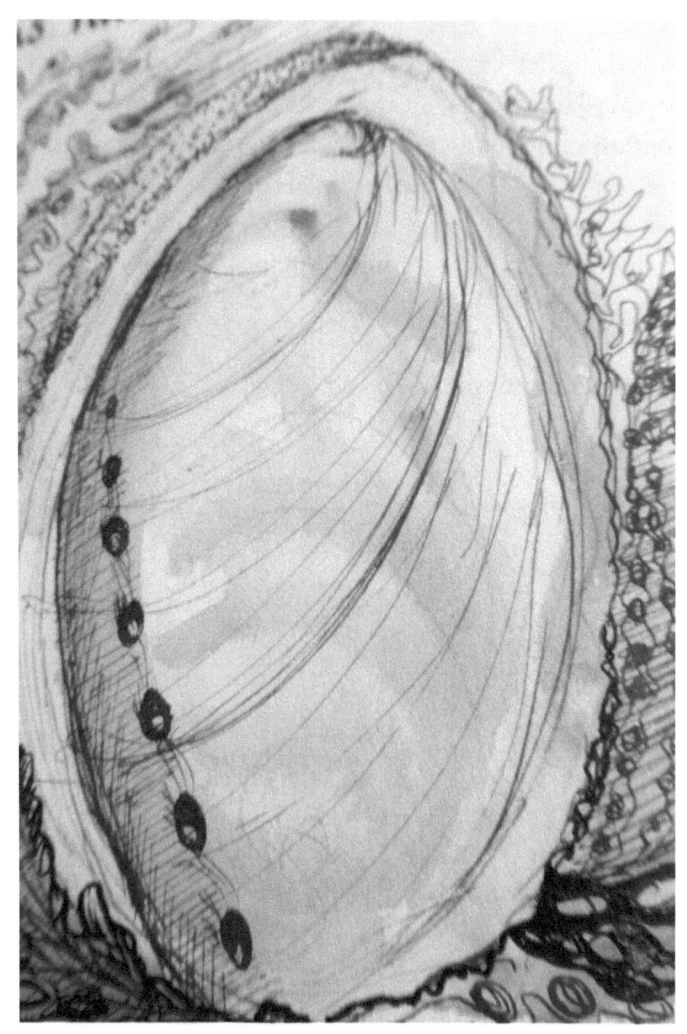

Ormer Shell by Janice

Contents

Contents	v
Introduction	vii
Sources	ix
Why the Channel Islands are British.	xi
The ENEVOLDSEN family, 1940-45	xiii
The TORODE family 1940-45	xiv
Chapters	xv
Map 1 — The Channel Islands.	xvii
Map 2 — Lancashire	xviii
Map 3 — Clowbridge & Cotton Row	xix
Map 4 — Guernsey: St Peter Port region	xx

Introduction

In June 1940, after the German army seized Cherbourg on the north coast of France, I was evacuated with my mother and sister from the Channel Islands to England. I was two years old and my sister was five. The British government had decided to demilitarise the Channel Islands and boats were sent to evacuate whole schools, men of military service age, and women and children. The choice to leave or to stay was left up to each family. My father, like many men, decided to stay on the island. We left on June 20.

Hitler realized that he had a small piece of the British Isles close at hand and, after bombing and finding that they were de-militarised, landed troops on the islands. He wanted to occupy them before sweeping across the Channel to take England. He expected the islanders to express their contentment under German rule, and at the beginning the Kommandants were honourable men who were perhaps well chosen. Later, things changed.

In this book I have tried to tell two stories. The first is my story: how our shipload of women and children found ourselves in an old hospital on the Lancashire moors in late June, 1940. Our arrival presented both a challenge and an opportunity to local villagers. Later, evacuees were worried about what was happening behind enemy lines in Guernsey, especially after D-Day, and questions in the House of Commons gained no clear answers. But we felt that we were part of a united community in Britain.

The second story is about my father's life during the Occupation of Guernsey. I have put together scenes of how he and his new "family" coped under the enemy. Forced out of his home, he joined his parents and sister until German tunneling made their house unsafe. The bombing which preceded D-Day forced them all to move again. Soon the supply routes from France were cut off and slow starvation was the norm for most islanders. With a Nazi Kommandant and his 10,000 or more German troops eating available food supplies, food was worth more than anything.

Living under wartime conditions, ethics are sometimes reversed; laws may be ineffective or disregarded; trusting a neighbour or fellow worker becomes questionable; some will take advantage while others strive to be reasonable. With shortages of food, the Bailiffs sought help through the Red Cross via German telephone connections. Well planned escapes took the real facts out of the island to London. Churchill was unwilling to send in Red Cross parcels which he presumed the Germans would grab, so how could lives be saved?

Much of both stories is told through scenes where a meal or a visit is happening. I knew all these characters and still hear their voices in my head. Their reactions and comments reveal their concerns and motivations. I hope that this makes them come alive to you, dear reader, as you get to know a Lancashire hamlet and a Guernsey family group. I have tried to keep the British vocabulary and spelling. Some background history of the war is presented in boxes of information.

Sources

My own and my sister's memories, talks with my mother, her own 1941 diary, letters from Aunt Annie, supply me with many details about the war years. I am indebted to my parents for the memories they passed on; to my sister Janice Parkington whose support, family research and art work has been invaluable; to my cousin Bert Enevoldsen, who has given information and advice, and who wrote a book of his own war experiences.

I am indebted also to diarists: to Ruth Ozanne and Violet Carey, who kept writing their journals during those five hard years of the Occupation; to Dorothy Higgs who published wartime cooking suggestions; and to Leslie Sinel, a Jersey Evening Press reporter who kept a secret diary in the sister island of Jersey. Charles Cruickshank wrote the official history of the Occupation of the islands at the request of both bailiwick governments; it was published in 1975.

I have relied on these and other sources to create a picture of my father's life on the island. A list of these publications follows. Other references are added as footnotes.

I wrote this book during the years of pandemic, 2020 to 2023. During this time I was greatly encouraged by the WHWN (Write Here Write Now) program, which was part of Bishops University Lifelong Learning Academy, at Lennoxville, Quebec, Canada.

If you would like to receive a monthly newsletter, and ask questions about the writing of this book, please send an email to the following address: splitbywar4045@gmail.com

Carey, Violet, Guernsey Under Occupation, ed Alice Evans (2009)

Cruickshank, Charles, The German Occupation of the Channel Islands (1975 OUP)

Enevoldsen, Bert, A Guernsey Schoolboy in Wartime (Published privately)

Higgs, Dorothy, Life in Guernsey under the Nazis 1940 - 45 (1979)

Le Huray, C.P. The Bailiwick of Guernsey (1952)

Ozanne, Ruth: Life in Occupied Guernsey, the diaries of Ruth Ozanne 1940-45, ed William Parker (2011)

Sinel, L.P. The German Occupation of Jersey, Jersey Evening Post, 1945; & London, Corgi Books 1969

Toms, C., Hitler's Fortress Islands, London, Four Square Books.

Currently, an "occasional blog" by N. le Huray at island-fortress.com offers well-researched information.

Why the Channel Islands are British.

Most British children know—or used to know—the date 1066, when William, Duke of Normandy sailed across the English Channel, defeated King Harold's army, and became King of England. His possessions included Normandy and the islands off its coast which call themselves The Channel Islands or Les Iles Normandes. Jersey, Guernsey, Alderney and Sark are the largest of the group. From this time the islands remained loyal to the British monarch. Island laws originated in Normandy and are different from British law.

The islands comprise two bailiwicks: Guernsey's bailiwick includes Sark and Alderney, although Sark's local government is of a hereditary nature and Alderney had its own independent ruling body. The second bailiwick is the largest island, Jersey, about 46 square miles in area.

Guernsey has an area of about 24 square miles and is shaped like a triangle. Almost attached to it on its west coast is tiny Lihou Island. Three miles east of it are two small islands, Herm and Jethou, also part of its Bailiwick; beyond them lies Sark. Further north is Alderney, situated just 10 miles from the French coast.

The capital of Guernsey is St Peter Port, which has an excellent harbour on the more sheltered east side of the island. About 40,000 people lived on the island in 1939 and over 17,000 were evacuated in June 1940 before the Germans landed on June 30.

The islands have always had their own government, known in Guernsey as The States of Deliberation, or simply, The States. Only matters such as civil aviation and foreign affairs are dealt with by the British government. Acts of Parliament in London do not apply to the Channel Islands unless expressly indicated.

The monarch is represented by a Lieutenant Governor in each Bailiwick. Linking him to the island's administration is the Bailiff, who is appointed by the Crown. Two other important posts are: the Attorney General and the Solicitor General. In 1939 the States consisted of 18 Deputies who were elected by the people, 10 Rectors of Guernsey's 10 parishes, 15 elected representatives from parish councils or douzaines, and 12 Jurats who were elected by this group of officials for life. Guernsey law is based on the law of Normandy.

In June 1940, as the Germans advanced through northern France, Whitehall dithered about whether to de-militarise the islands. The bailiff of Jersey, Alexander Coutanche, had asked for the evacuation of women and children to be considered. The response from London was that it was undesirable, and soon after: that it should be considered. Who would pay the cost? Ships had to be found from the Portsmouth region.

On June 18 Jurat Dorey, representing both bailiwicks, told Home Office officials that there were men of military age on the islands and also about 30,000 women and children - counting both Bailiwicks - who should be given the chance to leave. Evacuation was agreed to and he phoned both islands. On June 19 the War cabinet officially de-militarised the Channel Islands. It was left to the local governments to organize the evacuation.

In Guernsey a new Lt Governor had arrived on June 7, 1940, and he had little time to know the local authorities before he was recalled to England. The Bailiff, Victor Carey, was an elderly islander and it was left to the Attorney General, Major Sherwill, to make decisions about evacuation amidst the confusion of those days.

This is where this story begins.

I have drawn four sketch maps to help you visualise the geographical surroundings of the places where we all lived.

The ENEVOLDSEN family, 1940-45

Pa (b. 1863. 3.11) was usually known as **Eric Enevoldsen**, but he was christened Lars Peter Enevoldsen, born in Denmark.

Ma was Guernsey-born **Emilie Louise le Page** (b.1863.7.10)

They married 1890. 3. 30. and had eight children, listed below by date of birth.

"Louise" Jay's real name was Frances.

Names of people who appear frequently in the book are underlined.

Born	Child	Married to:	Children (birth year).
1891	Emily	James Jay	"Louise" (1916)
1893	Elsie	Edwin Carter	Eric (1920), Daisy (1923)
1895	Eric (to USA)	Matilda	6 children
1896	Charlie	Elsie	Marion (1929)
1898	Herbie	Doris	Peter, John, Clive, Olga
1900	Otto	Nellie Torode	Bert(1929) Nancy (1930) Sheila (1934) Alan(1940)
1902	Arthur	Frances Torode	Janice (1935), Lynette (1938)
1905	Walter	Mahala	Molly (1934?)

The TORODE family 1940-45

Grampy (b.1879) was born **John Torode**
Gran (b——) was born **Elsie May Wheeler**.

Born	Child	Married to:	Children(Birth year)
1899	Elsie	Art Frampton	Lionel (1920), Ruth, Vera.
1901	Nellie	Otto E.	Bert (1929), Nancy (1930), Sheila (1934), Alan(1940)
1902	Jack	Ellen	2 daughters
1904	Edith (d.1937)	Jack Workman	Graham (1929), Rose (1931)
1906	Frances	Arthur E.	Janice (1935), Lynette(1938)
1908	Mabel	Bob Masterman	Patricia(1937?)
1912	Violet	Fred Cowling	David (1940), Margaret (1942)
1917	Frank	Adele	
1919	Bill		
1921	Joyce	Ken Denziloe	
1922	Geoff		

Chapters

1	Evacuation—Arthur	1
2	Evacuation—Frances	10
3	The Walk from Crown Point	17
4	The Move to Hawthorne Road	24
5	Visitors at Hawthorne Road	30
6	Goodbye to Vi	36
7	Flitting Burnley	44
8	Settling in at Cotton Row	53
9	Autumn and Christmas 1940	62
10	January 1941: Family Visit and a Blizzard	71
11	Feb–March 1941—Sickness & Snowstorm	82
12	April–May 1941—Bolton Visit & Bombings	90
13	Late May–June 1941: End of the Blitz	100
14	June 1941: Fortifying Guernsey	109
15	The Russian Front—Summer 1941	117
16	July–Sept 1941: A Week in Bolton	126
17	Sept 28–Nov 15, 1941—Deportations	136
18	Nov–December 1941—Pearl Harbour	147
19	January–March 1942—Snowstorm	168
20	March–May 1942—Goodbye to Nellie	177
21	June–July 1942—Police trial	185
22	August 1942. Island on Alert—Dieppe	194
23	Sept–Dec 1942: an Accident and Monty's Victory	201
24	Jan–April 1943: Losing Ma and Moving again	211
25	May–Sept 1943: Russian Victory; sending photos	221

26	August–Dec 1943. Custard tarts for a Birthday	231
27	Jan–April 1944: Allies make progress	239
28	April–June 5, 1944: Invasion jitters	247
29	June 6–Sept 1944: D-Day Invasion	256
30	Islanders despair; Oct–December at Cotton Row	264
31	Guernsey Nov–Dec 1944: Facing Starvation	272
32	January–May 1945, at Cotton Row	282
33	Guernsey Jan–April 1945: Trying to Survive	289
34	Victory in Europe and Guernsey's Liberation	298
35	Summer 1945: Evacuees Prepare to Return	302

Afterword	314
Poem: Mum	315
Poem: Meeting.	316
Acknowledgements	318
Questions for discussion.	319

Map 1 — The Channel Islands.

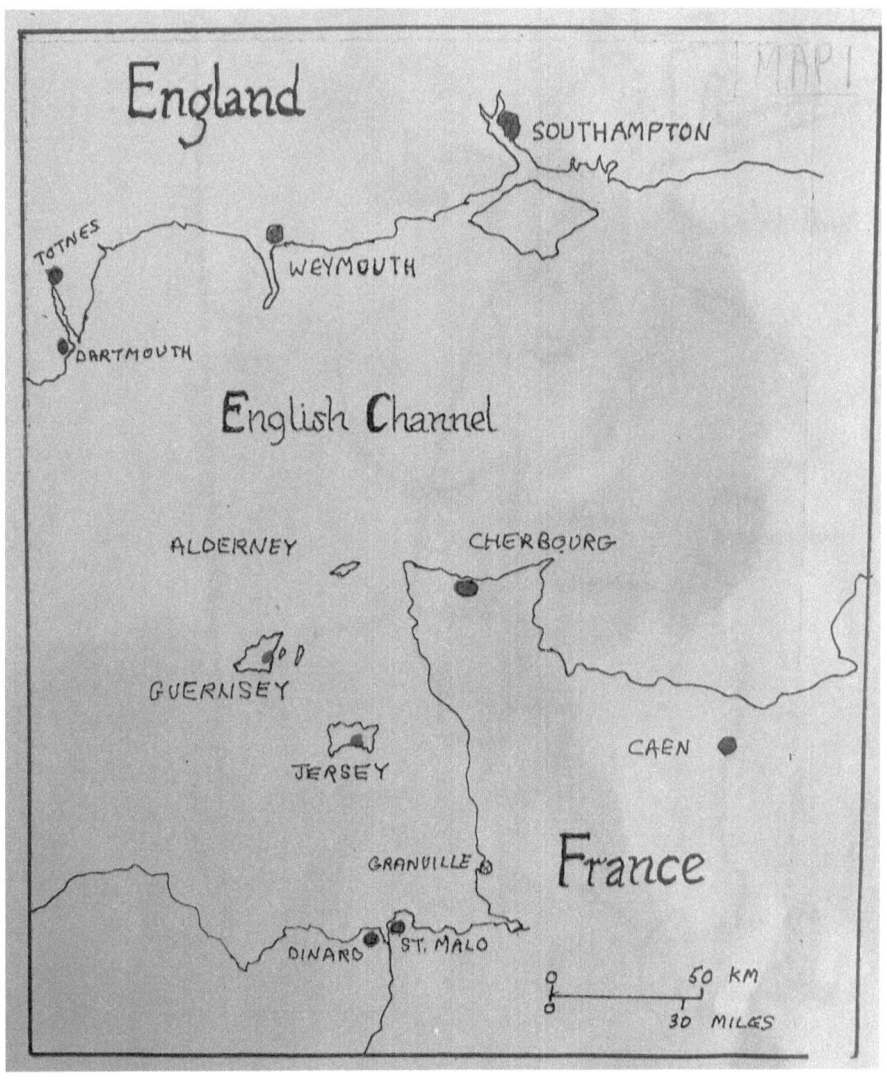

Map 2 — Lancashire

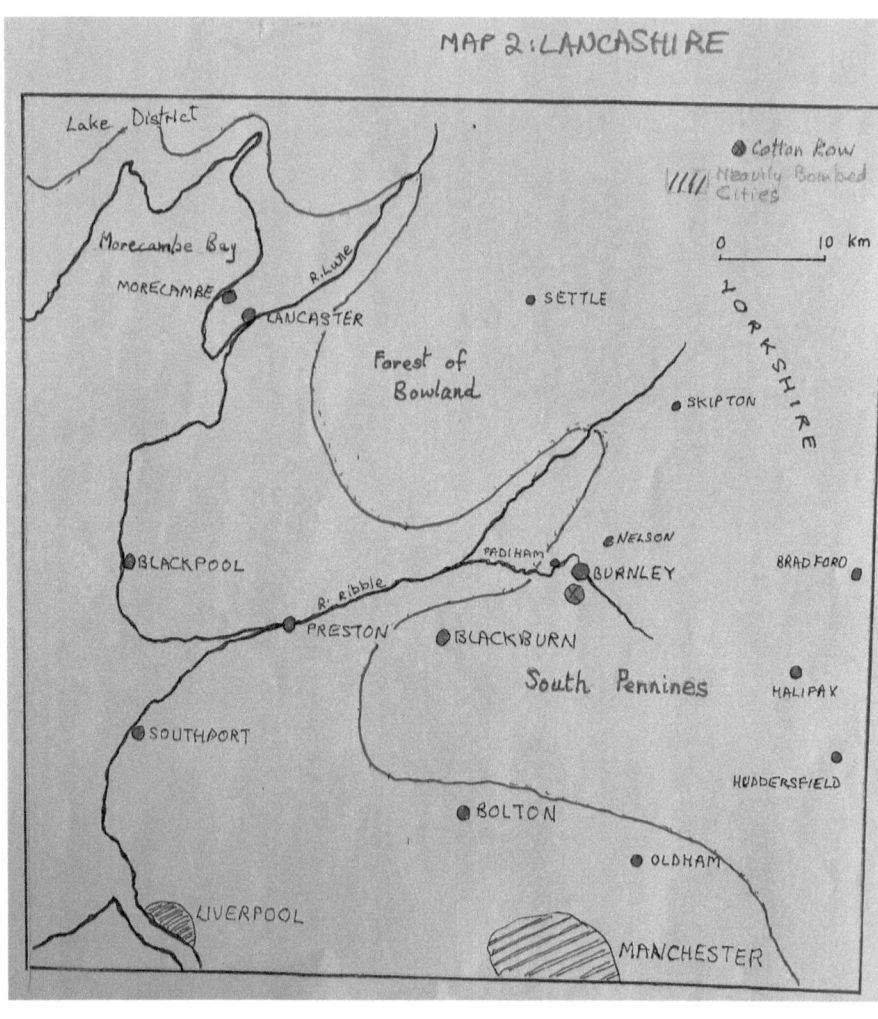

Map 3 — Clowbridge & Cotton Row

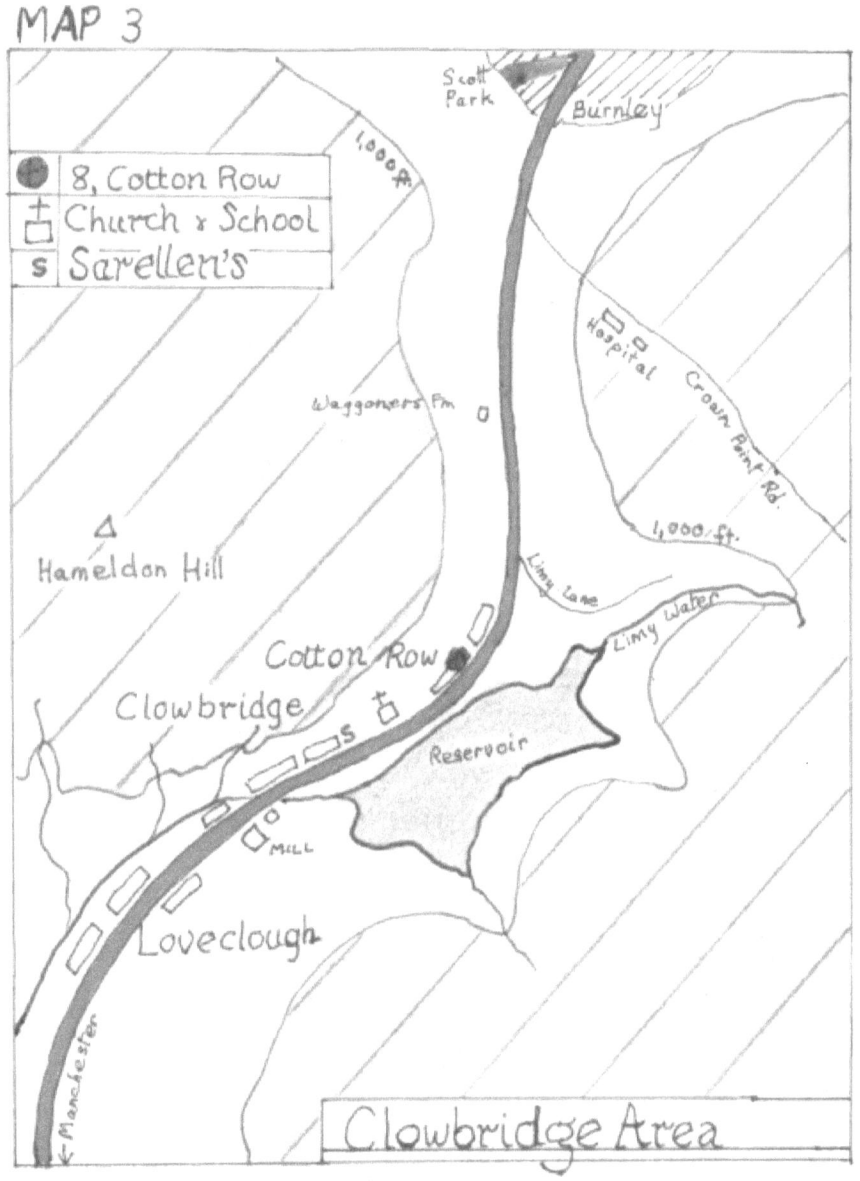

Map 4 — Guernsey: St Peter Port region

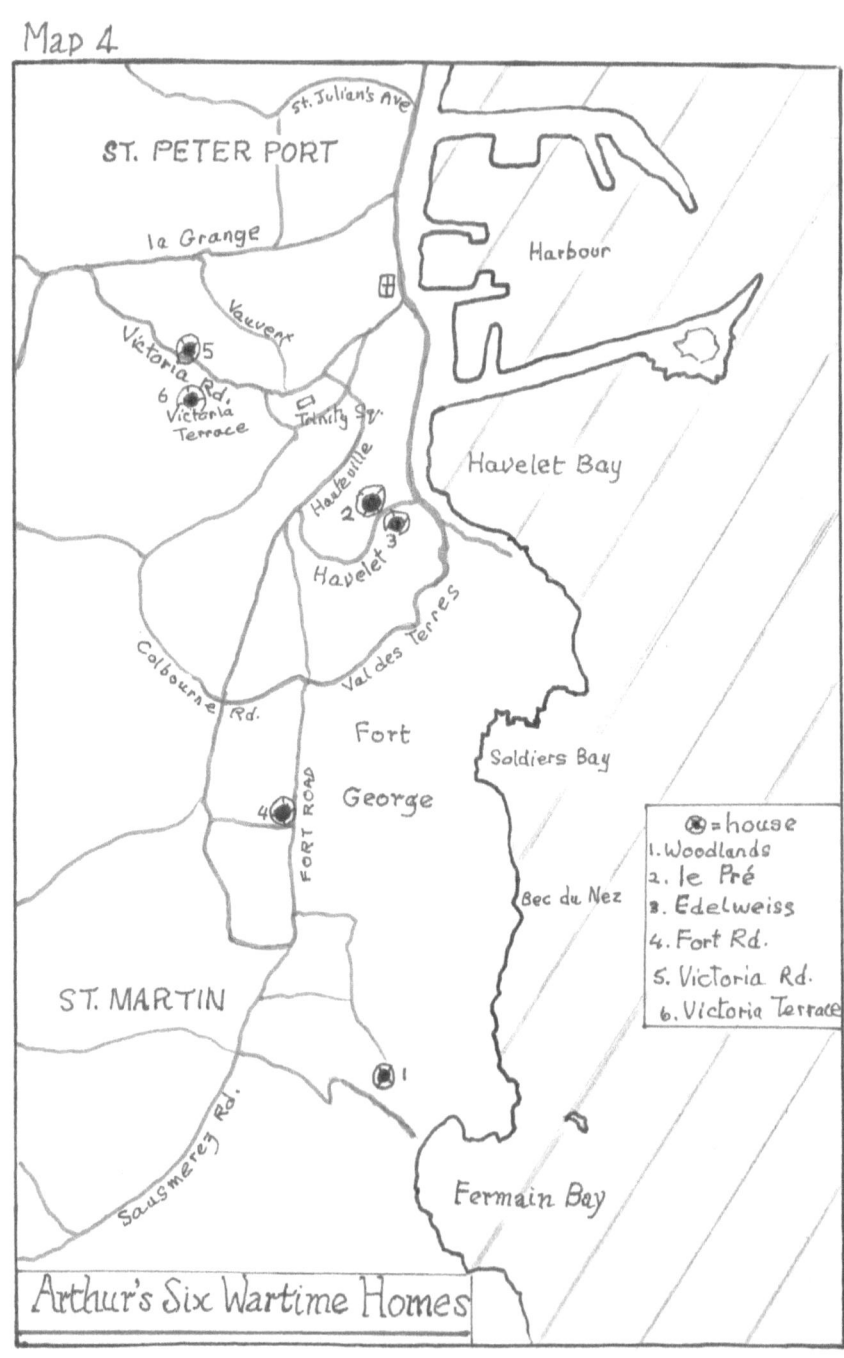

1: Evacuation—Arthur

*A restless night—The previous day—Evacuation morning—
Trinity Square farewells—Arthur has a surprise at home*

A restless night

Arthur realised he had been awake for quite a while, thinking in the silence of the night. Now he was aware of a chink of moonlight making the bedroom a little brighter than usual. Of course, it was a full moon night. Not a rustle from the trees, hardly a sound from the beach where the waves were breaking quietly. It was as if the whole island was in shock, the moon watching and savouring the peace before the frenzy that tomorrow would bring. And if you were the moon, you could see the destruction the Germans had done in Cherbourg, only forty miles away.

He slid away from Frances. She had been exhausted by the time they came to bed after midnight, and too anxious to settle down, but she was sleeping soundly now. He pulled back the sheet and blanket gently and took his body's weight off the bed. With his shorts and shirt over one arm, he paused and cast a long glance at her. When would they be together again?

He moved silently across the hall, through the living room, moonlight showing the way to the kitchen. He switched on the light.

Their local newspaper, *The Guernsey Evening Press*, in its strange small format, was still on the kitchen table. Wednesday, June 19, 1940—it was a date he would probably never forget, with the oversized headline: "Evacuation of Children." Their two girls were fast asleep: Janice, now five years old, in her regular small bed; and two-year-old Lynette in her cot. They had been told they would be going out for the day tomorrow with Mummy.

Women and young children would leave early in the morning on the mailboat for Weymouth. School children should also leave tomorrow with their teachers, as other boats arrived. Frances had walked up to St. Martin's Parish School, where Janice was enrolled, to tell them that her daughter would definitely not be leaving with her school class. Now it was today, this morning, the twentieth. He would be saying goodbye to all three of them.

Their suitcase was ready in the kitchen. They were each supposed to have one complete change of clothes, but Frances had squeezed in enough for at least two, plus their basic washing stuff. She had been hovering over that suitcase for the last ten days. "It's just in case," she had insisted.

The weather promised to be a beautiful summer morning, but evacuees had been instructed to wear winter coats. Luckily a friend had been able to provide Frances with a coat for Janice, who was now too big for her last winter's coat.

The previous day

Arthur's older brother Otto had walked up from St. Peter Port, or "the town" as everyone called it, yesterday evening, with his eleven-year-old son Bert[1]. Otto and Arthur had married two sisters, Nellie and Frances, and they had remained close friends as their families grew. Otto and Nellie had three children in Vauvert school in the town, and Nellie was expecting their fourth.

Frances had taken Bert indoors so that the two men could talk outside. "I've got some *gâche-melée*[2] left," she told Bert. "I bet you could eat a piece after walking up from town."

Bert was only too happy to join her and the children around the kitchen table.

"What have you been doing today?" she asked him.

"Mum took us to buy some stuff we need to take with us: some soap, and a new toothbrush, and pencils…" He paused to eat. "I've got to help her pack my clothes when Dad and I get home, then we sleep for two hours, and we must be at the school at 11.30 tonight."

Why tonight? Frances thought. *Why make them wait all night in their classrooms?* Out loud, she cheerfully said, "So you'll be camping out at school tonight with your friends."

"Yes." Bert's tone was not at all cheerful. Frances could picture her sister's anxiety.

Outside, the men talked quietly.

---

1 Enevoldsen, B. *A Guernsey Schoolboy in Wartime*, p 10.
2 A sticky apple cake.

"I took the family to Herm[3] last Sunday," Otto said. "We had a swim and noticed smoke over France in the afternoon, and we wondered if the Germans were bombarding Cherbourg."

"*The Press* says the French marines blew up the harbour installations there that evening."

"That's right. You could smell the fuel burning in town. They say that every family in Cherbourg fled long before that."

"Frances has signed up to evacuate on the early boat with the women and children. I told her that whatever she feels is best, is ok with me."

"Nell's going with the three children and the whole of Vauvert school. She offered to be a helper and she's been accepted. She's expecting, so I want to be sure she has a place. They're packing at home. They all have to be at the school tonight and wait there. At least Nell will be with the three of them."

They talked about the Great War. They had been a bit older than Bert when it started, Otto 14 and Arthur 12. There had been no need to evacuate children then. Island men had signed up with the British Army, and quite a few had lost their lives, but the war had stayed on the other side of Paris, two hundred miles away, and life on the island had continued. Sending the schools away was a shocker.

"I called in to see Ma and Pa," said Otto.

"Do they still want to stay? I was talking with them yesterday."

"Yes. He won't leave his boat. He said as long as he can fish and grow potatoes...."

Arthur nodded. "They have the garden and Pa has a good boat. He's always had fish to eat and fish to sell. I have a mortgage to pay. Frances will leave with the children, but I'd prefer to keep on at my job and wait and see. Why would the Germans bother to land here?"

"I don't think it'd be worth their time to stop here. Cherbourg's probably nearer to England than we are."

"It's only women, children and the schools going tomorrow, isn't it?"

"Women and children, and men between twenty and thirty-three who signed up for the army. If you want to leave, you'll have to wait for some more boats to come from England, maybe in a couple of days."

---

3   Herm Island lies 5 miles east of St. Peter Port.

Now, in the moonlit kitchen, Arthur thought about his parents, who were simply known as Ma and Pa to everyone in their large family. Eric and Emilie were both born in 1865, Eric in March and Emilie in July. They would have been planning a beach party for Emilie's birthday in about three weeks' time.

Eric Enevoldsen was born in Denmark, one of six children. He had resisted efforts by his parents to have him train to be a minister of the church. He wanted to travel, and worked on ships that sailed all over western Europe and as far as South America. At some point Eric's father advised his children to leave Denmark: "Sail away, sail away to a safer place," he had said, "before Germany tries to take more territory away from Denmark."

In the 1880s, four of them sailed away: Eric, Karl and Frederik headed for the Channel Isles and were shipwrecked on Guernsey's rocky west coast. Nils went to the USA and settled in Oregon. In Guernsey, Eric met Emilie le Page, and they married and started their family. Henceforth he would earn his living as a fisherman. He was one of the first to have a fishing boat with an engine; his registry number, GU 91, was well known. He designed better nets in his spare time. Emilie, or one of their two daughters, would sell his fish twice a week in the busy indoor fish market in St. Peter Port.

Arthur and Otto had left school as soon as they could. They worked on the sea with Eric and knew the coast like the back of their hands. At one time, they were part of the lifeboat crew when oars were still in use. Otto was now one of the registered pilots for island shipping.

Otto and Arthur had also been to the USA. They worked in a logging camp in Oregon near Uncle Nils, with their cousin Eric, just to see what life in America was like. Nellie had gone with them after she married Otto. Now Arthur thought of Uncle Nils and his cousins, far away and safe. Today it seemed that only Nils had gone far enough.

The official announcement that Guernsey would be demilitarised was there, on the front page of *The Press*, signed by the Bailiff, Victor Carey:

The Government of the United Kingdom has decided that this Bailiwick is to be entirely demilitarised... All persons in possession of firearms must forthwith hand them to the Constable of their Parish...

He must remember to hand in his rifle to the Constables, the two parish officials.

If they were demilitarised, why would the Germans come here? Guernsey had no war industries, no strategic airfield. Surely invading England was the German goal now.

It was 3.45 a.m. He filled up the kettle and put it on the gas to heat.

Evacuation morning

They had set the alarm for four o'clock, and when it went off Frances was upright in a flash. Arthur's side of the bed was empty. No noise from the girls—that was good. They would need their sleep. She would wake them before five, when it would be daylight. One of Arthur's workmates was coming here at 5.45 a.m. to drive them down to their evacuation meeting point at Trinity Church in the town.

She dressed in the clothes she had prepared just a few hours ago and added an apron to keep them clean. She wouldn't have much choice of clothes for a while now. Her new white summer shoes were by the front door, ready to put on when they left. She wasn't going to leave them behind.

Arthur was standing by the kitchen table. He had made a pot of tea already. He didn't look as though he'd slept at all.

"Did you pack the ration books?" was his greeting.

"Yes, I did. Did you sleep?"

"Not much."

She moved towards him, and they held each other close, drawing strength for the day to come, exchanging waves of uncertainty.

They ate because it was the right thing to do, and then it was time to wake the girls and give some semblance of a normal day. Frances gently woke Janice, who still had cards from her fifth birthday around her bed. Two-year-old Lynette preferred to stay asleep but wasn't allowed to. The girls' breakfasts and milk were eventually stuffed in a jar or a paper bag because they didn't want to eat. More food to carry! But they would need it.

"No, we aren't going to the beach today," Frances told them. "We're going on a boat trip to England. Daddy will meet us there." It echoed what she wished for.

She told them to choose a small toy to bring and stuffed their selections into the shopping bag. Frances noticed later that one of Janice's birthday cards had been slipped in as well. She made no comment, and quietly rescued four more cards from the bedroom, and Lynette's small bunny, and put them in as well. They would make a welcome surprise if the day was hard on them.

Five-forty. Arthur took the suitcase and large zippered shopping bag containing toys, sandwiches, apples, milk, cold tea, and toddler provisions, up the four flights of steps to their gate at the road.

Frances slipped into her new white shoes, ushered the girls outside, and closed the door. She was too warm already inside her winter coat. She looked down at Fermain Bay. It was calm, the water almost turquoise over the golden sand that would be uncovered at low tide. Small waves dropped on the pebbles, pulled back, and dropped again, like a caress. The valley sloped down to a hidden stream, a forest of sycamores greening it on both sides. Remember this, remember, she told herself, and please God, keep us all safe.

Trinity Square Farewells

Arthur came down and scooped up Lynette. "Jim's here already," he said. "He's watching the bags."

Frances took Janice's hand, and they steadily climbed the steps up to the road. Jim was talking to Arthur by the van. He looked exhausted. "You're the fourth lot I'm picking up," he said, "and I've got two more before I'm done."

Frances got in the passenger seat and took Lynette on her lap. Her handbag and the shopping bag were on the floor beside her. Jim closed the door gently and looked at her worried face through the open window.

"It's not quite five forty-five," he told her. "We're in good time. Don't worry."

She smiled at him as best she could. She heard a blackbird singing and willed it also to stay in her memory.

Arthur and Janice crept into the back of the van on their hands and knees, past the suitcase, and edged their way up to the front between boxes of plumbing supplies that didn't seem to want them there. It wasn't designed to accommodate people and there was little head space. Jim closed the back door.

"Hang on to the back of Mummy's seat," Arthur said to Janice. "I'll have my arm around you as well."

He made sure that the suitcase was near him and put his arm firmly around her, feeling her warmth through her winter coat. She pushed back against him to make sure he was there, her face full of questions, but in the presence of a stranger and the lack of jollity, she kept quiet. Nothing seemed normal, and not at all like the day's outing that the grownups had talked about.

Frances pointed out things to the children as though it was just a regular day: the cows along the Fort Road, a bird, the sunlight, flowers. Jim was driving carefully as they twisted down the curves of Colborne Road to the town. Soon they were in front of the big church at Trinity Square.

Arthur had brought her and the children here yesterday during his dinner hour, in the lorry that he drove for Leale Ltd, Ironmongers & Engineers. They had to register for evacuation in their parish, and Woodlands was just inside the parish of St. Peter Port. It had been a scene of anxiety and near panic when Frances arrived, women carrying infants, asking questions, and officials with few answers.

After registration, she had bundled the girls and Lynette's pushcart into a bus going past Fermain in the opposite direction, to St. Martins, where Janice went to school. Frances talked with the teachers and found everyone as upset as they had been at the church. She took Janice's name off her class list for possible evacuation. There was no way that she would let her five-year-old daughter leave with a school group. Luckily Lynette slept in the pushcart as they walked home. Bus service was becoming unreliable by then.

Now Arthur was out of the van with Janice. He saw a blue bus and two lorries lined up under the tall trees of Trinity Church Square, as though ready to take on passengers. A small crowd of mothers and young children passed a checkpoint and were climbing into the blue bus. A few men stood at a distance, watching, silent.

They were out of the van and in the queue. Those ahead of them were checked off against the parish lists. Husbands kissed their little ones and then their wives and stepped away. Arthur picked up each of the girls, hugged them, and gave them a kiss. "I'll see you soon," he told each one, knowing he could be lying.

He hugged Frances. Her face was all eyes. "Please, be careful," she whispered, taking an intense last look at him.

"Take good care of yourselves," he whispered.

Frances showed her papers at the table. He saw Janice struggle up the bus steps, someone helping her with the heavy shopping bag. Frances came after her, carrying Lynette and her handbag. The bus driver passed up the suitcase, and they were swallowed up into the interior.

Eventually, the driver got in and the motor started. The fathers waved and called out, "See you all soon!" and "We'll join you in a few days!" Their words floated on the air, the tone anything but joyous. Arthur waved, but his voice was silent, remembering the instructions he had read in the newspaper last night:

It will not be possible, on account of the danger of air raids, to permit masses of people to congregate at the harbour… parents must say goodbye to their children at home or at the schools or churches…

Praying that there would be no sound of aircraft over the island that day, the fathers uneasily returned to their empty homes.

Arthur has a surprise

Arthur started to walk home. That evening he would cycle down to his parents' house, which overlooked the south end of the harbour. Otto would probably be there, unless he had been needed to help pilot one of the ships doing the evacuation. He would have been around the harbour all day, and would have all the news.

While they were waiting for the blue bus to leave, someone told Arthur that the Vauvert students and staff had stayed most of the night in their classrooms until buses arrived at 4 a.m. to take them to the harbour, where they would have to wait on the long arm of the White Rock jetty for a boat to arrive. After that, the buses started to pick up women and young children waiting at parish church centres around the island. They would be boarded first on the regular mailboat. As other vessels arrived, the schools would board according to capacity. Men wondered if enough boats would turn up from England.

The sound of a motor made Arthur turn. He waved down the car, was given a lift, and was back at home sooner than he had expected. There had been no sound of aircraft, and he was thankful. Frances hadn't closed the front door properly. He put the kettle on. His mind was like a camera, full of the morning's images.

He opened the cupboard to get the tea caddy and was surprised to see how little they had left in the cupboard…Wait a minute, there had been half a pie, a full bag of sugar, and two tins of his favourite soup. Frances had shown him what was there. It looked a bit messy…Someone had been in their cupboard while they were gone! He was disgusted. Pilfering already. And the enemy hadn't even arrived yet.

He felt relieved when he went outside for milk in the safe near the back door and found that the jug was still there. Set against bare granite in the narrow space between bedrock and the bungalow's back wall, the safe acted as a small refrigerator. It had a screen front and kept food cool enough to save from spoilage for a few days. Frances had left him a packet of sandwiches from her food preparations the night before. He took one almost with reverence: when would she next prepare food for him? There was milk, cheese, and a packet of sausages. At least the thief had missed this lot.

Back to his tea. Yesterday's *Press* was still on the kitchen table. Someone had told him that it, or *The Star*, had been delivered free of charge to every house on the island early yesterday morning. So that was why it had arrived early, and in a smaller format than usual. He decided to sit down with his tea and read every detail. He couldn't afford to be ignorant of instructions or information.

He re-read the paragraphs under "Evacuation of Children" to see if they had done everything that was needed. They had almost committed it to memory the day before. There was a list of names of volunteers leaving to join the British Army, the news of the devastation in Cherbourg. Jersey and Guernsey boat owners had taken their boats to rescue British and French citizens fleeing from France.

And to think that only a few days ago he had been driving a lorry around the island with signs on it saying *Don't Panic, Be Calm*, at the request of the States of Guernsey. Ironically, he saw one small paragraph with the heading "Be Cool and Calm" at the bottom of the front page. *There is no need to be flurried and put out…* it continued. Today, that seemed to be very old news.

2: Evacuation—Frances

*Sisters at the harbour—Slow Boat to Weymouth—Train ride north—
Arrival at Crown Point*

Sisters at the harbour

Squeezed on one seat in the blue bus, the girls and the suitcase packed around her, Frances was relieved that the driver was helpful and that the women were helping each other. She felt so vulnerable now that she had the luggage as well as the children to manage. She was hoping that two of her sisters would be on the boat: Violet, usually known as Vi, who was very pregnant, and Mabel with her three-year-old daughter, Pat. They both lived near the Route Militaire on the flat northern part of the island.

The bus arrived at the White Rock, the long north arm of St. Peter Port's harbour, and slowly drove along it. There were school groups sitting on the elevated walkway parallel to the quay, waiting for a boat that hadn't arrived yet. She wondered if Nellie was among them with her three children: Nellie, who was pregnant. Now she could see the mailboat against the quay. A crowd of women and children were filtering through barriers to board it.

The bus stopped and again the driver was helping everyone. Frances struggled out of the bus: three packages and three females of various sizes. Scarcely were her feet on the ground when she heard a man's voice call out her name and saw Fred, Vi's husband, striding towards her.

"Frances, let me take the suitcase and luggage. Hello girls. Let's get out of the crowd. Vi's over there, Frances, sitting down."

He carefully gathered her suitcase and bags, and she was able to carry Lynette. Janice held on to her coat.

Fred walked close to her. "Frances, I wanted to ask you, can you travel with Vi? Together? She's over seven months pregnant now."

Frances nodded. "Yes, of course, Fred. We'll stay together."

He looked relieved. "I've signed up. I'll be coming over to England, maybe today. Your brother, Frank, is with me. We signed up together. We're waiting further down on the pier for a boat, but it's not in yet."

"I thought Frank would sign up. I'm glad you two will be together." Now they were out of the crush of women and children, and she saw her sister sitting on a bench. Vi's face lit up when she saw them coming.

"Here I am, Frances!" she called out. "I was just hoping that you or Mabel would turn up. Come on here, Janice, and sit by me. I have some mints that I think you like."

Janice accepted a mint happily.

"We're all going for a boat ride together," Vi said to her. She turned and whispered loudly to Frances, "If you say you're expecting, like me, we can be in the same section, and I can help you with the children, too."

A sister to share this with! Frances relaxed a little. "Yes, I can do that."

"Mabel should be on the boat as well, with Pat," said Vi. "She came around to see me yesterday. But I haven't seen her yet."

"She won't be with your expectant mothers' group, though," said Frances.

"You mean with *our* expectant mothers."

Frances smiled. It was lovely to smile at something.

"Let's get you all on board," said Fred. "You need to find a place to sit. Load me up with all the bags and let me be useful. As soon as I'm in England, I'll find out where you are."

Slow boat to Weymouth

June 20 stretched well beyond its twenty-four hours. This unusual morning, followed by a few hours' wait before the steamer left the harbour, was tiring enough; but that was just the beginning. Vi was given a berth and Frances found a few feet of deck space next to some shallow steps and put her suitcase down behind her. She wasn't far from Vi and she was relieved to find a mother and child from Janice's school near them. They arranged to keep an eye on each other's children and bags.

At some point before they left Guernsey, Mabel and Pat called to them from the other side of a barrier, and Frances managed to talk with them. They would all get together in Weymouth when they landed. Frances wondered if Nellie and her children were also on the sea with their school, somewhere behind them. They had seen two ships heading for St. Peter Port as they left.

Late in the afternoon they approached Weymouth. Suddenly there was a shot, as though from a cannon, and the boat swerved sharply. Some women screamed. Frances grabbed the arms of her children…she heard no more shots. An officer yelled that things were all right, and she breathed again and waited, and it really was all right. After an hour's delay they entered Weymouth harbour.

There had to wait for almost an hour before they were allowed to leave the boat: six hundred women and children, struggling with bags and suitcases, were directed into a huge warehouse. Tea, milk, and sandwiches were supplied by the Red Cross.

Frances made sure that Vi had a chair by a long counter, which served as a table. She stood and waved her arms hoping that Mabel would see her through the crowd. Eventually they made contact, and Mabel and Pat pushed through.

"Look, Pat, here's Auntie Vi and Auntie Frances and the girls. Vi, how are you feeling?"

Vi was on her feet handing milk to the girls. "I'm all right, Mabel, I think. Come over here, Pat. I have some milk for you." There were a few quick hugs and tears as they found chairs, looked after the children, and claimed tea for themselves. Someone handed them a plate of sandwiches to share, and a second plate held a variety of biscuits[4].

Mabel sipped her tea and closed her eyes. "Just to sit here and be safe…" she murmured. "I was so frightened when they shot that gun before we came into Weymouth. Do you know what that was all about?"

"I overheard the deck hands saying the Weymouth harbourmaster wondered if our boat was controlled by Germans," Frances said. "I suppose they had to radio each other to make sure we were friendly."

"We weren't the only boat arriving," said Vi. "One of the stewards said that there was a boat of wounded soldiers waiting to enter, and it had to go ahead of us."

"There were several other boats waiting to dock after us," Mabel added. "I was hoping Nellie and some of the schools would be on one of them, but I suppose they'll be a few hours behind us."

There were announcements over a loudspeaker: they were welcomed in England; they would have a brief medical check; and then they would be put aboard a train for the next part of their journey.

---

4   Cookies

Frances tidied the plate. "There's a couple of sandwiches left here. Let's eat them up or take them with us. We don't know when we'll get more food."

Train ride north

There were trains somewhere, and eventually enough carriages were linked together and the next phase of the journey began. They found themselves in a long carriage with tables set between seats, and managed to secure most of a table between them. For some women, this introduction to trains was another challenge, as there were none on the island, and some children were scared to go near these noisy, mechanical monsters. Frances and Mabel had lived in Toronto with their aunt for almost a year in 1923, and now felt fortunate to have had that prior experience.

"We're going to travel in a train!" they told the three girls, and any other children within earshot. "We're going to sit by a big window, and we'll see all kinds of nice things—farms and horses and sheep."

And, once inside and seated, it started to be quite a novelty, with strange things like rivers and black and white cows for them to look at. Yet, after dark, with windows sometimes blacked out and the dimmest of lighting, or none at all, it became increasingly difficult. Sleep didn't come happily. These children were used to beds and quiet places to sleep, not this strange mechanical noise, even if it did have a rhythm of sorts.

Arrival at Crown Point.

Around two in the morning, they arrived somewhere in pitch blackness. Frances thought she saw the name Burnley on a poster. They boarded buses, counting bags and children. The buses had dimmed lights, and only moonlight allowed the women to see that the buses climbed up out of the town to a treeless moorland. They stopped outside a large building, and someone read the sign: *Crown Point Hospital*. They wearily disembarked and found it chilly; but there were Red Cross staff and the WVS[5] ready to help them carry bags and suitcases. The youngest children were carried by their mothers from the gloomy outdoors to brighter lights inside.

Outside, a WVS lady approached Vi, who had Janice by the hand.

---

5   Women's Voluntary Service.

"*Madame, voulez-vous de l'aide?*"

Vi looked startled. "Sorry. What did you say?"

"Oh. Can I help you?"

"I have this suitcase and bag," she said hesitantly, and the WVS lady looked relieved. "I'll carry it in for ya, luv."

"Ee by gum. They do speak English, after all," she heard a second lady say.

There were more strange accents around her, but she was relieved that she understood most of it.

Frances stood with Lynette asleep on her shoulder and her bag and suitcase were placed next to her by the driver.

"Ello, missis. I can 'elp thee with that," a voice said, and a smiling WVS lady picked up her bag and suitcase and led the way into the building.

They sat at long tables. Warm or cold milk was available for bottles and cups, and strong tea was poured from large teapots. "Ow dju like thee tea?" Frances was asked, and opted for extra hot water and milk. "Tea and water—'ere you are, luv," came the reply.

These helpful ladies had waited since late evening for their arrival. Their smiles and helping hands were truly welcoming.

More milk, more hot tea, and food appeared. Some children were awake enough and hungry enough to tuck in, and others were too overwhelmed. They were taken to large rooms—old hospital wards they were told—where mattresses were laid out either on the floor or on camp beds; each had two grey blankets on it. Gently and patiently, mothers did what they could to quieten small children and soothe them into sleep. Tea continued to be served.

Frances pushed three mattresses together and did her best to create a bed for each child, two layers of blanket under and two to cover. Washing and toilet facilities were scanty, and wiping faces with a damp facecloth was about all that any child could tolerate. Finally, they were asleep, Lynette on the middle mattress with her bunny near her hand, and Janice clutching a doll.

Vi brought her mattress close to Frances, Pat being between her and Mabel. They were all in their nightdresses now. Frances sat on her mattress, and Vi carefully lowered herself down opposite her.

"I'm glad I could rest in a berth coming to Weymouth," she whispered.

"I hardly slept last night. I slept a bit on the boat, and I know it helped me get through the day."

Mabel tiptoed around the mattress and squatted down by Vi. The ward room was now full of sleeping children and murmured conversations.

"Did you have much room on the deck where you were?" she asked Frances.

"No, we were crowded. We were sitting by a set of steps. It's a good thing it was a nice day."

"Well, you weren't any better off than I was then," Mabel whispered. "When that shot was fired near Weymouth, some women were screaming, and we were all on our feet wondering what to do."

"We nearly fell when the boat swerved," Frances replied, as quietly as she could. "I'm glad the captain sent a message fast to say we were friendly. It just shows how worried they are in Weymouth about the Germans trying to invade."

Frances omitted to say that she had placed herself and the children as near as possible to a lifeboat. It was the nearest one to the bunk where Vi was resting. When the shot was fired across their bows, she had grabbed both children and was about to yell to Vi to come with her, leaving bags and suitcases behind. But Vi and Mabel didn't need to know that.

"I'm just glad we're together," Vi whispered.

"Being together was the best thing of the whole day," said Frances. "Just being able to take it in turns to sleep on the train…And you spotting that nun with the bottle of milk, Vi. I don't know how I would have stopped Lynette from crying without that half cup of milk."

"The nun was with the Catholic school children, I think."

"Well, I hope we'll never have to sleep like that again, leaning on a table, with no food or drink on the train," said Mabel.

"Did either of you talk with Mum and Dad on Thursday—to see if they were leaving?"

"Yes," Mabel whispered back. "When I called in, they weren't sure if they would leave or not. Dad said he had a good crop of tomatoes ready to ship and he didn't want to leave. But he wanted Mum, Joyce, and the boys to leave. So, I don't know if they'll stay or go."

Frank, Bill, Joyce, and Geoff were the four youngest siblings in the family, and still lived at the Torode home. The boys worked in Guernsey's well-developed horticultural sector, growing tomatoes and flowers. Joyce was the youngest sister and worked in a shop in St. Peter Port.

"Joyce would have been working in town today," said Vi, "and Geoff and Bill in the greenhouses."

"I know. I doubt if the buses were running…or if there were enough boats…"

"And Bob's definitely staying on the island?" Vi asked, trying to keep her voice down. Mabel's husband had been adamant about staying in Guernsey the week before.

"Yes, he wanted to stay in our house and look after it. He didn't change his mind about that, but he wanted me and Pat to leave. He said he didn't think the war would last long."

She looked at her watch. "My gosh, it's almost four in the morning! We'd better get to sleep."

They whispered their goodnights.

Vi pulled a cardigan over her nightdress and eased her way under a doubled blanket.

"Wasn't it funny though, they thought we might speak French," she whispered to Frances.

"Yes, but I found some of those Red Cross people were hard to understand, didn't you?"

Frances pushed herself down under the blanket and then re-emerged and reached for her cardigan and pulled it on. Vi had made no reply, and her eyes were closed. Frances looked at both her sleeping children, pulled the blankets up around her shoulders, closed her eyes and was asleep in an instant.

3: The Walk from Crown Point

*A walk to Sarellen's—Meeting Annie & Hilda—Sharing a house—
Making jam with Annie—Bad news on July 1*

A walk to Sarellen's

Two days later, Frances walked away from Crown Point Hospital, firmly pushing a rickety pushcart that she had noticed among several near the entrance, a precious find. Lynette sat in it, a small blanket arranged around her. Janice danced ahead, looking for flowers.

It was a narrow, quiet road, with one low farmhouse in the distance behind them. She would explore in that direction tomorrow. Today, they were headed the other way, to the main Burnley-Manchester Road, which ran north-south. One of the WVS ladies had told her that there was a village less than two miles away if she walked south, and it had a bakery and post office.

She stopped and looked around. It was an obvious place for an isolation hospital, with treeless moorlands humped around, and a reservoir occupying the lowest portion. She could see the beginning of the village on the other side of the water. She turned back and looked at the hospital. It was currently the home of a young and lively population, but it had been built for smallpox cases in 1901, and had been in use until about ten years ago. From outside, it had the aura of a gloomy history.

However, there were no enemy planes above, and the summery weather told her to be outdoors with the children. And she needed to be quiet, to think over the last two days, to wonder if Arthur was on his way, or still waiting for a boat…or not coming. This morning, the lady in charge had told them that they may be moved into Burnley, if empty houses were available.

They reached the main road and turned south. By then they had seen a curlew and two magpies, and Janice had picked a bunch of buttercups. There was a road sign, Crown Point Road. That would be easy to find on the way back. A red double-decker bus trundled past. Mabel was going to enquire about fares, and they would try a ride into Burnley, perhaps on market day. They had been given a small allocation of money until they were placed in a house. Then they would receive an allowance for rent and food. If they needed more, the women must find a job.

She walked south along the road. Opposite the small reservoir, they came to two separate rows of four small houses. Each row had four identical front doors, chimneys, and small gardens with iron railings around each one. She pointed out to the children the roses climbing around the door at Number 8, the first garden flowers she had seen. There was little of interest in the other front gardens.

They continued on and the stone wall curved around a schoolyard and a small church—and there was the village. They walked past a row of houses, and on the corner of the next row was a small shop. Above the door was an old sign saying *Bakery*. A notice in the window indicated that it was also a Post Office. This must be what the WVS ladies called "Sarellen's."

The owner, Sarah Ellen, was behind the counter, and Frances was received with a hesitant welcome. Local people were not sure about these southerners who had been brought to the hospital. There were evacuees from London in the next town, who had been disorderly; but this woman looked respectable and had clean and quiet children, and looked like she might be a customer.

"Yes, Missis?"

Frances replied awkwardly. "I wanted to buy a bun or something, for each of us."

"I've some custard tarts over here. They were baked fresh this mornin'. And I've some plainer oven bottoms as well. Those may be easier to 'andle."

Lynette was pointing to the custard tart. Janice and Frances opted for oven bottoms.

"We're evacuees at Crown Point," Frances said, "and this is the first time I've walked here. What's the name of the village?"

"Clowbridge." Sarellen spelled it out and then wrote the name on the corner of the brown paper bag which held the buns.

"Thank you, and I'll buy five stamps and some envelopes while I'm here."

The transaction was completed and she received her change.

"I dare say you have your letters picked up and delivered up at the hospital?"

"Yes, that's what we've been told. Thank you, Missis…"

"Just call me Sarellen. That's what everybody calls me."

"Thank you, Sarellen. Come on, girls." Frances turned the pushcart around. The two women managed a quick smile to each other as Frances left.

Meeting Annie & Hilda

On the way back they passed Number 8, right opposite the reservoir, and Frances looked at the flowers and thought of the roses in her garden at Woodlands.

"Can we eat our buns now?" Janice asked for the third time. "I'm hungry."

"All right. Let's sit on the wall across the road and look at the water."

Before she could turn the pushcart, a woman came outside and a conversation started. In a few minutes a second woman appeared, and a spoon was found to help with the eating of the tart. Janice was given a small garden seat among some orange poppies. The pushcart was brought up the path so they could supervise Lynette's efforts with the spoon.

The three women shared their first names: Annie and her sister Hilda lived there; and the conversation went from Sarellen's bakery to flowers to evacuees to the weather and back again. Frances learned that the two groups of houses were jointly called Cotton Row, and had been built by the owners of the Landless Cotton Mill at the far end of Clowbridge, for their employees. The women both worked shifts at the mill.

"Now, I have a problem. I wonder if you can help me with it." Annie said to Frances, having ascertained that she was a respectable housewife. "Do you ever make jam?"

"I usually make all my own jam."

"Well, I've been trying to make apricot jam, and it won't set."

"Add some chopped apple, like a Bramley, a cooking apple," said Frances. "That should help."

"Apple. Would you be able to help me with it, if I bought some apples?"

"Yes, I could. Make sure you buy Bramleys."

"I'll have them here the day after tomorrow. We can have a cup of tea after."

"All right. As long as it's a fine day again, I'll walk down in the afternoon around the same time."

Lynette insisted on getting out of the pram and was walked around the small garden. Annie explained to Janice why the orange poppies had protective hats on before they opened and then re-explained it to Lynette, who by then was more intrigued with the pattern of the iron railings. She clung to the spoon and was allowed to keep it. Goodbyes were said, and they continued their way back to Crown Point.

It hadn't been too hard to understand each other, Frances reflected. It felt good to talk with local people, and the two sisters seemed friendly and even sympathetic. She was glad that she had something different to do, the day after tomorrow, to take her mind off this situation that she had no control over.

Sharing a house

On June 25, the morning's news that they might be put into houses in Burnley led to a lot of discussion. Frances, Vi, and Mabel talked it over while Janice and Pat played ball in a group. Lynette was hugging a teddy that a WVS lady had offered her.

"If we can be together in one house," Mabel said, "Frances or I can get a job to help pay for the rent, and the other will look after the three children. Vi, you'll be having your baby and we need you because Fred's in the army now."

"I don't know why one of us has to have a husband in the army so that we can rent a house," said Frances.

"It's to get a better house," Vi corrected. "I suppose it puts pressure on Guernsey men to join up. Otherwise, they don't have to."

"I wonder what kind of work is available," said Frances.

"Maybe there are things like cleaning or housekeeping," said Mabel. "I've been trained for that. There won't be any tomato packing jobs here like we have at home. You were in charge of Collins' sweet shop, Frances. And remember when we were in Toronto? You worked with Bell Telephone and I helped in a shop. We managed all right."

"Yes, but we went there with Aunt Ada and lived with her and Uncle Peter."

"I remember you going," said Vi. "I was only about eleven, but I was the oldest one after you all left, and I had to help look after Frank and the others. Geoff was only a year old."

Mabel giggled. "That's why it was so good to get away."

Frances laughed. "At least we were too old for Aunt Ada to shut us in a cupboard if we didn't behave properly."

Mabel smiled. "Yes, just as well we weren't young children. It was all exciting, but I was too homesick. It was good to come home."

Making jam with Annie

After the midday meal, Mabel watched the children while Frances wheeled Lynette down to Annie's house. Vi would see a visiting doctor. Annie had bought apples and had her jam jars lined up on the table in the kitchen. She noticed that Lynette had the teddy bear in her arms.

"Well, is that your nice Teddy?" she asked.

Lynette nodded.

"Just a minute. I think we can find him a blanket." She took a small kitchen towel off a shelf and offered it to her. "You tuck him up like your mummy tucks you up in bed. And you can make him a bed in this, if you want."

She reached for a basket on an upper shelf, put it on a low stool, and Lynette was enthused and busy.

Annie turned to Frances. "You know, we don't see many small children around here. My brother Tom and his wife have one boy and he's eleven; my other brother has a little girl, but he lives near Bolton. I have two married sisters with no children, and two of us—Hilda and me—not even married."

Now that Lynette was fully engaged in caring for Teddy, they peeled, quartered and grated a couple of apples and started the cooking. In an hour, the apricot jam was setting nicely and the job was done. They made a cup of tea and it was time to walk back.

"Drop in any time you're passing," Annie said. "It's nice to talk to somebody different, and your children are so good. If I'm not at the mill, I'm usually here."

"I will," Frances promised.

Walking back, with Teddy sporting a new blanket, she reflected on their afternoon. Annie's sisters lived mostly in the village. Dora was married to the manager of the cotton mill, where Annie and Hilda worked. Another sister lived two doors away at Cotton Row. Annie's brother Tom and his wife lived a few houses away from Sarellen's. The sisters seemed to keep in touch with each other just as Frances did with her sisters.

She had a feeling that Annie had probably not had much schooling, and had little work experience beyond her village life, but she had a frankness and curiosity about her, wanting to know the whole story of the evacuation and where they would go from Crown Point.

Vi was sitting outside when she returned.

"Good news, Frances. The WVS people are looking for a house for the three of us," she said, "and they should find something for us in a week or two."

Mabel came along with Pat and Janice. "The children have all been playing outside," she said, "and I've talked all afternoon. How was your doctor's visit, Vi?"

"He was very nice, and everything's normal. He works at the hospital in Burnley and when I have the baby, I'll go there. I think it's called the Victoria Hospital. They're trying to find out where Fred is, too."

"It probably won't take them long," said Mabel. "Don't worry. We're all on a list, and they know where the train went from Weymouth. He'll soon find you."

Demilitarisation of the Channel Islands[6]

In June 1940, the British government considered sending two battalions to protect Jersey and Guernsey; but on June 12, seeing that the Germans controlled the coast of France, they reconsidered. By June 15 they were pondering the demilitarisation of the islands, and the evacuation of any military personnel. On June 17 and 18, Jersey yachtsmen helped to evacuate British and French soldiers escaping from St Malo, ferrying them to transports which took them to England.

On June 19 the decision to demilitarise was made. This meant that the Guernsey militia and defence volunteers were demobilized and arms handed in. Three thousand young men had just become liable for service and should be allowed to evacuate.

---

6   Cruickshank, pp 15-23.

> The British government did not want to announce publicly that the islands were demilitarised. They felt it would be like an open invitation to the Germans to land there. Unfortunately, not knowing this, the Luftwaffe attacked the islands to see if they were armed. Planes bombed a line of lorries waiting to unload tomatoes at St Peter Port harbour, on June 28. They killed about thirty men and injured over thirty others.
>
> It was only on June 30 that the German government was officially informed of the demilitarisation of the islands, through the US Ambassador in London.

Bad news on July 1

The WVS volunteer who gave out the news on the morning of July 1, left the worst part until the end. She regretted to inform everyone that Guernsey was now occupied by German forces, who had landed at the airport the day before. There was a complete hush from the adults as she repeated the announcement; even the children became quiet, absorbing the mood. It was almost like a day of mourning as each woman worried about who she had left behind and felt more dependent on strangers for help.

Mabel went to Burnley and bought a newspaper, but it didn't tell them much. She knew that Bob was now behind enemy lines; Frances feared that Arthur might never have left the island; Vi only hoped that Fred really had left the island and would be located soon.

In Guernsey, married women didn't work. Each of the evacuees had to face the fact that she was no longer a woman protected by her working husband. Each woman would receive an allowance of fifteen shillings per adult and about half that amount per child, but it was a minimal amount. Women would have to share accommodation, and find some kind of work.

So, as Mabel said to Frances, one of them would find work and the other would look after the house and the three children. Vi would be fully occupied with her baby; and they presumed that by then Fred would have turned up.

4: The Move to Hawthorne Road

*A house in Burnley—News from Fred—A profitable visit to the WVS—
Back to Sarellen's—A long chat with Annie*

A house in Burnley

A few days after they knew that Guernsey was occupied, Vi was told that a house had been located for them, and they would move on July 9. The sisters had swapped addresses with other women who had already moved into Burnley. Scott Park, situated on the south end of the city, would be their meeting place.

Thankfully, the weather remained warm. Twice they took a bus to Burnley to find the market and the park, and to register for rations. From the Crown Point Road bus stop, the Manchester Road sloped up for a while until it was near the highest part of the moors, called the Summit, and then plunged down steeply past Scott Park to Burnley's centre.

From the Summit, the view of Burnley was obscured by a smoky haze; the tall chimneys of the cotton mills near the river created an industrial landscape. Shafts of coal mines were less evident. As the bus descended, they passed the park on their left, and rows of terraced houses on the slopes of the moorland on the right.

Their new address was Number 5, Hawthorne Road, which was not far from the Manchester Road and Scott Park. The house was part of a row of narrow, two-storey houses with a bay window on the ground floor. Across the street, an identical row stood like a reflected copy.

Each house had a small space between its bay window and a low wall running along the whole block of houses, but there were no gardens, no flowers. The houses looked solid but colourless and were darkened by the smutty air.

After Vi was given the keys, the sisters moved in with minimal furniture: single mattresses with sheets and blankets, three bed frames, and one table. Cutlery and dishes had been rationed out. There were about twenty chairs, which they had to cope with for a while. As soon as they could, Mabel, Frances, and the children set out for the WVS Centre to see what they could find in second-hand donations from Burnley's population. Vi stayed at home to rest. This was a working-class town and people didn't have much to give, but they tried to help.

At the WVS, Frances noticed a child's small chair and a buffet—a soft cushiony stool —which Janice and Pat could use.

"Could we have these?" she asked one of the WVS ladies. "We have three children and only adult sized chairs. And the floor's very cold for them to sit on."

"Well, of course. That's what they're here for. We have somebody who'll bring it to your door. Just tell me your address."

"Five, Hawthorne Road," said Frances. "I can write it down if you like."

"No, I'll remember it. We've so little paper nowadays, there's nothing to write on."

Frances thanked her and told Mabel.

"Oh, that will make a difference," said Mabel. "Let's not tell the girls before they bring them to the house. It'll be a nice surprise."

It really was a surprise, because a man stopped at their door two hours later and delivered a bundle of sheets instead.

"We were given sheets when we moved here," Mabel told him. "We're all right for sheets. But I think I know where the sheets should be delivered. I heard the woman across at Number 4 asking for some. She didn't have any at all."

The man frowned. "That's the second wrong address I've been given. I'll take it across to number four. Thank you, Missis."

"We were expecting a chair and a buffet."

"Well, I haven't got that."

The chair and buffet didn't arrive. In the meantime, they brought a mattress into the living room for the children to sit and play on during the day. They had a small fireplace in that room, and the coalman was helpful, leaving them a second bag of coal when rations dictated that they should only receive one.

News from Fred

Next day, Mabel, Frances, and the children walked to Scott Park, while Vi went for a checkup at the hospital. Lynette was able to walk to the park, but had to be carried part of the way home after playing for an hour. The children enjoyed seeing their friends from Crown Point, and their mothers discussed making clothes, knitting patterns, accommodation, and finding work. The park was on the slope of the Summit, slightly higher than the town, and they agreed that the air felt a bit cleaner.

"I think I'd do well as a housekeeper," Mabel said to Frances, as they walked home. "I've been trained for that, and I could start early morning and do the meals, and come back after supper, if you looked after Pat with your children; but I don't think people around here have the money to pay for a housekeeper. Even up here near the park, the houses are small. It's all working class and factories from what I've seen. And there's a lot of dirt in the air."

"It's the factory chimneys, I suppose. But most workers have to do war work, so a housekeeper might be hard to find. People with money must live around here somewhere. It's just, how do we make contact?"

As they returned, they saw Vi walking back to the house from the hospital. She was waving to them, smiling.

"They've found Fred!" she called, as they came near to her. "He'll come and get me after the baby arrives!" She was beaming. "Frank helped him to find where we were; and Fred phoned the hospital. Fred's mother was evacuated to Bradford, somewhere in Yorkshire. He's rented a small house there. I'll have the baby here, and then he'll be given a couple of days on leave to come and fetch me. His mother will look after me."

Frances and Mabel glanced at each other. They felt relieved at the news, but also realised that their right to live in the Hawthorne Road house might disappear as soon as Vi moved away. Frances was content, knowing that Vi would be taken care of. Two years ago, Vi had taken care of Janice for several weeks after Lynette's birth, which had been complicated, and she owed Vi for her help and support. It seemed that Frances and Mabel would have to find a new place to live, and one of them must find a job as soon as they could.

A profitable visit to the WVS

Next morning, the two of them were back at the WVS and Mabel informed one lady that the small chair and buffet hadn't arrived. She said she would try to find out what happened to it, just as a second lady called Frances from across the room. "I think we have what you're looking for, luv," she said. "Wasn't it you that was asking for a pushcart? Wait here a bit." She disappeared and came back with a pushcart and wheeled it to Frances. It looked in good condition and Frances was overcome with gratitude. It would help with shopping and all their walks, and Lynette could even sleep in it. Pat and Janice came running over.

"Look what we've found for you," she said to Lynette, who was already trying to climb into it. Frances picked up a red velvet dress that she had already selected. Once Lynette was seated, it served well as a blanket, and she patted it down all around herself.

Mabel laughed. "Well, look at you," she said to Lynette. "Aren't you posh with your red blanket? And look, Frances, you've got a wire basket underneath. You can take along a picnic or carry some shopping."

Frances was pleased with the red dress. Made of velvet, it would make good material to sew a warm, bright dress for Janice for Christmas. She would have to sew it by hand, but she had brought needles and scissors and only needed to buy the thread. If Guernsey was occupied by the Germans, they wouldn't be going back home before this coming winter. Both she and Mabel were looking for anything that they could transform into winter clothes.

She found a blue cardigan which she could adjust for Janice, and a striped wool jersey for Lynette, a bit on the small size, but it would do for a while. She wasn't a knitter, but she would learn. They shopped carefully at the Saturday market where there was both wool and needles. There were also ends of rolls of various cottons and heavier materials that came from local factories.

Back to Sarellen's

On Saturday, July 20, Frances decided to take the children to Clowbridge and stop at Sarellen's again. It had been a pleasant walk from the hospital and now it was an escape from the grey houses and smutty air of Burnley. The weather remained warm and dry and with the pushcart they could walk further.

She only had to ask the girls one question to get an enthusiastic response: "Who wants to go for a nice walk and buy a custard tart or a bun?"

The bus ride on the red double-decker was a new adventure, and the conductor stowed the pushcart under the stairs. They got off the bus at the south end of Clowbridge near the big cotton mill, where Annie and Hilda worked shifts. There was a grocery and a fish and chip shop near the mill.

They walked past one row of houses, finding the shop at its usual corner. Sarellen was slightly more friendly. "I hear you're all in Burnley now," she said. "How are you getting on?"

Frances told her that she was still with her sisters, but wondering if they would have to move again. She mentioned that she or Mabel would be looking for a job. Better to let people know as soon as possible. Sarellen probably knew every person in the area. She bought one oven bottom and two custard tarts. They would eat them on the wall by the reservoir. Seeing the water seemed to help. Two bus fares and some fresh baking made it seem like a day out.

A long chat with Annie

When they reached Cotton Row, Annie was in her garden, and the reservoir was forgotten. Hilda brought out chairs, and they met Annie's dog, Dinah, who was curious but gentle. Annie admired Janice's tiny bouquet of daisies and laughed when Lynette produced the spoon for her tart from Frances' handbag. She went to get one for Janice. Like Sarellen, she was curious about how they managed in Burnley. "And how's your sister doing—the one that's expecting?" she queried.

"Vi? She's been checked by the doctor. They've managed to locate her husband. She'll have her baby soon, and then they'll go to live in Bradford."

"Bradford! And what happens to you after that?"

Frances explained that she or Mabel would have to find a job and move again.

"They've been asking people around here if anybody's interested in taking an evacuee and children into their homes," Annie told her. "Billeting, they call it. Have they told you about that?"

"Yes, they mentioned it. But up to now I don't know of anyone who's done it. I suppose we don't know enough people yet. We have an allowance if we're billeted somewhere."

They talked about the occupation of the island and agreed it may not be a short war. To Frances' surprise, Annie had been on a group visit to Jersey a few years before.

"We were just listening to the news," Annie said. "They don't tell you much, but we hear that there's a lot of bombing going on down south."

"Do you hear the sirens going in Burnley from here?" asked Frances. "We've just had a couple of warnings, but it was frightening."

"Oh yes, we get the warnings and the 'all clear' afterwards. Just make sure you don't show any bit of light at night. We don't want any bombers up here."

"We're careful. They showed us how to make sure the curtains are drawn when we moved there, and one of us goes outside to make sure we're not showing any light."

"Well, be careful, the air raid wardens will be knocking on your door if there's any light showing. One man at the Sutcliffe factory in Burnley was fined ten shillings for not closing the factory blackouts properly."

They looked at the flowers, and it was time to say goodbye. Annie seemed to phrase her last words carefully. "Let me know if things change for you. If you prefer to be out of the town, there's folk around here that might have room to billet some evacuees."

Frances looked at her. Annie and her sisters probably knew everyone in the village.

"Thank you," she said. "I'll keep in touch. I'd certainly prefer to be out of the town."

5: Visitors at Hawthorne Road

A surprise visit—How to find work—Mabel looks for a job

A surprise visit

During the next few weeks, Frances was tossed through an emotional storm of relief, anxiety, hope, and near desperation. It all started with an unexpected visit.

On Sunday, July 21, they all went to Scott Park in the morning, Janice and Pat taking turns to maneuver the new pushcart. Back at Hawthorne Road, they were preparing a meal when both Janice and Pat suddenly yelled: "Mum! It's Gran and Grampy!"

There was a knock, and Mabel opened the door. There was her mother, smiling, and a man who was unmistakably Grampy to the children: John Torode, dressed simply, wearing his trilby hat and his round, brown-framed glasses.

"You didn't expect us, did you?"

"Dad! Mum!" said Mabel, hugging her mother. "Come on in." She was almost crying, and so were Vi and Frances. The children watched the excitement and waited for Gran to greet them. Grampy observed, but didn't greet, small children.

"You were hard to find. We were in touch with the authorities through my work in Bolton," he said. "I found a job there through a contact from the Guernsey Tomato Export Board. But you changed your address, so it took a while to know where you were."

"Yes, we left Crown Point Hospital nearly two weeks ago."

Gran disappeared with Violet to ask her how she was.

They still had eight chairs and were quite glad of them today. Grampy put his hat and coat on one and they arranged the rest around the table. Mabel put the kettle on and counted cups.

"When did you get away from Guernsey, Dad?" Frances asked. "Was it the same day as we left? I thought you didn't want to…"

"We all left the day after you, the twenty-first," he said. "That was a long day. We had to walk almost half the way from home to the harbour, carrying our stuff."

"And what about Joyce, and Frank, and Bill, and Geoff?" Frances had mothered those younger siblings at weekends and every evening after her school day. She was especially close to Joyce, who was now nineteen.

"Well, Frank joined up. So, he probably came over here with the other volunteers."

Frances nodded. "Yes, we saw Fred. He said he and Frank were leaving together."

"Good. Anyway, next day, Bill and Geoff were at work in the greenhouses, so we called them in before dinner and we all decided to evacuate. Joyce got home from work, just as we were ready to go. She had to race around. We started walking and she caught up with us."

Gran was already back from talking to Vi and squeezed in a few words: "We were told: No luggage. Jump in any boat."

"We didn't bring much," Grampy continued. "I intended to settle your mother and Joyce and the boys in Weymouth somewhere, and go back home. Then we were all pushed into a train and landed up in Bolton. By the time I could turn around and go back to Guernsey, I was told there were no more boats leaving England. I had my tomatoes all ready for export…A really good crop this year…"

There was a sympathetic silence. He was top of the line as a tomato grower, and most of his year's income had just disappeared.

Mabel measured tea into the teapot. "Bolton? How far away is Bolton?" she asked.

"Towards Manchester. It's a bit more than an hour to get here. We managed to get on an Express bus this morning. But it was crowded."

"So, you're only an hour or so from Burnley," Mabel echoed. She made the tea and Vi and Frances put dinner together: scrambled eggs and bread, some cheese, sliced cucumber and radishes, and raisin buns. The guests and children were served first, the dishes quickly rinsed, and a second service was made for the sisters.

"You said you were working, Dad. What kind of work are you doing?" Mabel asked.

"Yes, it didn't take me long. We used to export tomatoes direct to Bolton. I've got a job looking after the Bolton cemetery gardens, five days a week. It's a huge area, on a hillside. Beautiful gardens. And Bill and Geoff are working there too, under me. They've added new land, they have a greenhouse, and they want us to plant vegetables wherever we can, so it's part of what they call 'war work.' The boys are underage for the army yet. And Joyce will find a job."

"So, there's five of you in your house," said Vi.

"The house has three bedrooms, and there's five of us right now."

"But we'll be seven soon," Gran added, "when we have Rose and Graham. They evacuated with their school. We found out where the school is, and they'll join us soon, so we'll have to stretch things a bit. We're not allowed to have more than seven people living there."

Rose and Graham were the children of their daughter Edie, who had died in childbirth in 1937. Gran and Grampy were their official guardians.

They ate, sipped their tea, and thought about things.

"Is this your day off, Dad, on Sunday?" asked Vi.

"Yes, but I can take most of the weekend off. We had to get up early to get a seat on an Express bus. I wanted to see how you girls were doing, as soon as we found your address…"

"And have you heard where Nellie is?" Frances asked.

"Yes. I was coming to that," Grampy said. His tone was a little hesitant. Both Mabel and Frances stared at him. "There's not something wrong, is there?" Mabel asked, almost in a whisper.

"No. Nothing wrong." He looked at Frances. "Now, Frances, Otto came to England on the last boat, on June 30th, just before the Germans took over. He managed to sign up as one of the crew. There were no more places for men or women on the boats. He traced Nellie and the children to Glasgow."

"Glasgow!" Vi gasped.

"So, Otto's here," said Frances. "And Arthur? Does he know anything about Arthur?"

"Well, this is what I was hesitating about. He said Arthur is still on the island."

Frances couldn't speak. Couldn't Arthur have signed up as crew also? Now she had to abandon her hope that he might still appear and rescue her from this whole evacuee nightmare.

Mabel patted her hand. "My Bob's there on the island too," she said. "And we're all here together."

"We've had a house full," her mother said. "Otto and Nellie and the children came to Bolton when they knew we were there. He has a contact in Nottingham and he went there and got a job. He and Nellie and the three children are all there now."

"So she'll have her baby in Nottingham," said Vi. "I hope she gets good care. They've been really good to me here. Fred wrote to say he'll have two days leave about a week after I've had the baby, and we'll go to Bradford."

They seemed to need another break to let all the news sink in. Mabel tidied away the dishes. Vi went to put her feet up on her bed.

How to find work

Mabel came back to the table and sat down. She lowered her voice. "Is Bolton bigger than Burnley, Mum? Dad, do you think jobs are easier to get there? We only have this house because Vi's living here and she's married to a soldier. When she leaves with Fred, Frances and I will have to move out."

"Fred's rented a small place in Bradford," Frances explained. "Vi will live there with the baby and Fred's mother. It's not big enough for us as well."

"Do you think we could find a job in Bolton?" Mabel asked her father. "Frances and I can share a place as long as one of us has a job, or we could be live-in housekeepers in different places."

"I heard that there are a lot of openings because the men are in the army," Grampy commented. "You couldn't live with us, though. We'll be stretched as far as we're allowed when Rose and Graham arrive."

"But if you want to come soon," said Gran, looking at Frances as well as Mabel, "either of you, while we have the space, you could stay for a couple of nights while you look for something. You'd have to bring your rations, though."

Frances felt her stomach turn over. More moving, more decisions.

Her father was looking at her, too.

"I'll look for jobs for you both, right away. If we find a likely job for either one of you, I'll write and let you know. The postal service is excellent and you'll get my letter in twenty-four hours. You must write back straight away or send me a telegram so I can try to keep the job open for you."

"One of you must stay with Vi, though," said her mother. Frances nodded. "Yes, I promised Fred. I'll stay till he comes."

"If you want to live in Bolton," her father continued, "it's best to find a live-in job because they're using houses in the slums for evacuees now, putting three or four women in one house. I don't think you should try that. We're also nearer to Manchester than you are here, and there are bombers flying over some nights. You have to go down the street in the dark to get into a bomb shelter. That's not easy with small children. The sirens go quite a lot."

They talked about the bombings and the buses. There were express buses almost every hour between Burnley and Bolton, and a slower route through Bury. Gran wanted to return on the six o'clock Express.

Frances and Mabel walked with them to the bus station, and looked at the route map indoors on the wall. Bradford was east of them in Yorkshire, separated by a vast round area of high moorland which the roads circled around. Bolton was south, just this side of Manchester, less than twenty miles away. Saying goodbye wasn't so difficult when you knew how to connect with each other.

Mabel looks for a job

On the following Wednesday, July 26, the postman stopped outside and looked at their number. Janice and Pat, always on watch, yelled, "Postman!" and Mabel was suddenly there and picked up the letter that dropped through the postbox.

"It's from Dad," she said.

Aloud, she read: "There's an older woman looking for a live-in housekeeper. It's all right if you have one child who's not a baby, but not more than one. All right for Mabel. Nice house. Frances, we'll look for something for you. Mabel, if you're interested, write back or send a telegram. I will let them know. If you want it, come on Friday and we'll see them Saturday."

Frances was in shock. She realised that if Mabel accepted the invitation, she would have to cope with Vi going in to hospital alone, as well as looking after the girls.

"Wait a bit longer, Mabel," she pleaded with her sister, "at least till Vi has had her baby. I can't cope with that and my two children as well."

But Mabel was firm: "I don't want to leave you when Vi's baby is due," she said, "but it might be the beginning of a job for me, and I can look for work for you. After Vi's gone with Fred, you must come to Bolton. Mum and Dad will make room for you for a couple of nights, like they said. At least we'll all be near each other."

Within an hour, she had sent a telegram to say she was coming. Then they all walked to the bus station so she could buy a ticket to Bolton for Friday morning. Pat would travel free. They discussed how Frances would manage while Mabel was gone, and also if she didn't return, and if she found a job for Frances. Anything was possible.

Next morning in the park, they talked to one of their Guernsey friends, Gladys. Her daughter June was the same age as Lynette and the two little girls often played together. She shared a house with two other mothers in the next street to them.

"Don't worry, I'll look after your girls when Vi has to go to the hospital," she said. "We're just around the corner." Later, they all walked back to the house that she shared so that the girls would be familiar with it when the time came.

Two days later, on Friday morning, Frances and Janice walked to the bus station with Mabel and Pat, helping them with their luggage, while Vi watched over Lynette and started packing her bag for hospital. She packed the rest of her possessions in her suitcase, ready for her move to Bradford.

Within a few days, a letter arrived from Mabel to say she had the job; and she and Grampy were looking for work for Frances. The next day, Vi started to feel birthing pains at dinner time. Frances took the girls to Gladys and went with Vi to the hospital. The following day, August 2, their next visitor arrived: a baby boy who would be called David.

6: Goodbye to Vi

*Visiting Vi—Fred comes to Hawthorne Road—A silent house—
Guernsey under Occupation—Commando raids*

Visiting Vi

For the next two afternoons, Frances visited Vi and was relieved to find her in good spirits and very absorbed in being a new mother. David was doing well. There were two new mothers from Guernsey in her ward, so they had been able to share their experiences of the last few months.

"We talk together a lot, Frances," Vi said to her on the second day. "I'm getting used to it all, so don't come tomorrow. You and Gladys have enough to do, and the nurses are very good."

"Well as long as you're sure, I'll look after June tomorrow afternoon and give Gladys some time off," Frances said. "I know she's looking for a job. I'll come in the day after that."

When Frances next went to the hospital, Vi told her that Fred would arrive in a couple of days, probably early in the morning, and he would take her and the baby to Bradford.

"His mother's there getting things ready for me," she said. "Now, I left all my stuff in my suitcase, ready for him to pick up at the house."

Frances nodded.

"I won't be able to come with him, and I don't want you to visit me tomorrow. You have enough to worry about. I want to say goodbye to you now and thank you for staying here and being with me. I hope you find a job in Bolton and then you can be near Mum and Dad and everyone."

They were both in tears.

"You gave me the address, Vi. I'll write to you."

"And once we're settled, you must all come and visit."

They hugged each other and Frances left to collect the girls from Gladys.

Fred comes to Hawthorne Road

On Wednesday, August 8, Frances was drying the breakfast dishes when she was startled by Janice calling: "Mum! There's a soldier coming here, and, I think, yes, it's Uncle Fred!"

A knock on the door confirmed that someone was there, and there were smiles as Fred entered. He was wearing his khaki uniform and had a huge grin.

Frances was overjoyed to see him, and congratulated him on the birth of his son, almost in tears.

"Frances, I can't thank you enough…"

"Fred, you and Vi helped me so much when I had Lynette, when you looked after Janice. I'm glad I've been able to help."

"You know, it seems like an age since you and Vi boarded the mailboat. I knew she'd be all right with you and Mabel. Now, Vi told me that you'll have to move again. If my tiny house was big enough, Frances, I'd invite you and the children to stay with us. But it's only got one bedroom, and we're stretching it for my mum to stay with us."

"I know, Fred. I understand."

"Now, just a minute, I've got something here…" He touched one finger to his lips and looked at the girls as though it was a secret from them, and quietly laid a paper bag next to the sink.

"There's two pieces of chocolate cake in there that I managed to get from the cafeteria," he murmured to Frances. "I know Janice likes that."

She smiled. "Nothing works better than that. They'll share it after dinner. Now, I'll put the kettle on. Can I make you some toast?"

"No thank you, Frances. I've been travelling all night and I went straight to the hospital from the train. They let me have breakfast in the cafeteria after I'd seen Vi. By the way, I have news of Frank for you. He located Adele in Halifax and he's rented a house there. Her mother evacuated with her. I think he and Adele are planning to be married when he can get a few days' leave."

"That's wonderful. Give them my congratulations when you see him, Fred. Halifax! That's not too far from Bradford, is it? Perhaps they'll be able to visit Vi."

"Well at least the bus services are better than in Guernsey! Now, you tell me all your news. I hear that your Mum and Dad visited."

She told him about their visit, and Mabel and Pat's departure.

"Do you think you'll be able to stay here, perhaps find somebody else to share with? Or will you go to Bolton?"

"I don't know. Bolton's nearer to Manchester and the bombing, isn't it? I just don't know. I wish Mabel hadn't gone."

Fred took both of her hands in his. "If only I could help. I'll tell Vi and my mum to look out for something for you in Bradford."

"How are you going to get to Bradford with Vi and the baby, Fred?"

"They've arranged for us to go by car with someone else who has to go there. We must leave at eleven, so I had better take Vi's suitcase and go back to the hospital."

He fished out two coins from his pocket, squatted down and offered them to the girls: "Here's sixpence each for Mummy to buy you a bun at the bakery."

Janice looked at Frances, who smiled and nodded. Lynette followed her and they approached the outstretched hands and shyly picked up the silver coins that were offered.

Five minutes later, a soldier left Number 5, Hawthorne Road, carrying a suitcase and a bag, and walked briskly down the road. Frances was on her own.

She vaguely answered the children's questions about when Uncle Fred was coming back with Auntie Vi and the new baby, and when they would go to the bakery. She wished she could cry and let the distress flow out of her. She must do something, anything, and stop thinking.

"We're going to have an early dinner, and then we'll go to the park," she told them.

She made dinner, and the chocolate cake was the high point of their day. After that she ordered herself around like a sergeant-major: pack the pram, talk to Gladys, perhaps look after June for the afternoon, go to the park…

A silent house

That night the house felt empty. Frances longed for a radio and envied Mabel being in a real home, Vi and Fred arriving in their new place with their first child, and Nellie with the children and Otto all together. Now, after the children were in bed, there was nobody to talk to in the silence.

"But who looks after me?" she had whispered to herself, when she watched Fred walk away from her that morning, carrying Vi's suitcase so easily. "But who looks after me?" The words repeated themselves all day like an echo in her head. She knew that Arthur wouldn't appear, and she could only count on herself. She must make the decisions, as Mabel had done, and find a place to live.

She knew where she didn't want to live. The rows of grey houses in Burnley reminded her of the rows of long greenhouses that she had lived amongst as a child, and that she had grown to hate.

Grampy had learned how to grow tomatoes from his father, whom everyone called Old John Torode. Like his father, Grampy lived in the flat northern part of Guernsey and worked as manager of a large vinery, a group of greenhouses dedicated to growing tomatoes for the English market.

Being a grower was what Grampy was good at. He even built two greenhouses on his own property, which took away the garden space but added extra revenue for his family of twelve children. His precious Muscat vine at the end of one greenhouse was pruned only by himself or by Frances, when she was older. The view from their home consisted of the road, low granite walls, and greenhouses in every direction. A few flowers might be squeezed into a corner.

Perhaps part of Arthur's attraction was that he wasn't a grower. Working with his fisherman father as soon as he was able to leave school, he liked fresh air and the view of a far-off horizon. Before he and Frances married, they had paid a deposit on a simple cottage overlooking Fermain Bay, in the southern upland part of the island. Surrounded by trees, and with a view across cliffs to the headlands near Jerbourg, and across the sea towards Jersey, no greenhouses spoiled the view. Perhaps that view of the bay was why she liked the walks by the reservoir.

Now Frances remembered what Annie had said to her, about finding a billet outside of Burnley. She knew she didn't want to share some run-down house in the grey city with unknown evacuees who had as little as she did. Sharing a house in a village seemed a better idea, if she could find someone willing to take them in.

She thought back to the big map at the bus station. Bolton was very close to Manchester, which was a target for German bombers. Vi had gone east to Bradford, which was very close to Leeds, another large bombing target. On the map the moorland had stretched nicely around Burnley in all directions, and there was a scattering of villages, including Clowbridge. Up on the moors the air was clean. She decided to return to Clowbridge the next day. She knew Sarellen and Annie, and would ask if they knew anyone who was interested in offering her a billet.

After the children were asleep, she went outside to make sure no chinks of light were showing between the curtains. There was a three-quarter moon. She remembered the full moon shining across Fermain Bay the night before they had left. It had seemed calm and quiet like tonight, but she was as troubled now as she was then.

Was Arthur outside tonight, looking across Fermain Bay and wondering what had happened to her and the girls? Should she have evacuated? Would it have been better for her and the children to remain on the island? Would they have been living a reasonable life, even with the restrictions that the enemy imposed?

Guernsey under Occupation

In Guernsey that night, Arthur was sleeping at Woodlands as usual, hoping that his presence would help to deter pilferers. There was a curfew from eleven to six, but that didn't stop anyone from snooping around houses, whether locals or Jerries[7].

He continued to look after his potatoes and carrots, planted on small terraces well out of sight of the house; but he had moved his chickens to Pa and Ma's house as soon as Frances and the girls left, and he ate all his meals with them.

His sister Emily had joined them after her house in the town had been requisitioned for the use of German officers. Pa's rented house, called *Le Pré*, was located on Havelet Road, where the higher southern half of the island sloped down to Havelet Bay and St Peter Port. It was conveniently near Pa's fishing boat, moored on the south side of the harbour. The four of them were registered for rations at the same shop and ate together. There was always someone in the house during the day to watch over food, the house, chickens, and the garden.

"With all these Germans on the island, I can't find bacon in the shops anymore," Emily had said that morning, when Arthur only had one egg on his plate for breakfast, along with a fried tomato. "But the tomatoes and grapes are cheap since they can't be exported to England now."

Arthur made no comment. Tomatoes were plentiful, but it was hard to

---

7   Common name for Germans.

eat even one of them after the tomato trucks had been bombed on June 28. He knew a couple of the drivers who had been killed.

"We might as well enjoy what's cheap while we can," said her mother. "What I don't like is this heavy bread that the bakers are selling us these days. It's hard to digest. It would be better to bake our own bread."

"There was no flour and no yeast in town anywhere yesterday, Ma, but I'll have a good search again next time. Perhaps they haven't organised imports from France yet."

"If we could get French flour, then I could make bread." Ma dipped a piece of bread into her tea to soften it. "I'll ask the others at the Women's Fellowship meeting at Trinity, tomorrow. There must surely be some other kind of bread being made. Who's looking after our food?" she asked.

"It's the Controlling Committee[8]," Emily said. "Sherwill—the Attorney General—is the President, because the Bailiff's a bit too old to cope, or so I hear. There's a committee to look after potato production, another for greenhouse production, and one for general farming."

"I hope they know what they're doing." Ma sounded doubtful.

"They're all Guernsey men. A couple of them go to Granville to export our tomatoes to France, and buy food that we need. The Germans seem to have arranged shipping from there."

"I don't think we'll see bananas or sugar or tea for a while," was Ma's conclusion. Emily shrugged her shoulders.

The conversation continued after Arthur left for work. Emily tried to be more cheerful.

"Well, Ma, at least Arthur's still got his job, and with four of us here we can manage our rations together. I know you can't get around on the buses to see your family in Cobo, but you've got your friends from Trinity around here, like I have. Thank goodness I have Louise's bike, and I can pick up our rations with it."

"That bike is a godsend. I hope Louise is all right with her school children in England. I'm glad they got away before the Jerries landed."

"Yes. She would have been furious to see Germans taking over our house."

"I hope they won't take over Otto's house as well."

---

8   The Committee replaced the States of Guernsey for the period of the German Occupation.

"Otto's house isn't big or central enough, and it's too near the rocky hill behind it; and Arthur's isn't big enough for them to use. I wish he'd sleep here though."

"Yes. I know he wants to look after his property and his potatoes, but I'd feel better if he slept here as well."

Commando raids

In July, British commandos landed at a rocky cove near Petit Bot Bay on the south coast of the island. Part of the two hundred steps leading down to the Bay were damaged after shooting occurred. Soon after, Arthur's younger brother, Walter, was told to move out of his cottage, which was below Woodlands and very near the beach at Fermain. Arthur and Charlie and a few others had helped Walter and his wife Mahala to move out. Their cottage blocked a proposed line of anti-aircraft fire, and it would be demolished.

Mahala was upset. "I'm glad Mollie was evacuated," she said. "She loved living near the beach and we'd made a little garden together."

"You'd better watch out for Woodlands," Walter advised Arthur. "You have a good view of the coast and you could be receiving signals from commandos up there."

Arthur agreed. From Woodlands he could see right across to Jersey on a rare, fine day. The Jerries already had a manned strongpoint on the headland opposite, and access to Fermain Bay for civilians was now forbidden. His own small boat had been taken from its sheltered moorings at Bec du Nez, just north of Fermain, and had been smashed.

He was still an employee of Leale Ltd, Engineers & Ironmongers, but there wasn't much demand for plumbers anymore. Sometimes he was called on to drive a company lorry to move furniture for people whose houses had been requisitioned for German officers or troops.

Some of the Jerries he had to deal with spoke English: "We enjoy being on your beautiful island," one had told him. "We will be in England in a few weeks, but I would like to come back here." He had grunted a reply. Every evening, German bombers met up and circled around over the island's airport before heading north to bomb English towns. They were expecting to achieve their goal of making England surrender.

He would soon have to handle the new currency—Reichsmarks—but he didn't want to touch it: *dirty money* was the word for it. Guernsey money seemed precious in comparison. Petrol wasn't easy to obtain now, and bus services had been cancelled or reduced. He relied on his bike. Fortunately, they still drove on the left-hand side of the road, but doubtless it would soon be changed to the right.

He had to be careful on the roads. The Jerries had requisitioned every car less than five years old and some of them enjoyed driving fast in the latest models. They might requisition lorries as well. They needed drivers like him: drivers who knew the island's narrow roads and their confusing French names. The Jerries offered a meal during the day as well as the best wages; but as long as Leale's could employ him, Arthur would avoid working for the occupiers. He must now play the man's part in his new family, and they must endure this together.

7: Flitting Burnley

*The question of billeting—Annie's proposal—Tea with the Howarths—
A tour of 8, Cotton Row—Flitting Burnley*

The question of billeting

Next morning the children reacted well to Frances' plan to go to Clowbridge. They had already decided that Uncle Fred's sixpences would be spent on custard tarts, and they liked riding on the bus. Frances promised that when they were bigger, they would ride upstairs on the double-decker. They got off at Clowbridge and headed for the bakery. Two customers were inside, and Frances waited for them to leave before she went in.

She bought four custard tarts.

"Who's the other one for?" Janice asked, not missing a thing.

"We might share one later."

This time, she had a longer chat with Sarellen, explaining that she was looking for a billet. Sarellen already knew the government allowance that went with it, and used the words, "Yes, luv," and said that she would ask around. Frances took note of the "yes, luv." It implied more sympathy from Sarellen than she had received before.

They planned to eat their tarts by the reservoir, unless Annie was in her garden. Beyond the church, they watched sheep through a large gate in the stone wall. On the other side of the road, the reservoir reflected blue, and a curlew flew by. Quiet, calm. The reservoir looked like a small, natural lake. She liked the view of the water.

Annie was looking at her rose bushes with Dinah for company. "I just came back from shopping," she said. "Our Hilda's gone out. Have you time for a cup of tea?"

Frances nodded. "I just bought some custard tarts," she said.

"I'll put the kettle on," Annie continued. "Yes, come on in, Janice, and I'll get you a spoon."

They took chairs outside, and the tea was welcome. Annie didn't want a tart but said she'd like to keep it to go with her dinner, so the gift was made. Frances was busy for a while cleaning up Lynette's efforts with her tart.

"Excuse me for saying this, but you've got a bit of a worried look about you," Annie said. "Did your sister have her baby yet? Is she all right?"

"Well, I am worried," said Frances, "but Vi is all right." She explained that Vi was now in Bradford.

"Mabel's gone as well," she continued. "My father found her a job in Bolton. I really don't want to stay in Burnley. I'd prefer to find a billet outside in the country. That's why I came along here today. You said last time you might know someone…"

"Yes, there's a few people interested…"

"I could go to Bolton also. My father and my sister are looking for a job for me there. I was just talking to Sarellen about it, too."

"Oh, yes? Well, she'd know a few… I'll ask around."

The children played outside the garden wall in the lane that led up to the hill behind. Janice was selecting stones and piling them between the railings according to colour and size. Annie asked about the government allowance, and where they shopped for their rations.

A woman came out of the end house and walked towards them with a boy almost Janice's age.

"This is our Alice-Ann," said Annie, "and Peter."

Peter had already gone to see what the girls were doing.

"Pleased to meet you," said Alice-Ann. "Annie, I'm just going up to the farm to see if they have any eggs to spare. Do you want a few?"

"You'll be lucky if he has any. I'll have up to six if he's got any, but one or two'll be good as well."

Peter preferred to stay and play.

"Can he stay for a bit?" asked Alice-Ann. "I'll be back in about ten minutes."

"Yes. That's all right," Annie said. She walked over to the wall and looked at Peter, who was walking a toy sheep along the wall, and in a slightly sterner voice she said, "Now, you play nicely, Peter. I don't want any trouble."

Peter nodded without a word and Alice-Ann disappeared up the lane.

"I like to make sure he's behaving himself," Annie said softly to Frances. "He's been really spoilt, that one. His father's a shepherd and not always at home."

They discussed food, and Frances told her that her father and brothers were growing vegetables in Bolton.

"They're talking about doing that in Burnley," Annie said. "They say more people should grow vegetables, and there are two big parks there. Is your father a gardener?"

Frances told her about her father's growing business and the lost tomato crop.

"Well, you should know a bit about gardening too," Annie observed.

"We all have gardens in Guernsey. But with small children you don't get a lot of time to work in them. Arthur does the potatoes."

"Well, your children behave well. There's not many that are as good as those two."

By now, they were outside in the lane watching the children.

"Anyway," Annie concluded, "I'll ask around for you. Now, where exactly are you living? What's the address?"

Between them, they found a scrap of paper and a pencil, and Frances wrote it down for her; then it was time to clean up the children, pack up the pushcart and catch a bus back to the house on Hawthorne Road.

Annie's proposal

Next day was Sunday, and Frances took the children to the park in the morning. They missed Pat and Mabel, and it helped to see Gladys and June and the others. Janice joined a group with a skipping rope. Someone had bought a newspaper, and it seemed that the Luftwaffe was bombing airfields and factories all over south-east England.

They had just returned to the house when Janice announced that someone was coming to the door: "It's that lady where we ate our custard tarts."

It was Annie.

"Can I come in?" she said. "I've got a proposal for you."

It was Frances' turn to play host. She welcomed Annie inside, where the eight chairs and one small table were duly noted.

"I'll put the kettle on," she said. At least she still had a kettle, teapot, cups, and some tea.

"Well, are those your cards? When was your birthday?" she heard Annie ask Janice. Four birthday cards were on display on one of the chairs, with a few choice pebbles. Lynette's bunny was lying on another chair under the small towel that Annie had given her two weeks ago.

Frances wondered if Annie was visiting on behalf of a friend or for one of Sarellen's contacts, trying to find out about her: did the place look clean? Were the children dirty? How did she respond to having a visitor? And what kind of place had the authorities entrusted to her and her sisters?

It turned out differently. Annie talked frankly with her, offering her a billet in her own house, in exchange for Frances' allowance and doing some housekeeping.

"Hilda will be moving out to get married at some time," she said, "and we have to work shifts at the factory in Clowbridge. I might have to start at eleven at night or seven in the morning. I don't want to have to come home and start shopping and cooking after that."

Of course, it would have to be registered with the authorities.

"Aren't there other jobs with more daytime hours?" Frances asked.

"Not around here; mebbe somewhere else, if you want to move. I don't want to move. My job is called war work, so I do it; and if I didn't like it, they could make me join the army or send me somewhere else to work."

"Where do you buy your food?" Frances asked.

"We have a Co-op in Clowbridge, near the mill," said Annie. "But we have to get our meat rations in Burnley like you do. And then we like to shop in the Burnley market on a Saturday. Listen, I understand you've got two children to look after as well. I can always pick up some food at the Co-op in Clowbridge after work and bring it home. My shift finishes at four at the moment."

Frances was glad to hear the children mentioned; but she knew that her allocation money would be paid directly to Annie, and they would need to discuss how it was spent.

"Well, Annie, I'm interested," she said. "Why don't I come to see you, and you can show me around your house, and we can talk again."

"Of course. For myself, I talked it over with my sister Dora and my brother Tom this afternoon. They thought it could be a good idea, if we want to work it out between us. They want to meet you and the children as well. And you'll be wanting to look over the house."

Tea with the Howarths

A few days later, when Annie had an afternoon off, the visit was made. Frances packed Teddy, some milk, and a doll, in the pushcart. Janice carried a bag with her small drawing book and four crayons. They got off the bus at Crown Point Road, and with the weather remaining dry and warm, Frances enjoyed the walk between the hills and the reservoir. By the time they arrived at Cotton Row Lynette was asleep, as she had hoped.

After being enthusiastic about seeing the reservoir and a lapwing, Lynette settled down and was asleep before they reached the house. Annie was watching for them, and they quietly put the pushcart inside the front door.

There was a murmur of conversation from two women at the table, and Annie introduced them as our Dora, her sister, and Mary, her sister-in-law. She had placed a biscuit and some milk on a small table for Janice, who settled down shyly to do some colouring, and some listening. Frances took her place at the table and a full teapot was brought into action. Conversation was a bit hesitant at first but soon flowed easily.

Dora was white-haired, delicate, and wore a lightweight black coat over her dress. Her clothes, well-made shoes, and a beautiful ring emphasised her marriage to the mill's manager; Frances would learn later that Dora had her own milliner's shop before she married. Dora was quiet, thoughtful, and seemed satisfied with what Frances said. Mary was more down to earth and friendly, but let the sisters do the talking. It seemed to go well. Janice answered a few questions, and Lynette slept through most of it.

A tour of 8, Cotton Row

After Dora and Mary left, Annie showed Frances around the house. The two rows of houses at Cotton Row had been built for the mill workers who paid rent to the company. It didn't offer much, but it was a home, clean, and lived in. Frances felt almost joyful when she saw Annie's sewing machine; and to see the radio was an added comfort.

The living room had two windows next to each other, with regular curtains and frames for blackout curtains. Hanging from the ceiling along the oppposite wall was a *maiden*, a long clothes rack that could be raised above the heads of the family. Clothing that had partly dried outdoors could be hung on the narrow slats until it dried completely or was properly aired. A sofa and an armchair filled the spaces around the table and chairs.

The most important item and focus of the room was a large and complicated black, coal-burning fireplace with a space in front of it that was surrounded by a polished metal grate. The fire in the middle heated a tank of water on the left, and an oven on the right. The narrow mantelpiece above it carried a clock.

"I noticed you were looking at my sewing machine," Annie said. "Have you ever used one?"

"Yes. I've got a Singer machine at home. Would you let me use it? It would be a big help to alter clothes for the children, whenever I can find some."

"Well, you're welcome to use it if you know what you're doing."

Annie took her into the kitchen, where they had previously made jam. There was a large dresser across the narrow end of the kitchen on the left. At the other end was a wide cupboard under the stairs. There was a white stone sink under the window and opposite was the gas stove, where they had made the jam. A table and two chairs were set in the middle, with open shelves nearby where Annie kept her baking trays.

"I worked at Sarellen's when I was young," Annie said. "The bakery belonged to somebody else then. But I can bake some pies and pastries when I have a mind to."

Frances was surprised to find that Annie was a little younger than she looked. She had a plain but open face, tied back her hair severely, and said she had turned thirty-two last January. Frances would be thirty-four in October. Frances guessed that Annie's family life in this small village had perhaps been tough.

They went out of the back door. The yard was walled in. Across from them was a small gate that opened on to a path that went right along the back of the four houses. Beyond the path was meadowland sloping up to the moor behind.

To the left of the gate, Annie showed Frances the outhouse toilet, concealed behind a full-sized wooden door. To the right of the gate was a stone-built shelter called the washhouse, where a large container, a copper, was housed. It sat on a firebox which burned wood or coal to heat the water. A heavy mangle stood next to it. The coalman delivered the ration of coal here in hundredweight (100 pound) bags, from which a coal scuttle was filled and carried to the fireplace. Between the washhouse and the kitchen door was a space with two or three hardy roses in it, and cement paths connecting things up.

They went back inside. "Now we'll have a look upstairs," Annie said.

A flight of narrow stairs led up from the end of the kitchen. She pointed to the cupboard-like space under the stairs. "If there's an air-raid, this is where we come," she said. "It's quick to get out of bed and just come downstairs here, and there's a bench to sit on."

By this time Lynette had woken up, and they took the girls upstairs with them. At the top of the stairs at the back of the house, there was a space just big enough to hold a single bed and a small chest of drawers, under the slope of the roof. One tiny window faced the field and moor behind the house. This was where Hilda would sleep, if she wasn't sleeping at Alice-Ann's. The floor seemed to have a slight slope.

Separated by a door, the front bedroom was relatively spacious, with both a double and a single bed in it. There was a small fireplace, a chest of drawers, and a wardrobe. The double windows faced east, overlooking the road and the reservoir beyond.

"Janice could sleep in the single bed, and Mary's got a small bed that we can put in here for Lynette," Annie said. "As I explained, you and I will have to share the double bed. I hope that's all right. In winter, it helps to warm up the bed, even if we've both got hot water bottles."

Janice looked at the small bed.

"You can lie down on it and see if it feels big enough for you," Annie suggested. "And then come over and look out of the windows. You can see right across the reservoir from up here."

Both girls tested the small bed and then looked at the view from the two windows.

"I can see the roses by your front door," Janice observed "and Dinah's down there. Where does she sleep?"

Annie laughed. She stays downstairs by the fireplace, and then she comes upstairs. She's got her own bed near the top of the stairs."

After that, they walked down the Burnley Road to the church, which was used as a primary school during the week. Janice would attend school here if Frances accepted Annie's offer. Annie showed her the entrance to the younger children's classroom on the moorland side.

Someone said hello to Annie and chatted with her while Frances followed Janice, who was wheeling her sister in the push-cart around the playground. Frances noted a line of flush toilets outside the building. On the other side was some sort of camouflaged air-raid shelter, half hidden by a grassy cover.

She heard a sheep bleating up on the hillside. Annie's conversation ended and the woman smiled towards Frances as she walked away. She was wearing clogs.

Frances wondered if she might be jumping out of the frying pan and into the fire, as her mother might have put it, but at least the fire seemed to be manageable at this point. She liked Annie's family ties with her sisters and her interest in the children, and she knew that her government allowance would be worth quite a bit to Annie and that might give her some leverage. At the worst, she would have to return to Burnley or go to Bolton.

They walked back and discussed the government allowance, Annie's contribution, food and rent, and pocket money. Frances noted down the main points of their agreement, and it was done. Annie said she would come to help her move next Saturday.

Flitting Burnley

Next morning, Frances took the girls to the evacuee centre to inform them of her intended move. Knowing of Vi and Mabel's departure, they had already sent a letter to her, saying that she would need to move by the end of the month. After that, they stopped in the park, and she found Gladys and told her the news while the children played.

That evening, she wrote to her father and described her agreement with Annie and gave him her address. She ended her letter: "I'll move in next weekend, August 24th. Can you come and visit us here in a week or two, as soon as you can spare the time?"

She badly needed him to visit, to have his backing and for him to meet Annie. At least she had found a way forward for now. Suddenly, she felt so relieved that she almost cried.

For the next few days, Frances looked for clothing at the WVS, and knitted after the children were in bed. At least she had a plan now. Sewing alterations could wait until she could use Annie's machine. She kept the letter from the evacuee office telling her to move because it was official, but it was now more of a souvenir.

Her father wrote back the day he received her letter. He would come to Cotton Row on the first Saturday of September. She was relieved. His presence would add that extra support she needed. It was as though someone was looking after her, after all.

A second letter, written in green ink, came from a WVS lady. She apologised for the non-delivery of the small chair and buffet. It had been sent to Number 4 Hawthorne Road by mistake, where there were several children.

Frances smiled. So not only did Number 4 receive sheets, but also the chair and buffet which they weren't supposed to. Well, she didn't mind now. It must have seemed like Christmas at Number 4 that day.

On Saturday afternoon, Annie arrived at Hawthorne Road as promised, bringing an empty suitcase. It was a good thing the Manchester Road bus stop wasn't far away. Gladys came to help them, and carried the Guernsey suitcase so that Frances could handle the pushcart with Lynette. Janice did her bit, carrying her winter coat and doll. A double-decker was there ten minutes later.

"Going for a holiday, are we?" asked the bus conductor, stowing the pushcart and suitcases under the stairs.

"Nay, we're flitting," Annie replied. "Moving this lady to Cotton Row. I wouldn't mind going on a holiday, though."

"It'll be a while yet before we can go on a holiday. There's been a lot more bombing and fighting in the south again. Battle of Britain, they call it. "

Frances marshalled the children on to a seat and felt a wave of relief knowing that they had left the rows of grey houses behind them.

8: Settling in at Cotton Row

*The budget—The blue pram—Grampy visits Cotton Row—Washing days—
A stolen crop, orders to move & an escape*

The budget

In the week that followed their flitting, there was plenty of discussion about shopping and meals. Frances received an allowance of 32 shillings a week: 15 shillings for one adult, and 8 shillings and sixpence for each child under eight years of age[9]. It would be paid to Annie. She would contribute one pound per week and Frances would manage it all to pay the rent, food, and coal as part of her housekeeping duties. If Hilda stayed on for a while, she would contribute a similar amount.

Annie said she really couldn't manage before, when it was just her and Hilda, and was glad to give Frances the job of housekeeping. Frances felt that Annie was quite capable of doing a good job, and probably intended to keep a close eye on what she did. Frances would do the major tasks of the weekly wash, preparing the main meal each weekday, and looking after purchases of rations in Burnley, and they would work out the rest between them.

Frances insisted on six pennies of pocket money for each child, and one and six (eighteen pennies) for herself, each week. Working out meals on a budget would be a challenge, but she had plenty of experience trying to live on Arthur's earnings as a fisherman when they were first married. She would find out what extra food she could obtain locally, like the eggs that Alice-Ann had gone to buy. With a ration of only one or two eggs per week per person, about 3 ounces of meat, and not much milk, she wanted to find more for the children especially.

The autumn term had already started. Annie was on the St. James school committee and knew the two teachers well. She went with Frances to meet Linda Taylor, who would be Janice's teacher. Linda was young, and she was sympathetic to their evacuee status. She taught the younger class, about

---

[9] G. Mawson: Guernsey Evacuees, p 45

twelve students of various ages.

Her schoolroom was attached to the moorland side of the church. It had a large fireplace on one side and a big blackboard in front. There were no pencils or paper: the children used slate boards, like a small, framed piece of blackboard, and wrote with thin slate "pencils" which left a fine mark on the slate. A cloth, or the side of one's sleeve, easily rubbed off slate marks. There were very few books.

A large door at the back of this room led into the church itself. Here the older children sat at tables behind several rows of pews. Miss Scanlon was the teacher, large and forbidding in long black skirts. She was strict and kept a cane which she used occasionally on a naughty boy's hand; adults knew her as kind and helpful.

Four times a day in the first week, Frances walked back and forth to school with both children. During that time Annie talked to Mrs Newsham, their neighbour at Number 4, whose nine-year-old daughter Margaret attended the school, and she walked with Janice from then on. Peter sometimes went with them but preferred not to be seen with girls.

The blue pram

There were no other young children at Cotton Row, and Lynette had few toys to play with. One day Annie came home from work with an old doll's pram under her arm. She quietly walked up the lane before the children noticed her, and went around the back to hide the pram in the washhouse. She had asked around at work for any discarded toys, and this had turned up. She cleaned it up quietly and on the following Saturday morning she secretly painted it.

On Sunday morning after breakfast, she produced a camera, having promised Lynette that there would be a surprise for her.

"I've still got a few pictures left on my film," she told Frances. "While the sun's out, let's get Mrs Newsham to take a picture of us all."

"I'll go and ask her," said Hilda, who had just dropped in. Taking a photograph was quite an event.

"And if it's all right with her, ask Alice-Ann and Peter to come, too."

Hilda returned with news that they would all be there in ten minutes. Outside in the field, Frances, Annie, Hilda, and their sister Alice-Ann posed behind Janice, Lynette, and Peter. Peter wasn't sure he liked doing this sort of thing.

Annie wanted another photo of her with Lynette and Dinah, and that was done, although from Lynette's expression she had had enough, and really wanted to see the surprise that Auntie Annie had promised her, and which was hiding in the back yard somewhere. Annie wasn't sure that the paint was fully dry yet.

It seemed to be a gift well worth waiting for. After she saw the pram, Lynette was so enthused that she had to find her Teddy and place him in it right away. Two more photos were taken of her tucking him up and beaming across at the photographer. She could invent a lot more games for herself with a pram. Frances saw how much pleasure Annie had, both from creating the gift and giving it, and that was encouraging.

Having a wireless was a luxury, after the silence of Hawthorne Road. Frances heard nothing about the Channel Islands but plenty about the bombing of British airfields and factories all over southeastern England, up to London and the Thames, as the Battle of Britain was fought. Even those accounts were delayed or vague, to avoid letting the enemy hear details of the damage it had caused. She soon learned the new vocabulary of war: the wonderful Spitfires and Hurricanes rescuing the country, and the nasty Messerschmitts and Junkers raiding and bombing.

Grampy visits Cotton Row

On the first Saturday morning of September, Grampy was due to arrive. The children were on the lookout, watching every bus from Burnley which appeared on the road. Just before eleven o'clock a bus stopped across the road, and when it moved on, Janice recognised a familiar figure wearing a trilby, glasses, and carrying a mac over his arm.

"He's here! He's here!"

The figure looked at the reservoir, at the houses and the moor behind, noted the number outside the door, and crossed over.

Frances opened the door, walked out briskly through the garden and met him on the pavement.

"Oh Dad, thank you for coming."

"Well, you're in the country all right," he said. "It's a lot cooler here. I almost put my mac on."

"We were told it's a thousand feet above sea level, when we were at

Crown Point," said Frances. She pointed north of the reservoir. "It's just up the road, up there."

"And that's where you first arrived? At the isolation hospital?"

"Yes. And there's the reservoir."

"Your bit of blue water. Well, it's all very good if you don't want to be bombed. I can't see anything worth bombing around here. Before we go in, is everything all right?"

"I think it's going to work out all right."

They had a look at the flowers in the front garden while the children watched at the window, and Annie appeared at the door.

"You must be Grampy," she said, and they shook hands. "I'm Annie, Annie Howarth. Come on in. Should I call you Grampy too?"

He laughed. "If you like. And what do I call you?"

"I'm Annie to everybody."

Frances had a hundred questions. "Dad, have you heard from Vi? And Nellie?"

"Now, let me sit down. Yes, a cup of tea would be fine, Annie, thank you. And I'll give you all the news I've got."

They had tea, and Grampy remembered he had a letter from Vi to share with Frances. She and David were doing well. Her mother-in-law was helping her and they were getting used to the dialect and to Bradford. Grampy said that Mabel had settled into her new job, and the woman she worked for had accepted Pat very well. Rose and Graham were now living in Bolton with them, so the house was really full. Bill and Geoff had settled down to work in Bolton's cemetery gardens, and Joyce had found a job.

"Have you heard anything from Frank?"

"Yes. He's located Adele and her mother. They were evacuated to Halifax. Since he's in the army, he's rented a house there. He and Adele are planning to get married when he's on leave."

"Yes, that's what Fred said. Have you heard any news from Guernsey, Dad?"

He shook his head. "It seems to be quiet there. Don't worry. We'd hear if there was something important going on."

They could hear Annie talking to someone at the back door.

He put his hands on hers. "Listen," he said quietly. "You're safe here. Just look after the children and yourself. Arthur's looking after your place in

Guernsey. Bolton isn't that far from Manchester, so we may not be as safe as you are here. Vi's not far from Leeds, and that may be another big target for German bombers. So she's not as well placed as you are either."

Dinner was as simple as all meals were these days, but it felt special to Frances, having her father there. He recommended they find a plot where they could grow their own potatoes and vegetables. Annie was intrigued with his tales of buying and selling produce when he took an occasional day trip to a French port near Guernsey or to Weymouth in summer.

"And did you buy apricots when you went to France?" she asked. "I like apricot jam."

He laughed. "So does her mother," he said, indicating Frances. "But I always bought a lot, wholesale, so we always had a good price. That was in Granville or St. Malo. I bought enough for several people, and they all made a lot of jam. I knew who my buyers were before I left home."

After dinner, Hilda came in with Alice-Ann and they were introduced. The children enjoyed the atmosphere. Tom and Mary called in, and since it was a warm afternoon, they all walked up the lane. Grampy was keen to know which vegetables did well in the north and had a good discussion with Tom. Frances and Mary felt more at ease with each other, and Frances realised that it was important for people to know that Grampy, Bill, and Geoff were all doing war work. It made a difference to people around here.

Her father wanted to get the six o'clock Ribble Express coach from Burnley and Frances put on her coat and waited outside with him for the bus.

"So what do you think, Dad?"

"I think you'll be all right," he said. "Always remember, they only have mill jobs. Getting your allowance is probably important to Annie. It's a good bargaining point for you. You're a good manager and a good worker, but don't let yourself be pushed too far. How old is Annie?"

"Two years younger than I am."

"You've accomplished a lot more than she has in her life. Look after your children first. Mabel and I can look for something for you in Bolton if you need to leave."

"Mabel…Mabel should never have left me alone with Vi going in to hospital, Dad. It was awful."

"There's a war on, Frances. It was a good job offer for her, and she may never get another one as good as that. She's done the best for herself and Pat, and you have to do the same. And don't forget, you're in a much safer place."

They could see the bus approaching. He put his arm around her shoulder.

"Keep a good account of the money, and see that your children are all right. And write to me every week. I'll write back to you, but only if you write to me. We're not far away."

She went back inside.

"You know, I really enjoyed talking with your dad," said Annie. "He knows a lot about business, looking after those greenhouses and selling and buying. I'd like to have a business of my own, eventually."

Later, Frances would learn that Annie's mother had been married twice and had been left on her own to manage her family. Grampy's concern for his daughters might have impressed her.

That night, London was severely bombed for the first of fifty-seven nights. The Blitz had started.

Washing days

The worst part of the week was doing the washing on Monday and the ironing on Tuesday; the best part was connecting with the evacuees in Scott Park.

Washing was a long business. In the washhouse Frances had to light a fire in the firebox to heat the water in the copper. She added soap to the water, put in the light-coloured clothes and placed the lid on top. A posser went through an opening in the lid. It was a wooden circle on the end of a stick and was used to push down on the linens to beat out the dirt. Once the whites were taken out and put through the mangle, the darker items would take their place.

Next to the copper, the mangle was at hand and Frances turned the large mangle handle to pull the linens through. They emerged as stiff sheets on the other side. The soapy washing water drained back into the copper. Once the clothes were rinsed and had gone through the mangle again, they were shaken out and pegged on the line to dry. Further airing was done indoors by hanging the damp items on the maiden.

It was difficult to manage half a day in the washhouse and look after a two-year-old at the same time. Annie and Hilda looked after Lynette, if they were not at work. As the weather grew colder, Frances started to use the stove indoors instead of the copper, and this would be the pattern over the winter months. By day's end, the maiden would be loaded with damp laundry. It was exhausting at first, but Frances reminded herself that at least she was in a home, with a radio and a sewing machine, and things could be worse.

The weather remained unusually warm and dry in both September and October and the evacuees enjoyed meeting in Scott Park when they could. Lynette played with June and other small children and Frances caught up on the news with Gladys and the others.

"I've got a part-time job working at the cinema," Gladys told her. "One of the other women I'm living with is sharing the job with me. It's either afternoons or evenings, and the one who stays at home takes care of the three children. None of them go to school yet. I envy you having a garden and the field behind you. The park is the only grassy place we've got."

"Yes, I suppose I'm lucky there. Next year, I hope we could have a garden and grow vegetables. They say that even potatoes are going to be rationed."

"We always grew potatoes in Guernsey, didn't we? Are there any farms near you where you can get extra eggs or anything? We just get what's on ration."

On the way home on the bus, Frances decided she would talk to Annie about having a garden next year if the war continued on. Some allotments had been created in the field further down towards the school. She wondered if Arthur had been successful with his potatoes and carrots.

A stolen crop, orders to move, & an escape

In Guernsey, Arthur's two terraces of carrots and potatoes at Woodlands had done fairly well. In late August, he pulled a few carrots one evening and they enjoyed them the next day for dinner at Pa's. Since he was only at Woodlands for the night, they all agreed that it was better to dig up the carrots and bring them to *Le Pré* where there was always someone to watch over their food stores. Two days later, he took extra bags when he returned to Woodlands after tea, and went to dig them up. He was surprised to see that the green feathery tops of the carrots looked wilted.

He pulled one up—and nearly fell over, because it came off the ground with no carrot firmly attached in the soil. The carrot had been cut off and the green top replaced carefully. Every carrot had been taken.

Furious and disappointed, he decided to dig the potatoes that same evening, working till it was too dark to see. He hid his crop in several places up near the house. He took a load to *Le Pré* next morning on his bike when he went for breakfast and managed to pick up the rest with his lorry during his dinner break that day, relieved that his bags of potatoes were still in their hiding places.

A few days later, he found an official warning on the door of Woodlands. The cottage was requisitioned by the Germans, which he had foreseen. He picked up what he considered was most valuable and moved it to *Le Pré*. When he showed Emily the notice that had been left on his door, she nodded. "That looks like the notice they gave to me when I had to move out," she said.

"You mean, from your house at Victoria Terrace?" Emily nodded.

"What about your other house, the bungalow just down the road here?" Arthur continued. "You called it Edelweiss, I think. What happened to that?"

"Edelweiss Lodge? I rented it to the Marquis family a few years ago. They've been good tenants; but in June they decided to leave. He joined the army the same day his wife and their little boy were evacuated to England. They both left very fast, like Frances and your girls. The house isn't being used right now, so I go and check on it occasionally."

Ma was glad to see Arthur move in permanently. "Welcome home, Arthur," she said. "I'm glad you're staying with us. I was worried that those commandos might come to Woodlands to ask for shelter, and you might be caught with them."

"I know. It'll be easier living here, but I'll worry about what they're using Woodlands for."

"At least you won't be riding up the hill every evening after tea," Emily noted.

"I won't be sorry about that."

"I was hoping we could go fishing at the weekend," Pa said. "Walter called in, and he'd like to come with us. We're limited to one mile out, or two miles if we have a Jerry with us on the boat. We have to watch out for the mines."

Arthur frowned. "There's not much to catch within a one-mile limit."

"Exactly. We'll try a Jerry and see."

Later that month, Arthur was looking forward to going fishing again, if they could get the petrol. The Jerry had spoken some English, and fresh fish had been a treat. But his father had a grim look when Arthur came home for tea on Friday. "We can't go fishing, Arthur," he said. "It's banned for a while. Someone escaped."

"Who?"

"I don't know, but the Jerries are really upset."

"Well, good for whoever he is, though I don't know what good it'll do for us."

"Exactly; now we're punished for it."

> **The escape**
>
> Eight men had escaped by boat from the north-east corner of the island on September 6. In spite of engine failure near Alderney, and four German Henkel aircraft dropping flares near them, they continued their journey and landed in England the next day.
>
> The consequences were that all boats in Guernsey had to be brought into St. Peter Port or St Sampson's harbour, even rowing boats used on the reservoir. Some boats had been laid up for the winter or were no longer seaworthy, which the Kommandantur hadn't thought of.
>
> After the ban was lifted, a permit to go fishing had to be obtained. It was given only to fishermen whose family lived on the island. Petrol was restricted to one trip, and it was forbidden to take on passengers. Fishing was not allowed when it was raining or foggy, and a substantial portion of the catch had to be given to the Germans.
>
> Later, a large security deposit was needed and a German escort went with a group of fishing boats. Needless to say, the number of fishing trips decreased steadily.

9: Autumn and Christmas 1940

Blackout and bomb scares—Capturing commandos—Christmas at Cotton Row—Christmas surprise at Le Pré

Blackout and bomb scares

Janice seemed to fit in well at school, and she soon wore clogs like every child in the village. Clogs had a steel piece under the toes, and she could make sparks by striking her toes against the pavement. Lynette was envious. The clogs had a wooden base to fit Janice's foot, a leather top, and were comfortable and durable.

Frances was making winter skirts for the girls from a large woman's skirt she had received from the WVS. She transformed the red velvet frock into a warm dress for Janice, with adequate seam allowances so that it could be used next year. Now Annie was asking around for some cast-off winter underwear for the girls: thick bodices were made of three layers of cotton, as were long warm combinations or underpants, simply called *combs*. There were none in the shops: manufacture of them had almost stopped because of the losses of ships bringing raw cotton across the Atlantic.

On chilly nights during the blackout, everyone went to bed soon after the BBC news at nine. At weekends, there were afternoon or evening card games, potato pie suppers, and local concerts to contribute money towards a new Spitfire or some other worthwhile goal. One evening, when Annie was out playing whist with some neighbours and Hilda was at Alice-Ann's, Frances was startled to hear a loud knock at the door. A man with a dimmed flashlight was outside.

"You're showing some light from the front window, missus," the man's voice told her. "Draw your blackouts properly."

"I'm sorry. I'll see to it right away." The last thing Frances wanted was a bad reputation about security.

"I'll wait and make sure," was the calm reply. After that, if she was alone, Frances always checked the blackout from outside.

Early in October, plans for the Harvest Festival were made. Annie had been practicing some songs and hymns with the children at Sunday School and she was part of the choir.

"I'll be singing with them on Sunday," she told Frances, "and all the children will do something. You and Lynette should come. You'll enjoy it."

"Our class is doing a song," Janice said, "and we're going to help decorate on Friday afternoon, and we're all making a picture to hang up."

On Sunday, the small church was decorated with sheaves of hay, vases of Michaelmas daisies and goldenrod. Children's pictures decorated the entrance and baskets of potatoes, cabbage, apples and pears were perched on window ledges and tables. The long blue curtains, drawn across the altar during school days, were now drawn back: flowers had been placed on each side of the altar. For the first time, Frances saw it as the village church.

The schoolchildren took part in the short service, and Frances listened to the broad accent of Lancashire with interest. It was becoming familiar. Next day, Annie took them back in the evening to buy some produce. The money would be used to pay for new electric lights in the church.

Lancashire speech challenged Frances several times. One Saturday morning, Annie was sleeping in after a late evening playing Whist. There was a knock at the door and Frances found their neighbour, Kit Hoyle, from across Wiles Lane. He was a tall, solidly built man. Kit said something that she didn't quite understand, mentioning Annie. He repeated what he had said as clearly as he could.

"Tell Annie…" and Frances nodded. "Tell Annie, as te owt agate?" Frances repeated the sounds she had heard and went and called up the staircase: "Annie, there's a man here and he's asking something about a gate."

"Nay…" Kit took his boots off and strode to the staircase.

"Annie, as te owt agate…" his conversation started. Annie was out of bed by now and they had a conversation up and down the stairwell. He was asking Annie if she was busy that day. Frances worked it out with Annie later.

The weather soon changed. It grew colder with grey, rainy days and little sunshine. Every evening they listened to the BBC news, as did millions of others. One evening there was a short pause in the reading, and then the reader continued calmly.

> **At 9 p.m. on October 15**, the BBC newsreader started to read. There had been a bombing raid an hour before, as the Blitz of London continued. After a minute of reading he paused, and that was unusual. There had also been the sound of a distant impact. Some people listening said they heard a quiet voice saying, "It's all right," and the reading of the news continued, although the reader was actually covered in dust[10].
>
> A delayed-action bomb had hit the building an hour earlier. Just after 9 p.m. it detonated and killed seven people. This happened a few floors above the news reader. The building was large and white, which helped bombers to locate it. Plans to darken the exterior had been made and were due to be carried out the next day.
>
> The nightly bombing of London continued. Hitler was not following the Geneva Convention, which stated that there should be no bombing of innocent civilians. Coventry was almost wiped off the map in a massive bomb attack in November.

In mid-October at Cotton Row, the high-pitched wail of sirens woke them all after midnight. They had practiced a few times, just in case. Frances flung on her coat, which had a torch in one pocket, grabbed Janice, and made for the stairs; Annie did the same with Lynette. Hilda had slept in the back bedroom and was already downstairs with a blanket. They squeezed into the cupboard-like space under the stairs where one large shelf served as a seat. They waited in the darkness until the "all clear" sounded.

About a week later, Frances took Lynette to the park. She was eager to hear what Gladys and the other evacuees had experienced during the raid. However, there had been no direct bombing in Burnley. The conversation was all about the eight Guernsey men who had escaped from the island in September. Someone passed around a brief report in the Daily Mirror, and another had the first of a series of interviews in the Daily Herald.

"The man interviewed was a signalman working on the White Rock,"

---

10 https://www.bbc.com/historyofthebbc/100-voices/ww2/bh-bombs/

one woman told her. "They escaped overnight in a twenty-foot boat, but they were stuck near Alderney for four hours with engine trouble."

"He said that on the island the Germans are grabbing everything," another woman added. "The jobs are handed out to men by the Germans and everyone gets paid about thirty shillings a week to work for them."

Eight men on a twenty-foot boat trying to get to England overnight, across eighty miles of rough, cold water. Frances hoped Arthur wouldn't try anything that risky.

Capturing commandos

In Guernsey, the Kommandant was still looking for the commandos who had landed on the south coast. He knew that there had been more than one commando raid.

> **The first raid had actually been a three-phase operation.**
> It began in early July. A submarine delivered one Guernsey-born soldier, Nicolle, to a rocky south coast beach to reconnoitre German strength on the island. He was successful. Two men landed a few days later as part of the second phase but were never picked up in the third phase, in which five launches were used; the operation was done in haste and was a failure. The two men eventually turned themselves in to Sherwill, the Procureur[11], who kept quiet about the men until he had found uniforms for them. Then he handed them over to the Kommandant, von Schmettow, and they were treated as Prisoners of War.
>
> Churchill sent two more men in September: Nicolle returned with a second Guernsey commando, Symes. This time, rough weather prevented them from being picked up and they hid with their families. The Germans declared that any men who gave themselves up by October 21 would be treated as POWs; if discovered later, they would be treated as spies and face the death penalty. Their families

---

11   The position of Procureur is equivalent to Attorney-General.

> would also bear the consequences. Nicolle and Symes gave themselves up. They were sent to France for trial with their families, fiancées, and also Mr. Sherwill[12].

In mid-November, the islanders were punished for the espionage attempts. The following notice appeared in *La Gazette Officielle*[13]:

The favouring of espionage in the Island of Guernsey makes further measures necessary. All wireless receiving sets of the Civil population will be requisitioned until further notice and deposited in a place of safety. In case of non-delivery, a fine of 30,000 Reichsmarks will be imposed or 6 weeks' imprisonment.

Christmas at Cotton Row

Annie made a Christmas pudding and cake on two different weekends in November, with ingredients carefully put aside by Frances over a couple of months. When she had finished preparing the mixture for the puddings, she called Frances to come into the kitchen to taste it.

"That's going to be good," Frances enthused, and the girls were allowed a taste as well. They all stirred the mixture a little and made a wish.

"You can't go wrong with the right ingredients," Annie said. "You did well to save enough sugar and butter. I had all that I needed."

"We've all been making do with less sugar, so we'll enjoy it at Christmas," Frances replied. "What we can't replace is the dried fruit that you had stored away. There's none in the shops."

"Well, we'll share out the cake and make it last," said Annie. "That's what we did when I was growing up. I want to invite Tom and Mary and their boy, Raymond, for tea one day, and we'll all be going to them for tea as well. And you know, you should invite your father here again after Christmas, and tell him to bring your mother and the others. Say I've invited them, and we'll have a nice day together."

The suggestion surprised Frances, but she had worked hard now for over three months, washing the clothes, buying rations, and keeping an account of how their money was spent. There had been no complaints about her accounting so far. Hilda was sleeping at Alice-Ann's now, but eating at

---

12   Cruickshank, p76.
13   Carey, p25.

Annie's, and she contributed less than Frances. Both Annie and Hilda had been helpful, watching over the girls and doing some shopping. Now the two sisters were called Auntie by the girls, and the Aunties seemed to derive a great deal of pleasure from it.

In December, the daytime temperature fell almost to the freezing point and every layer of clothing helped. Janice had been attending Sunday School, and she had a part in the St. James Christmas concert, which would be put on in the middle of the month. Annie was helping with it, and Frances used the sewing machine to make Janice's costume.

A Christmas card arrived from Vi and Fred, and another from Frank and Adele, enclosing a photo of their wedding. Nellie's letter said they had moved to Bolton after Alan was born in November. Otto had a new job there doing war work. She wrote that Frances must come and see them in Bolton in 1941, and that was like a precious Christmas gift for Frances to dream about. Perhaps she could find a billet in Bolton and be closer to her family? There was a card from Mabel, and Grampy's letter included an invitation from Joyce, who was planning to marry her Guernsey sweetheart on February 4th in Bolton: "Please come with the girls."

Frances received a dressing gown[14] for Janice through the WVS, and it made a good Christmas gift. Annie managed to buy one for Lynette, and she was delighted. Janice practiced putting her dressing gown on in the dark so that she would be fast if the sirens sounded.

Christmas Day was spent quietly together. They had half a chicken from Kit Hoyle and Frances managed to keep enough milk aside to make a custard to serve with Annie's Christmas pudding. She had saved four sixpences and had folded each one in a little greaseproof paper. In the kitchen, she skillfully inserted one into each of four slices of hot pudding before serving it at the table.

"Watch out for a sixpence in your pudding," she told the girls. "The lucky ones who find a sixpence can make a wish." When they found one, Janice paused to think of a wish, but Lynette wanted to eat her pudding first and had to be slowed down.

Later, before she slept, Frances remembered last Christmas: the smell of the pine branch that Arthur cut for their Christmas tree, and the joy of

---

14   A warm robe or housecoat to wear over pyjamas.

opening her Christmas suitcase, re-discovering the baubles and Christmas decorations of previous years. She hoped the suitcase would still be in the attic when the war was over.

On Boxing Day they went to tea at Tom and Mary's and met their son Raymond, who was about Bert's age. They played a few games around the table and Tom amused the children with some "magic" tricks. Frances felt grateful to be received as part of the Howarth family, and content that Cotton Row was beginning to feel more like home.

Christmas surprise at *Le Pré*

Late in the morning of December 24, Ma and Emily were doing their best to prepare for Christmas Day; but the chatter was about the two Guernsey-born commandos, Nicolle and Symes, and their families, in prison in France.

"What I don't understand," said Ma, "is why Mr Sherwill was sent to prison in France with the others. I mean, he's the Attorney General, isn't he? He's not one of those two families."

"From what I heard, Nicolle and Symes went to see him first, and he told them to stay hidden for a bit," said Emily. "He wanted to find British army uniforms for them because they'd arrived in regular clothes, meaning they could be treated as spies and shot. While they waited for uniforms, he probably didn't report them."

"I thought the Germans promised that they'd all be treated as POWs anyway, as long as they gave themselves up."

"I suppose they didn't trust the Jerries. Dressed in uniforms, they were more confident they'd be classified as prisoners of war."

"And why on earth were they sent from England in regular clothes? Those poor young men. And they weren't even picked up by the navy to go back to England!"

Emily shrugged. "Who knows what went wrong…with our tides, and the rocks and all. I'm glad they didn't land at Fermain. Arthur could have been in a French prison by now if they'd landed there and asked him for help. Sherwill found them uniforms and that may save their lives. Except that he's been sent to prison as well."

Pa had been listening. "Twenty people have been taken to prison in France, even the fiancée's parents, and the father's employer. How has that helped England with the war?"

"And we've all lost our wirelesses because of it," Emily added. "I could just do with some carols to make me feel a bit more like Christmas."

"At least we'll have the carol service this afternoon, Emily. Thank goodness you can play the piano, or we'd really be lost."

"There are so few children in the Sunday School, though. It's a good thing our Ladies' Fellowship is still pretty strong. We'll need every voice. What I miss is the entertainment that they always used to put on—the play, and the special songs. It kept Louise and me busy, playing the piano and rehearsing with the children."

Pa laughed. "You know what I came across this morning in my workshop? A long piece of chain. I think it was the chain I found for Otto when he played the ghost in *A Christmas Carol*."

"That was years ago!" Ma declared. "He was only about ten years old."

Emily was smiling. "Yes, I remember. He played two parts, and he was dragging that chain around here trying to act like a ghost."

"And Arthur played Scrooge as a boy," Emily added, "and he was also another ghost with Herbie. They were all rattling that chain around, and some piece of tin and phosphorous to make thunder and lightning."

"That's right. We had to have thunder and lightning every night here."

"And your Jimmy—Captain Jay as they called him—thanked everyone, and you played the national Anthem," said Ma.

They were quiet, remembering. Ma changed the subject. "I miss hearing the BBC news," she said. "I'm worried that the Jerries will think up some other new punishment for us after the RAF bombed their new airport hangar to smithereens last week."

"That bombing was done by the RAF," Emily replied. "It had nothing to do with hiding spies. I just wish we could change the clocks back from German time to English time. I'm fed-up making breakfast in the dark; and I can't see to do any sewing or cleaning in the morning till after nine. Plus, Arthur starts work late because of it, and finishes late, so we have to eat late too."

"Here's Arthur now," said Pa. "He's half an hour early."

Arthur came in, grinning. "I have some good news!" he announced, looking at the doubtful faces staring at him. Nobody had good news these days.

"Oh Arthur, don't be a tease," said Emily. "Here we are in a war, we don't have a wireless, people are in prison in France, and it's Christmas."

"Well, if you'll give me the wireless receipts, I'll go and get them."

"The wirelesses? They're giving them back?"

"Yes, Ma'am," was the reply, in Arthur's best American drawl. "I'm going to pick them up this afternoon for some of the upper class and I'll get ours also. The postmen are helping to deliver a lot of them, even tomorrow."

"Even on Christmas Day? Well, that'll be a good present for everyone," Emily declared. "There haven't been many Christmas cards for them to deliver this year."

"After I hand in the lorry, I want to check Otto's house but I should be here before dark."

Ma placed the bread and cutlery on the table. She was suspicious. "I bet they're not giving us back our wirelesses because it's Christmas. I bet they want to take more of our potatoes."

Arthur sat at the table next to Pa. "Well, there's more good news, if it's true: the families of those commandos—Nicolle and Symes—are being brought back from France, and Sherwill too."

"I'll believe it when I see it," Ma muttered as she served out the meal.

"There'd be a lot of bad feeling if they weren't brought home," said Pa. "It's not their fault that those Guernsey lads were sent from England. That was a good decision by von Schmettow."

Emily brought the receipts. "There you are, Arthur. My goodness. It'll be nice to feel more Christmassy. This evening," she continued, "I'm going to listen to the news and then maybe there will be some carols…"

Ma pushed the loaf and a bread knife towards her. "Come on, Emily," she said. "Stop dreaming about this evening. Cut the bread and let's eat."

10: January 1941: Family Visit and a Blizzard

*Visitors from Bolton—Commandos' news—January blizzard—Finding a doctor—
Two more uniforms—Diamonds outside*

Visitors from Bolton

On Sunday morning, January 5, a red double-decker stopped at Cotton Row and deposited five passengers. At a thousand feet up in the Pennines, it was below freezing at night and sometimes during the day. The reservoir opposite Cotton Row had started to freeze along the shoreline. It was icily cold.

Grampy led the way and Gran was behind him, hanging on to the arm of a young man in a merchant navy uniform. It was Lionel, their oldest grandchild and Frances' nephew. Rose and Graham, nine and eleven years old, had a good look at the reservoir and then followed the three adults to the door. They were glad to be welcomed inside by Frances and their two cousins, who had been watching for the bus.

Annie was pleased to meet Gran. "You'll find it a bit colder here than in Bolton," she said. "So come here by the fire. Now, let me get this right. Your name's Mrs Torode, isn't it? Did I say it right?"

"That's right. But if you call him Grampy, then just call me Gran."

"Very well, and I'm Annie. Annie Howarth."

"It was nice of you to invite us all," Gran said with a smile, "but Bill, Geoff, and Joyce have their own friends to see at weekends, and I think you'll find that five of us is enough."

Annie was very glad to see Grampy again; and especially pleased to see this young man in uniform. If the neighbours were watching—and why wouldn't they?—they were sure to spread the word around that someone in Frances' family was in uniform: seeing was convincing.

Once cups of tea were in front of them, they settled down to exchange news. Gran had quietly glanced around the kitchen with Frances, before they all took their coats off, and gave her an apple cake and some cheese and onions. Frances had eggs ready for her mother to take back. Gran reported that Vi and Nellie were both doing well with their new babies.

Mabel and Pat were well settled with Mrs Lawson.

Graham and Rose said they were glad to be with their grandparents, and school in Bolton was alright. Rose disappeared upstairs with the girls after a while, but they soon returned to the fire.

"We've got more evacuees from London now," Grampy said. "They're coming north from the Blitz. And then they started bombing Manchester and Liverpool, so there's been a lot of bombed-out people coming to live with their relatives."

"December was bad," Gran added. "It was one lot of sirens after another, and all of us out of our beds and going down the road to the shelter. And then on Christmas Eve there was a terrible bombing in Manchester. That was one night when we didn't sleep at all."

"We heard there were a lot of casualties," said Annie.

"Probably over five hundred killed," said Grampy. "It was a Christmas to forget."

"That's awful," said Frances. "Now I see how quiet we've been up here."

"With all this bombing of the docks, it's bound to affect our food supply," said Grampy. "We're going to be a bit short until they get some repairs done."

Annie looked at Lionel. "Now, Lionel, you're in the merchant navy," she said. "And you've been quiet up to now. How do things look to you?"

"Well, I can't say much," he said. "We're not allowed to. I'm just relieved to see so many of the family up here in Lancashire, and away from the biggest cities. My parents and my two sisters are still on the island. At least there's no bombing there."

"His mother is Elsie, our eldest daughter," Gran explained.

"Well, let's hope that no news is good news, as they say," said Annie. "Just remember, you're welcome to visit us here any time."

"There's a Channel Islands group at Stockport, near Manchester, and they've started a monthly letter," said Grampy. "A chapter has started in Bolton and they're going to send us the newsletter too. They've warned that there's a shortage of paper, though. Anyway, they gave a good Christmas party for the children. We all went."

"They're getting organised in Burnley as well," said Frances. "We had a Christmas party, a nice one. They had cake and sandwiches. I don't know how they managed the food. Next Friday, the mayor of Burnley has a party for the children, so we'll see the Guernsey evacuees there again. I haven't seen much of them since the weather turned so cold."

"And what did you have for your Christmas dinner?" Gran asked.

"There wasn't much meat that week. But we have a neighbour, Kit Hoyle, and he raises chickens. Annie will tell you."

They looked at Annie.

"Well, I've been doing this for a while," she explained. "Our neighbour across the lane, Kit Hoyle, has a withered hand. He's always kept chickens, and he sells a few eggs on the side and such, but he's not able to kill a chicken when he needs to. So, I do it for him. I used to do it for my mother. I was the boy in the family after my brothers moved out. I always manage to get a chicken, or half of one, now and again. We pay for it, mind you, but I'm head of the queue."

Grampy slapped his hand on the table. "That's the way to look after yourself."

"And we got another half a chicken off him for dinner today," Annie continued. "So, we can all enjoy that. Frances has made up a good chicken stew."

He grinned. "Good! We only eat meat about twice a week now, and it's only a couple of mouthfuls each time."

"We're warming up the stew already because we knew you'd be hungry soon," said Frances. "Guess where it's keeping hot? Here, by the fire."

"I thought that was a fancy-looking fireplace." Grampy got up to inspect it.

Annie showed them: to the right of the fire was a section like an oven, with a large kettle sitting on top. Using a thick cloth, she opened the oven door to show a large pot inside. The smell of chicken wafted under Grampy's nose.

It was a satisfying day. Rose enjoyed playing with the children. Graham used his imagination with the small metal animals that Frances had bought for a Christmas nativity scene. He was pleased when Lionel went for a walk with him up the side road, but it was too cold and they didn't go far.

In the afternoon, the Howarth family dropped in. Tom and Mary arrived with Dora and her mill-manager husband Chris on the bus, avoiding a cold walk from Clowbridge. Hilda and Alice-Ann came soon after but didn't stay long. The teapot was refreshed several times and the two families became acquainted. The Haworths left feeling that Annie's idea of billeting was working out well enough. Later, Graham kept watch for the Burnley bus outside so that they didn't have to wait for it in the cold, and they were in good time for the seven o'clock Express back to Bolton.

The afternoon had been planned for a while. Annie was not only pleased that it went well, but thrilled that Lionel had been there in uniform to impress her family. Rose and Graham were shown to be supported by their grandparents and Grampy was doing war work. This was a family whose friendship would raise her status a little.

There was a big, happy clean-up after the visit. Frances jotted down the event in the tiny diary she had bought for herself at Christmas, knowing it would cheer her to read it when she missed her family. She felt mentally stronger and decided to take life a month at a time. Some days were tough, but there were good days too.

On Friday that week, she took the children to the mayor's party in Burnley and chatted with the other mothers. The girls were happy to see their friends again. The children raced around the big hall, making so much noise that the mothers could barely hear the mayor's words of welcome.

Commandos' news

In Guernsey, on January 8, Emily bravely wheeled her bike up Havelet Road in the morning's chilly wind. At the junction with Hauteville she mounted her bike and enjoyed freewheeling down the hill slowly, down past Victor Hugo's house and other pleasant facades which looked a little short of care these days. As the hill flattened out, she turned left onto Pedvin Street, which led her on a more horizontal plane to Trinity Square. It was a familiar route.

At least there was no snow in the wind, like the day before, but she hated the sound of swastika flags flapping above some buildings. She pedalled around the square into Mansell Street, and was relieved to smell the fragrance of the bakery and to smile at a woman she knew who was just coming out.

The shop was warm, infused with the smell of fresh bread. Henry Machon, the baker, was in charge behind the counter. If news had to be circulated effectively, this was the place to bring it.

"Morning, Mrs Jay."

Before she could reply, he continued, more quietly: "We were discussing the news about the commandos."

Emily walked over, nodding at the three local people ahead of her. One of them was her friend Dorothy. "Good news, I hope?"

"Well. Kind of. There's good news: the Germans kept their promise and Nicolle and Symes are being treated as prisoners of war. Everyone else has come back to Guernsey, except one person. That's the bad news: I was told that the Jerries kept telling the parents of Nicolle and Symes that their sons had been shot, then reprieved, then shot…and Mr Symes was in despair and cut his wrists, and died. So, he has been lost."

They were shocked, silent.

"And what about Sherwill?" Dorothy asked.

"He's back, but the Jerries won't let him be Procureur anymore, and he can't be President of the Controlling Committee either." There was quiet chatter.

"Well, at least they kept their word about making Symes and Nicolle POWs," Dorothy commented quietly to Emily. "I was scared that they'd be shot for espionage. I respect von Schmettow for that."

"So do I," Emily murmured. "But the poor Symes family! Let's hope there won't be any more commando raids."

Dorothy promised to bring some brussels sprouts to *Le Pré* to exchange for potatoes that afternoon, and went on her way. Henry continued his news broadcast.

"Mrs Jay, did you know that we'll be having bread rationing soon? We think it'll start at the end of February."

"Will we have ration books for bread, Henry?"

"I suppose so. We'll have to make sure every loaf weighs the same. You'll have to register your whole family and pick it up twice a week."

Emily made her purchases, returned to *Le Pré*, and passed on the news to Pa and Ma. "It was so nice and warm at the bakery," she said, turning in front of the fire. "and it's the only place that seems to be normal. I cycle past abandoned houses, and the shops are closed or there's nothing in them. On the way back I went down the road and checked Edelweiss. It looks all right."

"Edelweiss Lodge? Your house down the road?' asked Ma. "I wondered when you'd last checked it. Your tenants evacuated, didn't they?"

"Yes. The Jerries haven't let anyone live there since they left. I think it's because it's like Arthur's house: it overlooks Havelet Bay and commandos could land and access it easily. I was just turning in to look around when a car screeched past me. I think some of the Jerries are having a good time speeding around in the cars they've seized."

"I think I heard that one racing down the hill," said Pa. "Perhaps they're fed up with waiting to invade England. Do you remember, some Jerries were saying last year that they were only here for a few weeks before they landed in England? As though they were having a bit of a holiday here first? They're still waiting to invade. Of course, they're hoping this blitz on London will make Churchill surrender."

"Thank goodness we don't live there with that bombing every night," said Ma, slicing the bread. "Now, here comes Arthur, so let's sit down. We've got carrots and parsnips with the beans, and tomorrow we'll have some brussels sprouts for a change. If bread's going to be rationed, let's eat plenty while we can."

That evening, after Ma and Pa had gone to bed, Emily and Arthur sipped a final cup of tea near the dying fire. The old photo album had been left open on the table and Emily picked it up. "Ma was looking at these photos of her birthday parties on the beach. This one is July 1931. Do you remember it?"

"Yes, I do. That's Eric and Daisy, isn't it?"

Emily nodded. "They must have been around twelve and ten; and Bert and Nancy are just little tots! Louise is about fourteen, sitting by me and Jimmy. She loved her dad; and she loved Ma's beach birthday party because she knew her own birthday was just a month later."

"Jimmy's right next to you. Jimmy Jay, he was a good man. Didn't you meet him at Holy Trinity?"

"Yes, he was an auctioneer back then; but he spent a lot of time working for the Boys Brigade at Holy Trinity."

"And you were playing the piano for the church plays and meetings."

"That's right. That's how we met. We were married in 1914, just when the Great War started, do you remember?" She laughed. " You didn't want to wear a suit."

She turned a few pages and closed the album. "Those were good beach parties, weren't they? Then Jimmy started cancer, and two years later, we lost him."

Arthur nodded. "He learned how to play *boules* on the sand at those parties. All we managed last year for Ma was that little picnic outside with Walter and Nun."

"…and we just talked about the children we were missing: your girls and Louise and Mollie, and the schools had gone…Today Ma said she was hoping we'd be able to meet on the beach again some time, but I can't see it happening."

"No, I can't. They're full of mines for a start. It's going to take time."

Emily picked up the cups and said goodnight. It was time to sleep.

January blizzard

Around the middle of January, a few inches of snow fell. Frances took Lynette for a walk to get to know this strange white stuff. Double pairs of socks had to be worn inside rubber boots that were designed for rainy days, and it was slippery.

On January 18, market day, the snow returned as a blizzard. It was accompanied by a wind that piled up the snow, and by late afternoon it stopped all travel along the Manchester Road. Frances, Annie, and Hilda had brought in coal and tried to seal every crack that let a draught in. Between two and three feet of snow fell and was whipped into high drifts. Much later, journalists reported that this was the worst storm since 1888. Newspapers were not allowed to report on storms for a couple of weeks, because the information could be helpful to the enemy. Until then, nobody knew how widespread the storm was.

Next day was a Sunday, so Hilda watched the children while Frances and Annie made their way slowly through the snow along the main road past the Waggoners Farm towards Crown Point Road, where two large Rawtenstall Corporation buses were stuck in a drift. It would take hours of shovelling to clear the drifts, and it would be a long wait for the Burnley snow plough. Several local men had done some shoveling already.

On Monday, nobody could get to work, and the milkman left them double rations. Plans were being made to deliver the milk to Burnley in large churns on sledges on Tuesday morning, but by then the Burnley plough had cleared the way. Everyone struggled to go shopping for the rations they were short of, before supplies ran out.

Finding a doctor

The stress of evacuation, the harsh winter and poor nutrition began to tell on Frances' health. She developed a sore throat that was very painful. A chemist recommended garlic and ordered some for her. On Friday, January 24, Annie had a day off and took her to see the evacuee doctor in Burnley. He prescribed a bottle of tannic acid, and she had to paint her throat with a long, angled brush, to coat what seemed to be an abscess. The dark brown tannic acid was extremely bitter, but she made herself paint her throat every hour to gain some control.

Next day, Annie took over the household tasks and went for the rations in the morning, while Hilda watched over the children, and Frances stayed in bed. Her throat prevented her from sleeping much at night, and she had no energy. Annie was worried about her. She had proved herself a reliable and honest companion and her billeting money gave Annie some peace of mind.

Frances couldn't help thinking back to her childhood, when she had diphtheria and felt this deadly tiredness. Guernsey law stated that anyone with diphtheria must be isolated, and Grampy had hidden her upstairs in the house, sending her younger sisters, and himself, next door to his mother's house, while Gran looked after her alone. Her father wouldn't send her to the Town Hospital, as decreed by the States, because he was sure she would never return. It was too deadly a disease. He was officially living with his mother, but he would sneak in through a window at night to reach his own bed, often watching over her during those long nights. Later, he was fined £5 by the authorities for keeping Frances at home, a high price in 1915, but better than jail time.

Diphtheria was happening again in England, and Frances kept the house as clean as she could, but she knew that the lack of fresh vegetables was partly to blame. She had discussed having a garden plot with Annie and planned to send away for a seed catalogue. Annie had asked her neighbours if anyone had a spare piece of land they could use.

That same afternoon, when Frances was resting upstairs, there was a knock on the door. It was Kit Hoyle, the chicken man, and he carefully stepped out of his boots when Annie invited him in.

"Annie, you were looking for a piece of land where you could grow some potatoes."

"That's right, Kit."

"If you want it, you can have some of my land behind my house. I've got more than I need and I'm busy enough with the chickens and all."

That sounded good. The plot was just across the lane, so they wouldn't have to go far to look after it. Annie called Frances to come downstairs.

What wasn't good, was that Annie had been catching up on some washing, and it was drying up on the maiden near the ceiling, Kit was a tall man and he lit up his pipe while Annie went back in the kitchen to check on something.

Frances came down, sniffed, and…

"Mr Hoyle! Mmm…" Her throat hurt too much to make any more sounds, but she pointed to a garment hanging from the maiden—which unfortunately was her vest[15]—and which had brown scorch marks on it. Annie pulled it down. It was scorched and smelled of tobacco smoke.

Frances was embarrassed at having a strange man near her underwear. Kit moved away and apologised. Later, he would talk about "burning Mrs That Woman's flannel." Frances addressed everyone as Mr or Mrs and their surname, as was the custom in Guernsey. Kit and the villagers tried to reciprocate but couldn't pronounce Enevoldsen. Their respectful reply was addressed to Mrs That Woman.

The scorching was soon forgotten, and the offer of the garden gratefully accepted over a strong cup of tea. The incessant bombing of ports and torpedoing of supply ships had shown how vulnerable Britain's food supply was. Fresh vegetables were almost unobtainable now, and having their own garden might be essential to survival if this continued.

Kit's wife came over a few days later and replaced the vest with a new one.

Two more uniforms

There was another surprise for them that weekend. On Sunday afternoon, two people in uniform got off the bus and knocked at Number 8. Annie answered the door and welcomed them in. Janice recognised them. Annie strode over to the bottom of the stairs.

"Frances, you've got visitors!" she shouted up the stairs. Frances had

---

15 Undershirt usually made of fine knitted cotton.

heard the chatter and quickly came down. Annie was in her element, inviting the two smart uniforms to warm themselves by the fire.

Daisy and Eric Carter, children of Arthur's sister Elsie, were happy to have found Frances and their small cousins. Eric was in his air force uniform, all six feet of him. Daisy had joined the Women's Auxiliary Air Force (WAAF) and was wearing her grey-blue uniform, her peaked cap now on Janice's head. Each of the girls held a chocolate biscuit, a rare treat, and were told that yes, they could eat them right away. A bar of chocolate from Eric would be shared another day. They had brought a whole packet of chocolate biscuits and a large triangle of Lancashire cheese.

"Eric and Daisy are from Arthur's side of the family, Annie," Frances explained in her whispery voice.

They could only stay for a few hours, but were happy to find this quiet hamlet where they could meet Auntie Frances and the girls. Annie was very pleased at having two more uniforms observed at her house. She was curious, though, how had they known where to find Frances? She left Frances to talk with them in her whispery voice, while she made tea for everybody.

They had come from Oldham, just north-east of Manchester, where Daisy was stationed. It was about the same distance from Cotton Row as Bolton. They talked about their parents, who had decided to stay in Guernsey instead of evacuating. They worried about them as Frances worried about Arthur.

"And has there been much damage from bombing where you are?" asked Annie. "Grampy—no, I should say, Frances' father—said they could hear bombers going over a lot in Bolton."

"It was awful in December, with Manchester being bombed so much," said Daisy. "Some of us went to help clean up."

"And how about Liverpool and other places?" asked Annie.

"We can't say anything," said Eric, "except it was very bad."

Frances was relieved that Annie took them and the children out for a walk. Whispering was all she could cope with. They left soon after, with a promise to visit in the summer when they had time off. Their visit and the news of Kit's garden plot cheered her, but it took another five days before her throat was back to normal. She felt relief as she wrote in her diary on January 28th: *Throat easier.*

Diamonds outside

During the last week of January, the weather gave them another surprise. There were rain showers which clothed the frozen surface in a layer of ice for three days. Even the rambler rose leaves around the door were suddenly bright and shiny. During the morning, shards of ice fell off the edge of the roof and in the wind, they were scattered over the snow on the front garden. It looked as though it was growing diamonds, especially when a feeble sun managed to shine for a while.

Frances seized the moment: "Come and see the garden. It's full of diamonds!"

Two faces gazed out of the window. Janice was at home because school was closed after more heavy snow. Frances layered both girls in clothing and they went outside to gather diamonds and use them to decorate a snow castle.

11: Feb–March 1941 — Sickness & Snowstorm

*Sick children—Blackburn Market—A surprise visit—February snowstorm—
First Aid courses—Pa and Arthur go ormering*

Sick children

On Saturday, February 1, Frances was well enough to tackle the bus ride to Burnley to buy the rations, but she came back early. *The bus went through high walls of snow which has been piled up*, she noted in her diary.

Unfortunately, the children were not well. By now she had abandoned any idea of attending Joyce's wedding in Bolton that week. She kept them in bed on Sunday morning to keep them well rested and tried a short walk in the afternoon. By Monday, both she and Annie knew that they needed professional help and Annie went to Burnley to find the evacuee doctor. He promised to visit the next day. He did come, and diagnosed bronchitis, perhaps developing into whooping cough. Janice's case seemed more serious.

Next day, Annie went to fetch medicine from Burnley. Frances kept the girls in bed and one anxious day followed another. As they improved, she tried to cheer them up with an activity in the afternoons: one day they chose a cotton remnant, and she sewed a *pinny* (apron) for each of them on Annie's machine. They were pleased. Next day she turned dusting into a game and they even enjoyed doing that. Lynette liked having Janice at home, even if they were both sick.

Annie showed the girls how Jack Frost painted fairy scenes on the windows overnight, and both children imagined that fairies might live in these frosty landscapes. Each morning they would try to interpret a new fairy scene before the magic of it gradually disappeared.

The following Sunday there was a little sunshine. Janice still had whooping cough, and Hilda said she would look after the children so that Frances and Annie could take a walk in the sun. The snow had almost gone. They walked up to Crown Point Road and stopped to chat at the Waggoners Farm. Annie then disappeared to have tea with a friend. Next day, she came home from work bringing two dolls for the girls. She didn't say how she obtained them; but it was like a mini-Christmas for the girls. Dressing, feeding and caring for Marigold and Daisy, helped them through more sick days.

Blackburn market

"We really need more fresh vegetables," Frances said to Annie and Hilda one teatime, "but I can't find any around here. It's mid-February and the snow's gone. Janice has improved a lot. If one of you could look after the children tomorrow, I'd like to go to one of the other markets and see if I can find some."

"I'll look after them both," Hilda replied.

"Is there a better market than Burnley?"

"I think Blackburn would have more," Annie said.

"Where's Blackburn? How do I get to Blackburn?"

Annie looked at Hilda. "If you can look after the children," she said, "why don't I go with Frances? Then we can bring plenty home. And I know Blackburn. It's only a half-hour bus ride out of Burnley."

They left early on Saturday and bought all they could from Blackburn's better-stocked market. Annie had a certain skill in beating down prices that made Frances almost cringe; but she had to admit that they got more for their money. Annie was also aware that evacuees were sometimes taken advantage of.

A surprise visit

There was a knock on the door soon after nine the next morning. It was Gran and Grampy, who had taken the early bus from Bolton.

"Well, what a surprise!" Annie exclaimed. "Come on in and warm yourselves up."

"Thanks Annie," said Gran. "We were worried about Frances. And how are the children?"

"They're still in bed upstairs. They didn't have a good night. Frances is in our new garden across at Kit's place. I'll go and give her a shout."

"No, tell me where it is," said Grampy. "I've still got my coat on."

Annie indicated Kit Hoyle's house and the garden behind it and he went across the lane. This would give him a chance to talk with his daughter privately to see how she and the children had been treated while she was sick. After a short conversation, he was comforted to know that Annie had been looking after both her and the children.

The kettle was put on and tea made by the time they returned to the house, discussing what they could grow in the garden. Frances beamed at her mother.

"Thanks for coming, Mum," she said. "I really was sick—my throat again. But today I almost felt like doing some digging when I went out."

Her mother shook her finger at her. "Don't you start gardening until you're well rested," she said. "Annie was telling me you had to paint your throat with that awful stuff. Remember how sick you were when you were younger." She insisted on having a look at Frances' throat and seemed more relaxed after her inspection. "Now, what have you got growing here on the windowsill?"

Frances had cut off and saved the tops of carrots, beets and swedes as she used them in a meal, and had let them sprout indoors. She had felt desperate for something fresh and green, and had snipped off the green sprouting bits to chew.

There wasn't much flavour but at least it was fresh. Nobody else would try it.

"I must go up and see the children, Mum. Janice needs to gargle."

"I'll come up with you. Then I want to tell you about Joyce and Ken's wedding. I've got some photos and a letter from Joyce for you."

After the children were settled, they managed to put a meal together, adding more fresh vegetables from their purchases the day before. Gran told Frances about the wedding and showed her the photos. Joyce would move down to Weymouth where Ken worked in the Post Office.

When Annie was brewing more tea in the kitchen, Gran said quietly, "Mabel seems to be getting on well with Mrs Lawson. Having Pat there doesn't seem to be a problem. In fact, she likes having her around. And Annie seems to enjoy having your girls here. Mind you, your two are well behaved."

Frances nodded. "Yes, that part has worked out well." She told her mother about the dolls Annie had produced.

Annie enjoyed chatting with Grampy, and they found that they both liked singing, and sang a few songs together. However, the weather was threatening snow, and the visitors left early, satisfied that all was well.

February snowstorm

Winter was not over yet. Two days later, on February 19, another snowstorm hit hard. It swept west from Russia and covered northern England with snow, right across to Liverpool on the west coast. In the northeast, six trains were buried under snow, and a thousand passengers had to be rescued. This "news" was not made known to the general public for a while.

On the moors around Burnley, the snow was piled into drifts everywhere. Frances took photos of Annie and Lynette, black figures in front of a huge mound of snow which hardly stood out from the blinding whiteness of everything behind them. Another shows Frances in the winter coat which she brought from Guernsey, holding Dinah on a leash. "*Lost in the snow 20 to 30 feet high*" is written next to it.

Soon after this, Lynette started to be ill, her face swollen, and she had a fever. Frances kept both children at home, frequently in bed to stay warm, till the end of the month. This second snowstorm was a shock. She had thought that winter was over and felt she had little strength to deal with another bout of it. The only thing that helped was knowing that they were far from the bombing raids on Liverpool and Manchester. She wrote nothing in her diary. It was a case of living one cold day at a time, one after another.

First Aid courses

By the middle of March, the temperature was above 40 Fahrenheit. Piles of snow had become smaller, curiosities that the girls jumped into for fun. Tea was made at any time, the heat of the cup transferred to the hands which closed around it. Finally, Janice was well enough to go back to school and Lynette was busy with the blue pram and her new doll Marigold, plus Teddy and a well-washed bunny.

Frances learned from Gladys that two evacuees had registered for First Aid courses given in Burnley by the St. John Ambulance Brigade (SJAB). She decided to register as well. She wanted to be in touch with people who could help her if the children were sick again. Proficiency in First Aid was also recognised as a voluntary contribution to war work, which was good for her status in the village.

She discussed it with Annie and Hilda.

"There are two courses being given this spring: First Aid, followed by

Home Nursing. Each one lasts a few weeks and then there's an exam at the end of them. They give the courses in the evenings, usually in Burnley, between seven and ten o'clock. It's to help us know what to do if we're bombed around here."

Annie nodded. "Yes, I heard about those courses. One of the women who comes to the Old Tyme Dances at the Astoria Hotel is a nurse. Her husband's a good dancer too."

Hilda butted in. "So, you'd need somebody to look after the children and put them to bed on those nights. I can look after them, Frances."

"And I can do that as well," Annie added. "Between the two of us there shouldn't be a problem, unless they call us both for evening work at the mill, which isn't likely."

Frances was relieved. "That's really good of you both. If you suddenly both have to work in the evening, I'll just not go. It's not as if it's a job that I'm being paid to do."

She knew that the sisters were worried about their jobs at the mill: imports of raw cotton continued to be unreliable. They might be assigned new jobs and do war work somewhere else.

Frances had also been thinking about gardening, and after tea one evening, she put some leaflets on the table.

"What have you got there?"

"I have some *Dig for Victory* leaflets," she replied. "They're free, from the Ministry of Agriculture. This one is how to grow peas and beans. They even suggest which type of seed is best."

"Good," Hilda nodded. "We were a bit short of vegetables last winter. I don't mind doing a bit of digging."

"I just fancy some fresh peas on my plate," Annie said. "I'd like to grow peas, and potatoes! I don't want to be rationed for potatoes again."

"Yes. There's even one on how to store them for eating or for seed."

"That's just what we want. And they've been bombing more ports again. —Portsmouth, I think, and somewhere northeast as well. Must be Hull. Like your dad says, we should try to grow some of our food."

"We must start digging up Kit's garden," Frances stated. "I went to look at it with Lynette this morning; but we'll have to shoo off the chickens."

Annie laughed. "Nay, you won't keep chickens off, once you start digging. They'll find plenty of worms there. Anyway, if we put our minds to it, we'll have it all dug up at the weekend. Mebbe I could be one of those *land girls*[16] if I lose my job."

Frances noticed that the Ministry leaflets came from a hotel at St. Anne's on Sea, Lancashire, and wondered if the London offices had been bombed. She wanted to get leaflets titled "Cabbages and Related Crops" and "Pests and How to Deal with Them." Unfortunately, there was no point in requesting "Tomato Growing is not Difficult" when they lived a thousand feet above sea level.

Pa and Arthur go ormering

In Guernsey, in the middle of March, when there was a full moon and a spring tide, Arthur and Pa went ormering[17]. Ormers cling to rocks underwater, revealed only at the lowest tides, and a curved ormering hook is needed to dislodge them. They left a couple of hours before low tide with hooks and buckets and hoped to find enough for a good meal to celebrate Pa's birthday, which had been a few days before.

Ma was making a carrot and potato pudding for tea. It was as near as she could get to making a cake. Emily was reading something she had cut out of the *Evening Press*. "The woman who writes about food[18] says that last year they were very successful at drying grapes to make raisins. I'd like to try that this year," she said. "Do you remember how cheap grapes were last year, with half the island evacuated? Last week I queued up for an hour to get that one pound of raisins at Plummer's. There were almost a hundred people waiting behind me right up along High Street."

Ma nodded. "I remember. Last year, grapes were only fourpence a pound. We should buy plenty. It shouldn't be that difficult to dry them. We have the space. Arthur will be happy to have raisin pancakes again, if only we had enough flour as well."

"I'd love some raisin pancakes," said Emily. "It seems so stupid. We're importing everything from France and it's much nearer than England, yet we can't get basic things like flour and sugar, and you can't buy cake anywhere."

---

16 Women who worked on the farms, replacing men, during the war.
17 The restricted harvesting of ormers, a type of shellfish, at very low tides.
18 Dorothy Higgs

"At the Fellowship yesterday, Dorothy told me that the ones who buy food for us in Granville have a hard job finding suppliers. And when they do have supplies delivered to the harbour, the dockers don't want to load it on the boats for us."

Emily walked across to the fire and put a small piece of wood on it. "Well, I suppose the dockers don't like to see French food supplies going to German-run islands. I hear they have to send a lot of their food to Germany already."

"I suppose the men on the Controlling Council are doing their best," said her mother. "They imported a lot of seed potatoes from Jersey last month, and as long as the growers have those, we should have plenty of potatoes this autumn. At least it's all Guernsey men on the Committee. Who knows if the Jerries would bother much about feeding us if they took over the food supply?"

"I'd like to try making syrup from sugar beet. They're planting a lot more this year. If we can't get sugar, we could give it a try."

"It takes a lot of boiling, Emily. But they said the jam factory people were looking into it and doing some testing. Perhaps we'll be able to buy it already prepared."

"You're right, Ma, and if they start rationing gas, we may not be able to do it. Anyway, they'll give us some recipes when they've done the testing."

"Dorothy told me that one of her neighbours in Hauteville had chopped up red beetroot and dried it, and it was nice and sweet like raisins. That's something else we could try."

A clattering outside told them that Pa and Arthur were back. Emily lit the gas under the pot of soup. Pa came in first and headed for the fire. "We've got around three dozen!" he announced.

"Praise the lord, Eric!" Ma exclaimed. "We'll have a good meal at teatime."

Arthur came in and showed them the bucket of ormers. "Brrrr. It was pretty chilly on the beach in the wind, but worth it."

Emily put soup bowls on the table. She glanced at her mother, happy to hear her being enthusiastic about eating. They were all losing weight and her mother was small and could least afford it.

Pa stayed close to the fire. After the soup, he and Arthur would cut the ormers out of their shells and Emily would help to pound them and start the long, slow cooking process. It would be a real birthday meal, except that there were no fresh vegetables to serve with them. The ten thousand strong Jerry garrison had taken everything. Spring crops like lettuce and celery wouldn't be ready for a few weeks.

Pa picked up *The Press* and glanced at it. "What's this about sixty men having to be on guard at night?"

"The Jerries said somebody sabotaged their radio wire last week,"[19] said Emily. "They've put the curfew at nine o'clock now instead of ten. They're making sixty men stay up all night to make sure nobody sabotages the airport."

Arthur warmed his hands by the fire and frowned. "What a stupid waste of time. Anyway, there's quite a few unemployed fellows who could do that job."

"Sabotage on a small island is stupid," said Pa. "We're lucky nobody was shot."

Emily ladled out the soup, and Ma cut the bread. "Come and get it," she said. "There's soup, bread and cheese."

Arthur was the first to sit down. "I'll eat whatever you put in front of me," he said.

---

19   A cow probably caused the damage and the curfew was re-set to 10 p.m. some days later.

12: April–May 1941 — Bolton Visit & Bombings

*Visit to Bolton—May Queen—Bombs at The Summit—Lionel Visits—
First Aid Friends—Guernsey is part of Hitler's Atlantic Wall*

A visit to Bolton

At the end of March, Frances received a letter from Nellie inviting her to come to Bolton during the Easter school holiday. Otto had found a house for them, and they would squeeze everybody in. Frances felt excited. She wanted to see what life was like in Bolton. She knew it was less cold than Cotton Row and perhaps there would be an opportunity to move there.

She hadn't left Cotton Row since she came to Annie's eight months ago. Surviving the cold, sickness, and the lack of fresh food had drained her mentally as well as physically, and she didn't want to face another winter like this last one. The only good idea at Cotton Row was the new garden, where they might grow enough potatoes and vegetables to maintain their health through the next winter.

Otto and Nellie were the couple that she and Arthur were most at ease with: two sisters married to two brothers. She hadn't seen them since June last year, when Nellie was pregnant with their fourth child. Otto was the last person in the family to have seen Arthur before leaving the island. She hadn't even seen Alan yet, already six months old. The girls were excited too; they would be able to play with a real baby!

Easter Sunday was April 13, Lynette's third birthday came two days after, so Frances replied that they would come on Thursday, April 17, and stay till Sunday. Annie and Hilda would manage without her for a few days. She hadn't written anything in her tiny diary for a couple of months, but her happiness triggered her to start recording her life again.

Annie had her own thoughts. She was worried that Frances might think of moving to Bolton and the billeting money would go with her. She never mentioned what was on her mind, but it hung in the air. There was another thing which no logic could explain: Annie and Hilda both enjoyed having the children around. They were both past the age of starting a family themselves and Annie, in particular, looked forward to seeing them when she came home and enjoyed giving them a surprise.

Once Annie knew when Frances was going to Bolton, she worked out her plan. Her friend Rose lived in Bolton, and she sent her a letter asking her if she could stay with her on Saturday night. Annie intended to drop in at Nellie and Otto's to get some idea of what was going on. She had to think of some way to get Frances to stay at Cotton Row.

Frances and the girls left early on Thursday morning, and while they waited for the Express bus in Burnley, Frances remembered being there with Mabel almost a year ago. The big map of Lancashire was still on the inside wall. Vi was in Bradford to the east, across the moors. Blackburn was almost next door to Burnley, their source of vegetables in February. Bolton was an hour's journey across the moors to the south, towards Manchester.

In the bus she took note of the hills and villages that they passed through, pointing out a bridge, or a village shop, to the children, who in turn would make sure their dolls saw it. With two children, a small suitcase and a bag of food, she had plenty to watch over while she formulated the questions she wanted to ask Nellie: how had she and the school children managed when they arrived in Glasgow last June? How had Otto found them? How was she treated in hospital when Alan was born?

They were in Bolton by ten thirty and found the bus to Nellie's. Otto came in soon after and they all sipped tea in the kitchen. Nellie looked a little tired and had lost some weight, but the new baby was doing well. Janice and her cousin Sheila, who was a year older, had always been good friends, and they disappeared upstairs. Nancy, who was almost eleven, broke the ice with Lynette, both watching over the baby. Bert was at the home of a scout friend.

Frances told them about the snowstorms and the buses that were stuck on the main road to Burnley. Otto laughed. "We all got to be good at shovelling snow," he said. "Even some trains in the north were stuck with passengers on board. Five or six trains, we heard."

"We heard about one being stuck," said Frances. "News is hard to get. At least we were at home, but I was worried we might run out of food."

"That's what worries me too," said Nellie. "But the worst was the bombing. We had a really bad night in January. We were used to bombers flying over to get to Manchester. Usually, they pass a bit to the south. But this one..." she paused and shook her head.

Otto glanced around to see where the children were and softened his voice. "We don't talk about it in front of the children, Frances."

She nodded.

"This one dropped bombs on both sides of the cinema," Nellie continued quietly. "We knew a man who had a shop there that we used to go to, and he was killed. It was a nasty business."

"Where do you go if there's a raid?" Frances asked quietly. "Is there a bomb shelter on your street?"

"There's a cellar under the kitchen—right here," said Otto, getting up and opening what seemed to be a cupboard door. "We never know if there's time to go to a shelter, so we feel this is our best place. We keep a thermos ready at night and we take blankets down with us."

Nellie smiled. "You know, we haven't even got enough blankets to leave just one down there. In Guernsey, we always had spare blankets, but you can't get hold of them anywhere these days."

"I know," Frances nodded. "I'm knitting Janice some vests because I couldn't find children's underwear." She looked at the cellar door and hoped she wouldn't have to bundle her children down there in the next few days.

"When Sheila grows out of her clothes, I'll pass them on to you for Janice," said Nellie. "Now, did you have any bombs dropped near you?"

"No, we've been lucky. We've had sirens going off and we hide under the stairs with the children until the 'all clear' sounds. We haven't got a cellar."

"Well, you're twenty miles further north," Otto said. "From what your father says, there's probably nothing that's worth bombing around where you are. You're in a good place."

Frances was realising that the solid block of chilly moorland that lay between Bolton and Cotton Row had its value.

That afternoon they walked to the large cemetery gardens where Grampy was supervising the vegetable plantings, and she surprised Geoff and Bill working in the greenhouse and had a short chat with them. On Friday they took the children to a park, and after tea, Nellie watched over the children while Frances visited her parents.

The next morning, Nancy and Nellie watched over the children while Otto and Frances took a bus to Stockport to visit Mollie, Walter and Mahala's daughter. She was with her school, supervised by her Guernsey teachers, and seemed to be well looked after. That day, Frances had ample time to ask Otto about Arthur and those last days in Guernsey. Otto had managed to sign on as part of the crew of one of the last evacuee ships, trying to join Nellie and the children. He said Arthur hadn't wanted to leave his property unguarded, and had been worried about Ma and Pa, who didn't want to evacuate. He also had the mortgage to pay. She had known all that but had felt her own need to be greater.

Annie arrived in Bolton on Saturday afternoon with a plan in her head. Luckily, Rose was a staunch friend and was able to provide her with a bed for the night. She turned up at Otto and Nellie's late in the afternoon and invited them to come to Cotton Row when they had a chance. She also made sure she visited Gran and Grampy.

Frances might not have been pleased to see Annie visiting her family. Her diary is blank for ten days until May 1. She was unable to keep her diary private and it would have been unwise to make angry comments in it. Visiting her family usually led her to use up all her diary space. The blank pages have to tell their own story.

Janice is May Queen

Towards the end of April, Janice returned from school with some special news: she would be May Queen this year. Frances had never encountered this kind of festivity, and Annie and Hilda had to explain it to her. Being May Queen was an honour, and an indication of how well Janice was doing in her class, and how well she had been accepted by her classmates.

It wouldn't be very warm on May 1, and Frances decided that Janice would wear the red velvet dress that she had made for her for Christmas. On the big day, all the girls in Janice's class came to Cotton Row after school and decked themselves out with daisy chains in their hair and around their necks. Frances had tea and buns for everyone. The other girls were now the Queen's Followers and carried her stool. One of them was in charge of the money bag. As Queen, Janice carried the Maypole with its long ribbons.

Frances and Lynette watched the start of it at the north end of Cotton Row. Neighbours came out and watched the performance. Janice sat on the stool, holding the Maypole. Each of the other girls held the end of a long ribbon attached to the Maypole and skipped around the Queen one way, singing the Maypole Song. They turned and unwound the ribbons, skipping in the other direction. The neighbours clapped and contributed a few coins.

The Maypole group went down to Clowbridge to repeat the show along the rows of houses. Later, the pennies were counted out and shared. Janice received one-and-nine (21 pennies) that evening, which was a grand amount. The next day they did it again after school but had fewer locations to visit, and her share was four and a half pennies.

Bombs at the Summit

On Sunday, May 4, clocks were put back for summer time. It was a warm day and Annie, Frances, and Hilda worked on their garden at Kit Hoyle's in the morning. After dinner, a younger Haworth sister, Agnes, came from Padiham with her husband, and they enjoyed tea together. It was a peaceful day.

The night was different. Sirens woke them after midnight and the two women quickly donned coats and slippers, and hustled the girls down the stairs. Bombs were dropped north and south of them in a raid which narrowly missed the bigger village of Loveclough, on the far side of Clowbridge's mill. Annie went outside and saw part of the moors on fire to the north, and they stayed awake well after the 'all clear' had sounded until there was no fire to be seen. Hot tea was a comfort; but they were too jittery to sleep much.

Few people knew that the RAF had built decoy sites on the moors, at some distance from the Manchester-Burnley Road. One was an artificial aerodrome; and the second, on a site beyond Crown Point, looked like a town. At night, fires might be started within these decoys to make them look like burning targets. That night, German pilots had bombed them with incendiaries, thinking they were target cities. Some of the bombs had fallen near the Summit, overlooking Burnley.

The day after the bombing, while Hilda watched the children, Annie and Frances walked to see the bomb holes at Loveclough. Next day, Janice had some news to share when she came home from school in the afternoon: "All the others in my class are going to see the bomb holes on the Summit after tea," she announced. "Can I go with them?"

"If everybody's going, then let's all go," said Frances. "We can walk up there. I'll take Lynette in the pushcart. We'll see if Auntie Hilda wants to go as well."

That sounded exciting, and Annie came with them. Frances noted:
Went with Annie and children to see damage at Summit. Clowbridge children picking up pieces of incendiaries on moors. Estimated 200 dropped.

The Summit was less than two miles from Cotton Row and just on the other side of Crown Point Road. It reminded Frances of Nellie's fears of a bombing raid, and suddenly the war felt that much closer. She had only just begun her First Aid courses and realised how important they might be. Luckily there were no houses where the incendiaries had dropped. In the days that followed she learned that Liverpool and its port had been bombed every night from the 1st to the 5th of May. The bombing around Cotton Row was comparatively light and inconsequential.

Lionel visits

Frances had a surprise visitor a week later on Monday, May 12, when she had already started the week's washing. Lionel turned up in the middle of the morning and stayed for the day. He didn't smoke and had exchanged cigarettes for a tin of golden syrup and some chocolate, which he brought for them all. After tea, Frances showed him the garden and they had a walk with Lynette in the pushcart.

Annie returned home from her shift early in the afternoon.

"I'm glad to see you again, Lionel," she said. She mentally added the visit of a uniform like a notch on her gun.

"Look at what he brought for us," Frances said.

"Golden syrup! We can eat plenty of that. Maybe I could make a parkin. That's a ginger cake, Lionel," she explained.

They talked over another cup of tea. "I came up from the south yesterday and London had a heavy bombing night again," Lionel said. "You said you were taking First Aid courses, Auntie, and I think a lot of women are doing that, and you can see that it's needed. Believe me, it's like another world up here. You said you had some incendiary bombing last week; but you should see the damage in London."

"And have you seen any action where you've been sailing, Lionel?"

"I can't say anything about it; but we've had to dodge around a few times. If only we knew where the U-boats were, it'd make it a lot safer for us to bring in supplies."

"Sometimes we hear that the RAF has been bombing St. Nazaire and

Brest and other French ports," said Frances. "I suppose that's where some U-boats set out from. Would they keep U-boats in St. Peter Port harbour?"

"I don't think the harbour's big enough in Guernsey, but I bet they sometimes hear RAF bombers flying over the island on their way to St. Nazaire."

"And now they're fighting in North Africa and the Germans are in Yugoslavia and Greece, aren't they? It just spreads and spreads."

"That's what I hear. I was looking at your maps of all those places stuck up on the wall here. You're lucky to live away from the bombs and the fighting."

Annie was happy to hear Lionel's comments and hoped it had an effect on Frances.

First Aid Friends

At the First Aid courses, Frances made several friends. One was Mrs Frost, a Red Cross nurse. One evening Frances went to an Old Tyme Dancing evening with Annie, and Mrs Frost and her husband were there. They chatted, and Mrs Frost invited Frances to tea at their home in Waterfoot, the following Sunday.

"Bring your children," Mrs Frost said.

"Waterfoot's a small town, just outside Rawtenstall," Annie told her. "Our Alice-Ann used to work in the big slipper factory there. It's a pretty place."

Apart from the one large mill, where everybody used to work, it certainly was a pretty place. Frances and the children found the Frost's house, not far from a stone bridge over a river. They were well received, and Janice was allowed to try on Mrs Frost's nurse's apron.

"You know, I was a nurse before I married, and now I'm really pleased to help in the war effort," she told them. "The SJAB and the Red Cross work together and we have Flying Columns to get to the scene of a bombing fast."

Janice looked up. "What's a Flying Column?"

"It's thirteen people who work together. One is the driver, one has a canteen and makes hot tea, and the others are nurses or assistants to help people who are hurt, or to make notes on what's happened. We all work together. Maybe you'll be a nurse one day."

Janice was delighted with the idea.

After tea and cake, they went for a walk along the river in a small valley. It was an afternoon that seemed to have nothing to do with war. The girls played with pebbles by a stream while the two women sat and chatted. Mrs Frost told Frances about how to be prepared in a war.

"If you suddenly have to cope with a bomb dropping near you, Frances, you need to know how to deal with burns or cuts, bleeding, or people in shock. You may need to ease the pain and wait for a doctor. You can't always move people, but sometimes you have to... But as long as you can remember your First Aid training, you may be saving a life."

"I'm glad I can follow these courses. I wish I could do more," Frances said.

"You have enough on your plate with your two children, but just keep coming to the training courses. We're hoping to have more people join us from the villages, so you could encourage other women to attend. Besides nursing, we have people overseas finding out what's happened to servicemen who have gone missing or if they're in some foreign hospital. A lot of families get their information from us."

They called the children and started to walk back.

"Now, I wanted to ask you, are you happy with your present billet? From what you said, you had a really bad winter. I might be able to help you to find a new one."

Frances hadn't anticipated the enquiry, and she found herself hesitating about making a reply. Moving to be near her family would be attractive, but a move within this same area needed thinking about. Every member of her family had been welcomed at Annie's no matter when they dropped in. Mrs Frost, or her middle-class friends, might not open their doors like Annie had.

"I think I'm more settled now," she replied. "Janice is doing well in school, and I'll be better prepared for another winter, but thank you for your thoughtful offer."

Hitler's Atlantic Wall

In 1940, Britain's air force prevented Hitler from launching his invasion across the Channel. In the spring of 1941, Hitler decided to invade Russia, which up to this point had been his ally.

He feared that as soon as his armies were involved in fighting the Russians in eastern Europe, Britain would attempt landings in the west, along the Atlantic coast of France and especially in the Channel Islands. Therefore, he must fortify those coastal areas so strongly that no Allied force could successfully land there. *The Atlantic Wall* was the name of Hitler's coastal defences, which stretched from Norway through Holland, Belgium, France, and down to Spain.

Early in June 1941, Hitler gave orders to strengthen the garrisons on the Channel Islands, and to increase food stores. Tanks were to be imported, and more guns were to be brought in, including twelve with a range of 25 km.[20] Similar guns would be stationed on the coast of France opposite the islands. They would control the whole Gulf of St Malo.

Later that year, he insisted on having guns with a range of 50 km. On the west coast the Mirus battery was completed by November 1942. Its four huge guns controlled the Gulf of St. Malo. Elsewhere, 54,000 mines were laid on the island cliffs and in the sea.[21] More ammunition, anti-aircraft guns, searchlights, escort ships were ordered. There would be over two hundred strong points on the island with walls between two and three and a half metres thick. Wired shell bombs were set up in fields and on the cliffs in case Allied paratroopers tried to land.

The Organisation Todt (OT) had built Germany's national road system before the war. It became part of the

---

20 Cruickshank, p 152.
21 Cruickshank, p.154.

war ministry and built fortifications. It used concentration camp prisoners as slave workers, and many of them died on the islands. Hitler seemed to be obsessed with making a fortress out of the Channel Islands. Losing them would be a huge blow to prestige. The Channel Islands absorbed one twelfth of all the Atlantic Wall materials—although they were only a tiny fraction of the Wall.

13: Late May–June 1941: End of the Blitz

Red Cross messages—Frank & Adele—Blitz ends—Weekend in Bolton
Annie's new job—A birthday party—Bismarck is sunk

Red Cross Messages

On Tuesday May 13, after tea, Janice saw Uncle Tom coming briskly to the front door and announced him loudly. He came in, waving a cutting from his newspaper.

"Look at this, Frances! This headline: '10,000 Red Cross Messages Received for Channel Islanders.'"

"Tom!" She looked at the cutting and read it out loud. "Thank you for bringing it."

"You can keep the cutting. I hope you'll be getting a message soon."

Frances wondered if she would receive one. Her heart had jumped when she heard Tom's announcement. One little message would be wonderful after a black silence of over ten months.

She wondered later: what could Arthur tell her? She would know if he was alive, at least. They had heard that messages went through German censors and then were routed through Geneva, so he wouldn't be able to tell her how they fared under the Germans. Was he well? She had dealt with evacuation and sickness, but one didn't send bad news. It needed simple facts. How much could they tell each other if it was censored?

Next day was cold and she was glad to be inside ironing, although it was a job she disliked, heating the iron on the stove. Suddenly, there was a sprinkling of snow on the hills. It had its own beauty, but she only stayed out for ten minutes with Lynette, and Janice was glad to kick off her clogs when she came home, and to warm her feet by the fire. The postman walked by without stopping. That evening was a First Aid night. The doctor's topic this week would be about sun and heat stroke! But she would bundle up and climb into a bus and get there. Perhaps she would hear that someone had received a message.

When Janice walked home from school at noon on Friday that week, she saw the postman ahead of her. He had just pushed letters through the letter box. Once inside, she picked up the letters and saw that one had a Red Cross marked on it.

"Red Cross Message! Red Cross Message!" she chanted. Lynette came running. Janice flopped on the floor and drew in her arms by her sides. "Lie across me, to make a cross," she commanded her sister. "We'll be the Red Cross." Lynette obliged, and they kept up the chanting. Frances had been tidying upstairs and rushed down.

She read the strips of paper glued on to the message form: "Ma, Pa, Emily, and I are well. Gardening in town with them," and a little more. At least Arthur was alive. Probably he was living with his sister and parents in their house in Havelet, growing some vegetables. A few words could suggest a lot.

But the excitement! Annie wasn't working that day and came back from Burnley on the bus a few minutes later for dinner. The children called out "Red Cross Message!" from their places at the table as she came in the door. She knew Frances had been hoping for this all week.

"Look—a message from Arthur!" Frances was rarely as excited as this.

"Now, will your family be getting messages in Bolton as well?" she asked.

"I suppose so. It said in the newspaper that Tom brought us, that they're being received everywhere."

"Well then, why don't we go over to Bolton right after dinner and see what's happening there?" Annie wasn't going to miss sharing this excitement.

"I was thinking of going tomorrow," Frances said, "but we could go today, I suppose. The children are eating already."

"We might even get the afternoon Express from Burnley if we're quick, and come back on the eight o'clock. I can help you with the children."

Once in Bolton, they found everyone in an excited mood at Grampy's. Nellie had a message from Ma to pass around, and Mabel had called in earlier to say she had received two at Mrs Lawson's. That gave them four messages and one hundred words from their families to analyse and discuss, let alone other evacuee friends and their messages.

Gran had another surprise for Frances: "I had a letter from your brother—from Frank—this morning. He's coming to see us on Sunday while he has a few days of leave. He'll bring Adele with him. If he has time, I'd like to bring them over to see you at Cotton Row on Monday."

"Oh Mum, please make them find time to come. When we left Guernsey,

Frank was at the harbour somewhere waiting for a boat, but I didn't see him. They'll be coming from Halifax?"

"Yes, that's where Adele and her mother are living; but he says they have to be back in Halifax on Monday night."

"Try to manage it, Mum. We all missed their wedding last year."

After all the excitement, they caught the eight o'clock bus back. The children slept on the way and Frances closed her eyes and let the words of the messages circle in her head. Annie hoped that her appearance with Frances made her seem like a family friend. She had repeated her invitation to Otto and Nellie and hoped that things were working in her favour.

Next morning was Saturday, and they walked across the moor to Burnley, and were caught up in shopping and exchanging greetings with fellow evacuees in the park. Frances learned that other messages from Guernsey said that everyone was well, that they were working in their gardens, but there were hints that people had moved from their houses.

Everybody in Clowbridge seemed to know that Frances had received a message. It had been a warm day, and after tea people dropped in to say how glad they were to hear the news. Frances was surprised and grateful for their support. She was also glad that Janice was thinking of her father, and that Lynette knew she had a father, somewhere. Receiving a message seemed to have completed her credentials as a married woman with a husband who was in enemy controlled territory. Below her diary notes, she added: *The weather is warmer and the cuckoo sings all day.*

Frank & Adele

On Monday morning, May 19, Janice went to school as usual. Frances had decided to postpone the washing until Tuesday, in case Gran was able to bring Frank and Adele to Cotton Row. She badly wanted to see him: a precious brother, born when she was eleven. He was now both a soldier and a husband, and she hadn't been able to wish him well at either of these important transitions.

Lynette was given the job of watching for the buses coming from Burnley; luckily, she remembered to watch at the right time. A bus stopped, and when it moved on, she saw a khaki-clad soldier helping Gran across the road, followed by another woman.

"Mum, I think they're here!"

Frances went outside to welcome them.

"Frank! I haven't seen you and Adele since…since…"

"I know." Frank strode forward and gave her a hug. She was the big sister who had looked after him so constantly when he was small.

"I saw you getting on the boat in Guernsey that day," he said. "You were with Vi and Fred. It was a rough time."

"It was very rough. Hello, Mum. Oh Adele, it's really good to see you. I'm sorry I wasn't at your wedding last year." She kissed Adele. "I don't know where we were then, maybe still in Burnley."

Annie was getting ready to go to work but stepped outside grinning when she saw Frank in uniform. "Come on in," she said. "I've put the kettle on. Now, Frances, you must introduce me to everybody."

"Well, you know me already," said Gran.

"I certainly do. And the first cup of tea will be for you."

Frank and Adele were introduced. Frank grinned. "We've heard a lot about you, Annie. I'm on leave till tomorrow night but we must be back in Halifax tonight, so this is a quick visit."

"Halifax!" said Annie. "Yes, that's quite a ride. Now, all of you sit down and then you can talk. I'll look after the tea, and then I have to go." She disappeared into the kitchen.

They exchanged stories about finding warm clothing while Annie brought in the tea things. Adele giggled. "Talking of clothing," she said, "you should see Frank when he's all dressed up." Frank grinned.

"What do you mean, dressed up?" Annie asked.

Adele laughed. "He wears a kilt," she said.

Frank smiled. "I joined up with the Black Watch." He produced a photo of himself in a kilt. That gave Annie another item to tell the Haworths, and she left after telling Frank and Adele to call in whenever they were near enough, and wearing a kilt would be welcome.

"I've managed to rent a small place," Frank said as they settled around the table. "Adele's Mum is there, so they're company for each other when I'm away."

"We're managing all right," said Adele, "now that we're getting used to the way people talk and the rations and everything. And there are quite a few Guernsey people there."

"Have you had any air raids ? Any bombs dropped? " Frances asked.

"There was one nasty incident last November. A huge bomb was dropped on a street near a pub, and about eleven people were killed, and others injured. It wasn't like bombing a factory that's producing guns or something.—Just a quiet street."

"But the Express bus schedule isn't working too well," Frank added. "We'll probably have to wait for connections; and they're reducing some bus services."

"We can chat while we have some dinner together," said Frances, "and as soon as we've finished, I'll come with you to the Burnley terminus, and you can get a start on your way home. Mum, I'll put you on a bus back to Bolton. I'll bring Lynette with us."

Gran nodded. "That'll suit me," she said. "I'll doze on the way home."

Frances felt as though she was flying high all day, even after they had all returned home from Burnley and she had taken care of Lynette and done the washing up. She had another trip to Burnley that evening for her First Aid course, but it had been a very good day.

Tuesday had to be washing day that week, and between her various jobs Frances wrote out a reply to Arthur's Red Cross message. She wanted to tell him about the winter, the sickness, and the bombing raid two weeks ago, which worried her every night when she put the girls to bed; but she told him that all was well, that they were gardening, Janice was doing well at school, and the children had played in the snow. Perhaps that would give a hint that they were in the north. It had to be squeezed into twenty-five words. When Janice came home after school, Frances helped her to write her own message to Arthur, and took both messages to the Red Cross office in Burnley next morning.

> After the middle of May, there seemed to be less news about bombing in London. It seemed that the **Blitz had ended** soon after the last attack that Lionel had described.
>
> It was later estimated that over a million homes had been destroyed in and around London and 40,000 people killed,[22] but few people knew the extent of the damage at the time.

---

22   https://www.historic-uk.com/HistoryUK/

Weekend in Bolton

Frances had promised Nellie that she would babysit Alan and Sheila in Bolton the next weekend, with Nancy's help. Bert had passed an exam which would give him a place in the Guernsey Intermediate Boys' School, which had been evacuated to Oldham. They wanted to take him to meet the teachers and see the school, which would use a portion of the Hulme Boys' Grammar School. They would also visit another Enevoldsen niece, Marion, who was with her school at Stockport.

Friday, May 23, was a chilly and wet day, with hail and rain beating down on the daffodils in the front garden. After school, they had a quick tea and rushed to get on a bus. It was nine o'clock before they arrived in Bolton and Lynette had fallen asleep on the way.

Next day, eleven-year-old Nancy helped Frances with Alan, and things went well. Otto and Nellie had a good impression of the school and its Guernsey teachers, who seemed to be very concerned about their Guernsey students. Later, they found Marion and she seemed to be doing well. They exchanged news of Red Cross messages with the staff on both visits.

On Sunday, Otto had to go to work at the factory, and the sisters had time for a private chat. Nellie told Frances that she was worried now about bombings in Oldham as well as Bolton.

"If something happens to Otto, what do I do with three children in school and a baby, all by myself?" she asked. "And Bert starts school in September in Oldham—which is just outside Manchester—but he wants to go."

"My worst time was last year," said Frances, "when Mabel left with Pat, and I had to look after Vi as well as my girls. But at least we had very few air raids."

"It must have been bad, feeling so alone. I think you made a good choice going to Annie's," said Nellie. "By the way, was she planning on coming to Bolton this weekend?"

"No," Frances smiled. "She won't be interrupting us. She's starting a new job tomorrow. Her factory's had to reduce the number of workers this year because they can't import enough raw cotton. She's not worked much this past week. She wants you to come over and see us, though. If Nancy's at home from school one day and could look after Alan, come over and see where we are."

"I'll write and let you know. The best thing for me would be to get out of this town and be somewhere peaceful."

The weather cleared up on Sunday and Frances took the girls for a walk to see Grampy and his vegetable gardens. Then it was time to catch a bus back home.

Annie's new job

On May 26, Annie started work at her new job. She had to report to a mill at Stoneyholme, on the north side of Burnley. This mill had changed its production from light cotton clothing to tarpaulins and haversacks for military use.

"I can use a sewing machine," she said to Frances when she arrived home after work. "But these haversacks are heavy material, and you need strong hands. I find it hard to manage. It helps with the war effort, and I can still live here at home, but it's hard on my hands."

"Perhaps they can change you to something a bit easier to handle," Frances suggested. "There's some good news from the garden anyway: our potatoes are showing up above the ground, and so are the swedes. So we've been successful there."

She left to start a new course in Home Nursing that evening, first taking a bus to Rawtenstall and then to a smaller town called Barleyhome. She left it to Hilda and the children to cheer up Annie.

A birthday party

On May 30 it would be Janice's sixth birthday. Frances had been grateful for the kindness shown to Janice in school and by the parents of her classmates. She had also been surprised at the way some villagers had congratulated her on receiving the Red Cross message from Arthur. They were more outspoken than people were in Guernsey, combining both respect and familiarity. She decided to do the best she could to have a birthday party after school on May 30, and invited all eight girls from Miss Taylor's class.

Wednesday and Thursday were spent cleaning the house and making a cake and a trifle. Eggs would soon be rationed, and she wondered if she would be able to make a cake at all in the future. She had saved enough of their sugar ration to make the cake. She managed to purchase a packet of chocolate biscuits earlier in the month. Annie produced an old box of Christmas crackers with hats inside them.

Fortunately, May 30 was a warm day. The children came after school for tea, pulled the crackers and wore the hats, ate trifle, cake, and chocolate biscuits. Annie took a photo of the group in the field at the back, and they played until various mothers walked up from Clowbridge to take their children home. Janice's closest friends were Sheila Marshall, whose father was in charge of the reservoir, and Eunice Westall. Frances felt she had entered a bit more into village life.

Lynette felt sad. She looked at all of Janice's friends. She had seen them sometimes on Sundays or at the Christmas party. She wanted to go to school and have some friends, too. Frances and Annie wondered what the solution could be and had a chat with Linda Taylor.

Linda was helpful; there were other children of Lynette's age in the village. On June 9, Frances noted in her diary: *Lynette went to school.* That was for the Monday afternoon only, with the hope that Linda could absorb a few younger children for half days in future.

The Bismarck is sunk

At the end of May, both Annie and Frances breathed a sigh of relief when they heard that the huge German destroyer Bismarck had been sunk. They had often thought about Lionel, who was on a merchant ship somewhere in the Atlantic.

> Between the 18 and 27 May 1941, the **brand-new battleship *Bismarck*** and the cruiser *Prinz Eugen* quietly left their docks in northern Germany and headed for the North Sea. The plan was to quietly enter the North Atlantic via the Denmark Strait, which separates Iceland from Greenland. From there, they would work with U-boats to continue Hitler's plan to destroy supply ships heading to England from North America.
>
> The *Bismarck* was the pride of the German fleet. Its movements had been noticed from an airplane over Norway, which was under German control, but the news was passed to the British consul in Sweden, who made sure

it was received in London.

British ships, including the huge battleship HMS *Hood*, were sent to prevent the German ships from entering the North Atlantic.[23] Moving around in fog, the *Hood* sighted what it thought was the *Bismarck* but was actually the *Prinz Eugen*. The *Hood's* manoeuvres made it a target of the Bismarck instead. The *Hood's* ammunition store was blown up, and it sank. Only three men of the *Hood's* complement of over 1400 were saved.

The British navy made a huge effort to corner the *Bismarck* and in the last week of May it was located in the Atlantic, over 500 miles west of Lands' End, ready to prey on supply ships. Aircraft from the *Ark Royal* bombed the ship, and the steering was damaged so that it slowed down. The ship headed for the French coast, probably to Brest, where repairs could be made. Next morning, the RAF and British cruisers put her out of action, and she sank.

---

23 https://www.forces-war-records.co.uk/world-war-two-timeline-of-events-1941#May1941

14: June 1941: Fortifying Guernsey

*Two more uniforms—Bike worries on a Fortress island—
Frances talks about Joyce—Newlyweds visit*

Two more uniforms

On Monday morning, June 2, Frances was sorting the laundry and Annie was still in her pyjamas playing with Lynette when there was a knock at the front door. She hurried over to answer it.

"Hello Auntie. We're surprising you!"

"You certainly are! Come on in. My goodness. Annie, you've already met..." She introduced Eric and Daisy Carter.

Annie got up off the floor and neatened her dressing gown. "Excuse me being in my pyjamas, but I don't have to go to work till eleven. Come on in and get warmed up."

They laughed and came over to the fire.

"Thanks, Annie. It's such a cold day," said Eric, "and yesterday we were too warm."

"We were picking flowers at the Bonk yesterday," said Frances. "That's an area down on the lower slope of the moors up behind Clowbridge village. There are little streams, and it was full of yellow marsh marigolds. The girls were wearing their summer dresses."

They had tea and when Annie had dressed and appeared again, Daisy said that she had five days leave next week and was it possible to spend it around here.

"If you have a neighbour who could put me up, I'd be happy to pay them, and of course I'd bring my rations and a bit extra. It makes such a difference to see someone in the family and be away from Manchester and the bombing."

Annie saw another chance to make her house the focus for Frances' family. Extra rations would be good too.

"Nay, you can stay here," she said. "There's the single bed upstairs, if that's all right with you. Our Hilda's sleeping at our Alice-Ann's most nights."

Daisy was shown around, and it was settled. She would arrive on Thursday night, June 5. Annie went off to work feeling content. In the afternoon, Frances bundled up Lynette and they all walked around the Bonk, but it was so cold that they were glad to return home. Eric and Daisy looked at the gallery of maps on the living room wall without comment. The news that Crete had been lost and Greece had been taken by the Germans wasn't cheerful, and they found other things to discuss. Later, the neighbours watched the two uniforms leave on the five-thirty bus.

After Daisy arrived on June 5, the weather turned warm again, and Frances prepared a picnic to take to Stoneyholme, so that Annie could easily join them for dinner when her shift had a dinner break at one o'clock. They enjoyed a walk along the moors after, with Lynette in her pushcart. Back at home, they inspected the garden. The scarlet runner beans were doing well.

On Saturday, they all had a picnic in Thompson Park in Burnley, and walked around to see how the leeks, beetroot and other vegetables were doing in the Italian Gardens. Frances took the children home while Annie and Daisy did some grocery shopping.

Frances and Daisy walked up to Crown Point on Sunday morning to see the hospital, which now looked empty and abandoned. Then they joined in a family service at St. James. All the school children sang a hymn and Lynette cried because she couldn't join in, but she was invited to attend school the next day in the afternoon. On Monday afternoon, Frances and Daisy walked the girls to school and took a bus to Burnley and enjoyed the market.

Daisy wanted Frances to see her WAAF lodgings in Oldham, and Hilda and Annie said they would look after the children on Tuesday if Frances wanted to go with her. They left early in the morning, and were in Oldham at noon. Daisy's WAAF friends gave them a special welcome; but Frances was anxious to return to Cotton Row by early evening. She wasn't comfortable leaving the children when it wasn't absolutely necessary, and there was still a risk of bombing around Manchester.

Bike worries

The weather over Guernsey was fine and dry early in June, and Arthur rode his bike home the long way round after work one afternoon, so that he could stop at a small bike shop. The owner, Frank Symons, grinned as he came in.

"Afternoon, Arthur. I've got something for you. You'll be happy. It's a spare tyre for your sister's bike."

"Good. Have you got one for my bike as well?"

"No, the Jerries cleaned me out. I put aside an inner tube for her bike as well, luckily. So you'll have at least one good bike between you. The Jerries just waltzed in and grabbed everything, and I don't know if I'll be able to get any more while this war's going on."

"I heard they might requisition more bikes. That's why I asked you to keep me one. We both need our bikes."

"I know. If I can find a spare for yours, even a used one, I'll keep it for you. Now, you and your sister have English bikes, and their tyres last longer than French bikes, so the Jerries are looking for those. It seems that you have to be an active worker to keep a bike. Tell your sister to always look busy, as though she's carrying rations home on it or something, or they'll find an excuse to take it."

"We bring in our bikes all the time now. It's too risky leaving them outside the house."

"I know. There are always Jerries snooping around, even in daytime. You'd better keep those spare parts well hidden."

Fortress island

At *Le Pré*, Pa was coming into the house for tea as Arthur arrived home. "The potatoes are doing well," Pa announced to everybody.

"The carrots and cabbage and beans should be good too," Ma replied from the kitchen table. "Emily and I did some weeding while you were out this afternoon."

Pa rinsed his hands. "I was watching the harbour for a while," he said. "There's always boats coming in with heavy machinery and full cargoes of cement. Now they have a huge French barge in the harbour with a crane that can lift up to a hundred tons, or so I was told. Arthur, do you know why that floating crane is there?"

"Emily and I saw Charlie in the market yesterday," Ma butted in, "and he said that French tanks from the Great War were being unloaded. Perhaps that's what the big crane is for."

Arthur took his place at the sink. "I heard about that. They'd need a crane to lift those huge things. But why would they bring tanks here? There's nowhere to go with a tank! I've heard them practicing with their anti-aircraft guns, which makes a bit more sense."

"Who's transporting all this stuff for them?" Pa asked.

"Their own soldiers. One of our drivers from Cobo said they're making gun emplacements on the west coast—one very big one. They're shipping a lot of concrete there. And on two days recently there was a lot of equipment being moved along the Forest Road towards the airport. I had to make a delivery along there and I had to wait a bit. A Jerry driver took a narrow road and he was knocking corners off."

"Do Leale's transport anything for them?"

"No. Local companies won't do it," Arthur said, "even if business is poor. I know Leale's have refused, because it's all for military operations."

"If Leale's doesn't have much business, does that mean your job's in danger, Arthur?" Pa asked.

"I'm all right up to now; but if they requisition some of Leale's lorries, I don't know what happens to my job."

There was a sympathetic silence.

"Talking about guns…" Ma began, "they've been practicing with them from up on the Val des Terres road, maybe from Fort George at the top. They make a terrible lot of noise."

"I don't know what they're practicing for," Emily observed. "I've heard RAF planes flying over two or three times this week, during the night, but the Jerries never seem to use anti-aircraft guns against them."

"I think the RAF planes are flying too high, probably headed for Brest and St. Nazaire," Pa replied. "Those are big ports, and I bet that's where a lot of those U-boats hide. I hope they're getting rid of a few."

They settled down around the table. Arthur told them about his visit to the bike shop.

Emily looked worried. "We registered your bike and mine, Art. I hope we won't have to give them up. You'd better keep yours well hidden, Pa."

"Well, I don't use my old bike much," said Pa, "but I like to have it to go down around the harbour, or as near as they'll let me."

"Your bike's old, Pa, but it's an English make," Arthur commented.

"I can't do without my bike," Emily stated. I buy a lot of vegetables some days, and bread, but I can't bring them home without the basket in front and the box on the carrier. Nobody delivers bread or groceries anymore."

Arthur remembered Frank's words. "Always have a shopping bag with you, Emily. If it looks as though you're riding around for pleasure, they'll take the bike."

"Arthur, I never ride around to amuse myself." Emily was indignant. "Remember, I do almost all the shopping for the four of us. I had to get our new fish ration cards this week as well."

"Emily, Arthur didn't mean…" Ma started.

Emily's voice softened. "It's all right, Ma. I know what you mean, Art. I think I'm going to put a few scratches on my bike and I'll dirty it a bit, so it looks old. I hope Louise doesn't mind when she comes back home. It's her bike, really; but there's no way I can manage without it."

Frances talks about Joyce

A few days after Daisy's visit, Frances received a letter from Gran saying that Joyce and Ken planned to come to Bolton in the middle of June while there was a lull in the bombing. Frances shared the news with Annie and Hilda. The newlyweds had gone south to live in Weymouth, where Ken worked in the Post Office, and he had a week's holiday.

"Invite them to come here," Annie said, when Frances shared the news with her. Annie didn't like her own job situation, and she was determined to keep Frances and her billeting money; better welcome the couple here than see Frances go to Bolton again, or even be enticed to Weymouth.

"I remember, they were married in February, weren't they?" she continued. "It sounded as though you were really fond of her."

"Well, I looked after the younger children at home," Frances explained. "It was my job. I wanted to go to the Intermediate School for Girls when I was about twelve—I'd passed the exam, but my parents refused and said I should go into service—working for a rich family. But I had really good marks, and my grandfather—Old John Torode they used to call him—liked a project I did on botany. He thought I could add some value to my father's growing business if I studied hard. He helped to persuade them, and in the end they let me attend the school. My mother gave me a job: looking after the younger children, after school and on weekends."

"How many were you looking after?"

"Vi was about six, then there was Frank about two years old, then Bill, and Joyce was a baby. Geoff wasn't even born yet."

"And did any of your other sisters stay in school?"

"No. Nellie wanted to go to secondary school like me, but Mum and Dad refused and she had to go into service; and so did the others. Actually, she was working for the vicar of Holy Trinity, which is how she met Otto. All his family attended Trinity."

"And did you stay on at school, to the end?"

"Yes. In 1923 I completed my final exams. Then my aunt arrived from Canada and I went back to Toronto with her, with my sisters Edie and Mabel. Nellie was already married by then."

"And Joyce?"

"She was only two when I went to Canada. I'd been like a second mother to her. We even slept in the same bed. Poor Joyce, she was devastated when I left. When I came back almost two years later, she didn't want to know me, and I was really upset."

"So, Joyce has been living with your parents up to now."

"That's right, and so have Bill and Geoff. Joyce was working in a shop in town in Guernsey. She's twenty now."

"You had a big family like I did. Why don't you invite them like your mum suggests. Hilda and me, we'll be back from work in the afternoon and we can meet them."

Frances wrote back to Gran and invited Joyce and Ken to come for the day on Wednesday, June 18. She would have them all to herself until Annie and Hilda came home.

There was some discussion about making dinner. Frances couldn't expect to provide for her guests out of the housekeeping budget, but she had no time to plan for this visit. At least whenever her family came to visit, they contributed some food. She had just made a nice tea for ten local children for Janice's birthday, and Annie and Hilda had some of the glory; but she hoped there would be an opportunity for her to earn a little cash somehow, in the future. For the moment, Annie was content to have Frances' family visit, but she kept a mental note of the family visits.

Newlyweds visit

Frances had a First Aid exam the evening before Joyce and Ken's visit and needed to study. She shared her anxiety with her diary: *I should not have left it all till now.* She started the washing on Sunday morning, completed it and the ironing on Monday morning, and had the next two afternoons to study her course notes, while keeping an eye on Lynette.

After the exam on Tuesday evening, tea and cake were served, and she was finally able to relax and chat with the others. It gave her a rare chance to talk personally with her instructors. However, the next First Aid course would start tomorrow, the evening of Joyce and Ken's visit!

On Wednesday, the weather was perfect and Janice stayed at home for the day. Annie and Hilda were working early shifts and wouldn't be back until the afternoon. Both children noisily announced the sighting of every bus from Burnley. Finally one stopped, and Joyce and Ken walked across the road to Number 8. There was a joyous welcome and after dinner they took a long walk down to Loveclough across the slope of the moors.

Ken said how good it was to come on the bus through villages that hadn't been hit by bombs. Frances told them about the terrible winter, that she had thought about moving, and told them about her First Aid classes. They talked about war work: Joyce and Ken were both Night Watchmen, patrolling outside at night, making sure that no chinks of light were showing. When sirens sounded, they directed people to air-raid shelters and checked their list of residents if a bombing occurred.

"There are so many volunteers helping each other," Ken said, "that you can't help but join in and do what you can."

"It was all right when I went there in February after we were married," Joyce added, "but they started bombing again in May and it was awful. There were raids almost every night until the middle of the month and we hardly slept. Ken had to go to work and he would fall asleep after tea and then we'd be up all night again. Since then, there's been only one night of bombing."

"Last year, Weymouth was bombed right through from August till the end of January," Ken added. "I'm glad Joyce wasn't there to experience it. Of course, Hitler thought he'd invade us last year. He thought it was just a walk across the Channel."

"Plymouth was the worst," Joyce said quietly. "It's quite a way west of us, but it was being bombed in April and May this year like the Blitz they had in London. Thousands of houses were destroyed. We've met some people who were bombed out. They say it's just rubble there."

"We wanted to come up and see you when the bombing slackened off," said Ken, "and here we are on a beautiful day in a peaceful place. Frances, you are lucky. Just the moors and these birds…"

"Curlews."

"…curlews, and the reservoir over there."

A photo shows Joyce and Ken with Janice and Lynette, sitting higher up on the moor behind Cotton Row, with the reservoir in the distance. When they returned, they found that Annie and Hilda had both arrived from their shifts and introductions were made. Hilda went to summon Alice-Ann and Peter, and they all sat out in the meadow.

They took a second photo: Joyce and Ken are sitting on a blanket with Janice. Annie is pretending to be asleep on a chair nearby, and Lynette is telling her to wake up and smile. Hilda and Alice-Ann are also part of the group and young Peter is on the blanket, on his best behaviour. The famous pram for Teddy is on one side. When the photos were developed, they became part of Frances' wartime treasures.

That evening, she took the bus with them to Burnley and said goodbye before they returned to Bolton. Annie put the children to bed and went to bed early to be ready for her morning shift. That evening Frances was pleased to learn that she had passed her First Aid exam. She tiptoed into the house feeling contented with her day.

Next day, when Annie came home from her shift in the afternoon, she wanted to hear all about the visit. "I think everyone in your family must have been here by now," she said.

"Yes, and you've made them all very welcome, Annie," Frances replied. "It's been such a relief to see each other and talk."

She felt much more settled after her family's visits. She worked to make the garden as productive as she could. She found twigs and string to support the peas and scarlet runner beans, transplanted some haricots, made broth with pea leaves and chervil, and found it added flavour.

Potatoes remained in short supply, however. She had to stand in a queue for half an hour to buy two pounds of potatoes for their family rations. Food imports had been seriously reduced with the loss of shipping. They realised that to have a garden in wartime might literally be a lifesaver.

15: The Russian Front—Summer 1941

The new Russian front—Otto's holiday week—Annie tries a new job—
Pa negotiates a fish dinner

Soon after Joyce and Ken left in June, there was news of a swift German advance into Russia, and everyone was glued to the radio again at BBC news times.

> **The Russian Front**
>
> It looked as though Stalin had been ready to attack Germany in 1941, but Hitler attacked Russia first.[24] Stalin lost hundreds of warplanes that had been left in vulnerable forward areas, and the Red Army was caught in a poor position.
>
> Russia was now suffering the onslaught of Hitler's war instead of Britain. A Treaty of Mutual Assistance was signed by Britain and Russia on July 12, and Churchill promised that the Royal Navy would escort ships carrying military aid and supplies to Murmansk, Russia's Arctic port. The USA had agreed to send material help to the USSR under a Lend-Lease Act. For Britain, it was a great relief that Hitler was attacking Russia instead of bombing Britain.
>
> German U-boats and bombers were ready to prey on convoys of supply ships heading for Murmansk as the ships sailed north, parallel to the Norwegian coast, and some ships and their crews and cargoes were lost.
>
> In May 1941, a German U-boat was captured intact. Its **Enigma machine and code books** were found and later de-coded. This, and a later capture of code books, gave the British information that would eventually help them and

---

24   Davies, p 1012.

> their allies to locate and destroy German U-boats
>
> After the USA was drawn into the war in December 1941, it established a second route to supply the USSR through Iran and helped to patrol the Atlantic more forcibly.

To Padiham and Goodshaw Chapel

Once there seemed to be less bombing in the news, everyone seemed to be meeting friends and family while things were quiet. Annie arranged a visit to her sister Agnes, who had visited them with her husband in the spring. "We're in Padiham, just outside Burnley," Agnes had told Frances at that time. "It's not like being up on the moors. We're in a valley and the countryside is beautiful. Come with Annie and visit us."

They went on a Saturday, taking a picnic, and took the pushcart. They had a pleasant day walking in the valley of the Calder River with Agnes, and went much further than they expected, but it was fine and warm. The diary notes:... *many trees, farms, bluebells, and honeysuckle in bud...*

On the next Sunday, June 29, Annie asked Frances to come with her to the Goodshaw Chapel morning service. This was the chapel that her mother had attended, and it was the anniversary of her death. Frances was touched by the sharing of this event and was happy to go with the children. They listened to the sermon and laid flowers on her grave. Janice liked the idea of placing flowers in a pot for someone you love and found some of her favourite harebells to add.

Otto's holiday week

It was warmer now and June 24 felt so summery that Frances declared it Midsummer Day in her diary and took Lynette to sit in the sun on the slope of the moors above the school. She wrote to Nellie, inviting her to come one day next week to arrange a family visit, which they had talked about some weeks ago.

Nellie sent a quick reply, and she and Bert arrived the next Tuesday. Annie was glad to see them when she returned from her shift in the afternoon. It took her mind off her job. She still found it hard pulling the heavy materials around her sewing machine to make knapsacks, and she was looking for other work. When she knew that Otto's factory would have its holiday the next week, she invited them to stay.

"I'd like that," Nellie responded. "It's so quiet here, and it would be lovely to come while the bombing has stopped. But, Annie, we're six people…"

"Nay, Hilda and me, we'll sleep at our Alice's," said Annie, "and maybe the girls too. It's almost next door. We can have a place for everybody if two of yours don't mind camping indoors…Your Bert's a scout…"

They talked it over and worked it out with Alice-Ann.

Next week, Otto and Nellie arrived with their four children, and it was almost as though the war had stopped. They walked through Clowbridge to buy custard tarts on the second day, but unfortunately Sarellen's and the Co-op were closed. The mill was having a week's holiday and the whole village had taken the week off. They happily explored around the reservoir and the Bonk, and met another Guernsey family, the Rookers, for a picnic. They climbed the moor behind Cotton Row one evening while Frances attended her Home Nursing course.

The best day was the fourth day, sunny and warm, and they took a picnic to Riley's brook, which was part of the Bonk, and splashed in the moorland stream. Annie's brother Tom came and enjoyed chatting with Otto, watching these southerners who frolicked in the sun on the moors. The marsh marigolds shone bright yellow, and the pools reflected a blue sky. Nancy enjoyed taking care of the younger girls, and Frances took a few photos. It was good to see the children in the sun.

Otto's family returned to Bolton on Friday, July 11, except for Sheila, who was allowed to stay on for a week to play with Janice. The arrangement suited both households and for the three girls it was a special holiday. Before leaving, they invited Annie to stay with them in Bolton after Bert had left for school in Oldham. Annie had achieved another goal.

When she was in bed that night, Frances thought about the visit and their conversations. Otto had reminded her of Arthur so many times, by the way he spoke, and his bushy eyebrows. Arthur had been to Oregon with Otto and Nellie, in the early 1920s. They visited their older brother Eric, who had gone to stay with Uncle Nils around 1913 and never returned. The three brothers worked in a logging camp.

Several memories had been recalled: the cougar story, when each man slept in a tiny tent near the logging camp, and a cougar had looked inside Arthur's open tent flap, as he lay there. Otto had recounted the story to Tom: "He held his breath as long as he could and played dead, and luckily it didn't come right inside the tent. I always say it was the smell of his boots that kept animals out. Anyway, he always closed his tent flap after that."

Nellie remembered the dance at Astoria that Arthur had attended with her and Otto. Some strong home-made brew had been available. Arthur certainly enjoyed the dancing, but coming from Pa's non-drinking family, he didn't deal with the hooch quite as well. "We were looking for him at the end of the dance," she said, "and we couldn't find him. Then Otto went outside and found him asleep in the grass!"

"That was his introduction to hooch," Otto added. "It was all home-made and illegal, but you could find it anywhere."

Had Arthur been with them that week, he would have been singing his favourite songs or doing some kind of dance. "Ain't Misbehavin'" and "Black Bottom" would have been conjured up; with a shock, Frances realised that Arthur would be thirty-nine at the end of August.

Three girls on holiday

Saturday of that week dawned hot and sunny. Annie had the day off and suggested going to the paddling pools in Nelson, just outside Burnley. She had achieved what she wanted: an invitation to stay at Otto and Nellie's in Burnley. She wanted the next week to be good for the three little girls, so that it would cement this new relationship with Frances' family; and she wanted Frances to forget the misery of last winter.

They had dinner at eleven and stopped at the Burnley fair on their way. The children had one ride on a roundabout; then an ice cream. The next treat was a short ride on the train to Nelson. The diary says: *had glorious bathes and the children paddled. Walked through a lovely park. Children had some pink spun sugar on a stick.* They reached Cotton Row at 7 p.m., just as a thunderstorm started.

The next week was pleasant, the garden providing new potatoes for the first time, as well as peas. Frances had plenty of washing and ironing to do, but Sheila and Janice kept Lynette busy, and it just seemed easier. She managed to attend two evening classes for her new SJAB Home Nursing course; and Hilda was happy to watch over the girls while she went with Annie to the Pot Fair, where they had their palms read.

By the time Nellie arrived on July 18, the girls had a little sunburn on their arms and legs. In Guernsey they were always very tanned. Nellie could see that the week had gone well. They talked about rations and the markets.

"One day last month, I saw some lemons in the market for the first time," Frances said. "I bought all that I could afford, twelve of them. I made lemonade—and it just happened to be hot for a few days—and I used the rest to make lemon curd to put in my store."

"Did you find any tomatoes?"

"There were a few tomatoes in the market in May, but they were eight shillings a pound! And the vendor wouldn't sell to evacuees, anyway. Now they're about three shillings a pound."

"It's the same in Bolton—a high price, but I bought a few."

Nellie wanted to know if Frances could go with her to pick up their niece Marion in a week's time, and would she and the girls like to stay with them all next week? Frances said she would have to discuss it with Annie. It would be nice to leave on Monday and stay the week, while there was still a break in the bombing. Nellie explained things to Annie later.

"Before Otto left Guernsey," she told Annie, "he promised that he'd find out where our nieces Marion and Mollie are—and that we'd see that they're all right with their schools. We've discovered where Marion is, and we want to get her away from Liverpool for a week. Then we can send a Red Cross message to her mum and dad to say she's all right."

Annie agreed to Frances' week off, but as usual, she worried that this might give Frances the chance to look for a place to live in Bolton.

Annie tries a new job

That same morning, a letter arrived for Annie from the Rawtenstall Bus Corporation. She had been determined to find a war work job which would free her from sewing knapsacks. Travelling to Bolton, she had noticed a few women conductresses on the buses. They looked very smart in a uniform and peaked hat, just like the regular male conductors. She applied for a job as a conductress with the Corporation.

The letter said her application had been accepted and she should report for the evening shift tomorrow. She would have a week's trial.

Frances caught up with shopping for rations next day. The evening was quiet with Annie working her first shift, and Hilda was at Alice-Ann's. She prepared rations for her and the children to take to Bolton and made sure the house was in good order. She knew Annie wasn't happy about her being away for the week.

"Annie, I wouldn't want to go to Bolton if there was bombing as usual," Frances said. "It's a chance to have a week's holiday—which I think I deserve—and the children are off school and the weather's good. It's only a week. I've left you a note with suggestions for meals. And since you're working the late shift, at least we won't disturb you when you need to sleep in each morning."

Annie managed to keep quiet.

Pa visits a pal

One weekday morning in mid-July, Pa cycled down to town and wheeled his bike into a quiet backyard where he occasionally joined some fishing friends. He wanted to arrange the purchase of some fresh fish the following week. The promise of part of his new ration of cigarettes would ease the transaction.

George was out there and agreed to do his best. "We never know which Jerry's going to come in the boat with us," he said. "We have to give them part of the catch, and sometimes we can keep a good bit for ourselves, and sometimes they watch us and make sure it all goes straight to the market."

"Why were all those barges in the harbour last week?" Pa asked. "Aren't those the sort of thing they'd use to land in England? There must have been thirty of them. I saw tugs bringing in three at a time."

"From what I understand, the barges were in France, all ready to invade England last year. Evidently the RAF started bombing them in France recently, so they towed them here, and maybe to Jersey as well. The RAF sank a couple on the way. Last week they had a big practice, landing them in Herm."

"Yes, I noticed them being towed out of the harbour."

"We wondered if they'd suddenly decided to attack England before they turn on Russia; England must be in a pretty bad way after all that bombing. But the Jerry we had on board was talkative, and he said they'd taken the barges back to France."

"And there were some of those S-boats cluttering up the harbour at the same time—schnell boats I think they call them."

"Yes, S-boats. Schnell boats. I think it means fast boats. Nasty things they are with their torpedoes. We call them E-boats-enemy boats. I think they went back to France with the barges."

"Perhaps they wanted to empty the harbour so they have room for the boats delivering all that cement and wire and tanks."

"Probably. The Jerry was chatty but we don't ask questions. This one had lived in England for a while. He was fed up with being here and said he was waiting for a few days' leave to go home and see his family. He had a job re-naming or numbering our roads, as well."

"Road names?"

"More like road numbers and colours. North-south roads and east- west roads, he said. Except that all none of our roads are like that, the way they twist around, so I don't know what they hope for."

Pa thought it sounded like an impossible task and was glad to smile at something before he started his ride back to Havelet.

Bream for dinner

A week later, Ma was in the garden early, picking beans. They would be exchanged for peas with Dorothy, Emily's friend.

Dorothy arrived on her bike. "Did you see a group of Jerries measuring things along the road?" she asked Ma. "Yesterday was the second time I've seen this group, as though they might be planning to build something."

"I noticed a group last week, on the road just below our house." Ma replied in the same quiet tone that Dorothy used. "I thought they were going to climb up that steep bit below the house and up into my garden. Then they left."

At that moment Pa came into view pushing his bike slowly up the hill, and the conversation stopped. Dorothy left and Ma went to tell Emily to start cooking dinner.

"I have some fresh bream!" Pa announced, as he came indoors.

"Bream? Fresh bream? Oh, Pa!" Emily took the parcel from him and carefully unwrapped it.

Pa nodded. "I paid too much for it," he confessed, "but at least we have a good portion each."

"Bream! We'll have that for dinner while it's fresh," Ma declared. "That's Arthur's favourite, and he said he's not working this afternoon, so we can take our time."

"I wanted some plaice, but the price was sky high. Jim bought a small bit. We had to meet them on the way from the boat before they took it to the market. The Jerries take twenty percent of whatever they catch."

"No wonder prices go up," said Emily. "Mmm, it's nice and fresh. So that's why you were out in a hurry this morning, Pa."

Jim said there's also news that Russia and Britain have signed a treaty together to fight the Jerries."

"Russia and Britain?" Ma echoed. "That'll change Hitler's plans."

Emily looked at her father. "Russia! That sounds a bit more hopeful. It would be nice if the Jerries would all leave the island and go and fight in Russia instead. It doesn't look as though the war's going to end this year, does it?"

"It gets more complicated, Emily. Nobody likes Stalin, but it's probably good news."

"I was at the women's Fellowship earlier this morning," Emily said. "We're planning to go and pick up acorns in September, to make coffee. The baker will roast them for us and then he'll grind them; and we'll give him some."

Pa looked up. "I wouldn't mind having something that tastes like coffee."

Emily reached for the frying pan. Arthur would be back for dinner soon. Twenty minutes later, they were all sitting down to eat.

"That is the most beautiful smell on earth," said Arthur, sniffing above his plate. "I think I'll have my birthday today, because this is like a birthday treat."

His mother laughed. "Good. We all know bream's your favourite, and Emily bought some of your favourite *mange-tout*[25] peas from France yesterday, and the beans are fresh out of the garden."

"We haven't had meat now for a few weeks," said Emily. "We could do with something substantial. It's worth every penny, Pa."

"Better than meat," her father grunted.

"What's new today, Art?" Emily asked.

"Well… Keep that spare bicycle tyre and inner tube safe, because now all spares have been requisitioned by the Jerries. That's the last one we'll have. And now they're pouring masses of cement into something in St. Saviours, a big gun emplacement, I think. I've never seen so many cement mixers in

---

25   Snap peas.

my whole life."

"Who's doing the work, Arthur?" Pa asked.

"It's the usual workers from the OT groups—the ones living in ramshackle huts over there."

"What are these OT groups, Arthur? Are they like those people living in some of the Hauteville houses, Spaniards and French and Polish people?"

"Yes. Some are here in town to unload boats in the harbour, and some are out in the country making cement or digging tunnels."

Ma persisted. "But why call them OT workers?"

Pa explained. "It's the Todt Organization, named after a Mr Todt who organised the building of the German highways, the autobahns. It's an engineering and building firm with German government contracts."

"Don't they have regular workers?"

"They're using prisoners of war," Arthur said. He didn't want to mention the way they were treated.

"I hear that they're damaging some farm land," Pa remarked.

"They've cleared the hedges and bulldozed the land, and you wouldn't know where one property finishes and another one begins," Arthur continued. "It's a huge work area. Today there was a huge gun on the back of a lorry, trailing behind it on a long wagon…going to the west coast probably. I was driving behind it for half an hour. They have guards all around. It knocked off a big rock on one corner."

"Jim told me that the Jerries are building a railway from the harbour to St. Sampson's to transport all this cement and wire they're bringing in," said Pa.

Arthur nodded. "Yeah, they've started it. They talked about that at work. Maybe they'll extend it down to the west coast. But mostly two of them were complaining because the Jerries had taken their wirelesses again."

"Was that because of the V for Victory signs?" Emily queried.

Pa answered that one. "Jim told me about that. Someone put up V signs near the Beaulieu Hotel, and every person living around there had to hand in their wireless; and two men have to patrol around all night to make sure nobody paints any more V signs around there. They called it sabotage."

He completed his thoughts in Danish, and Ma raised her eyebrows.

16: July–Sept 1941: A Week in Bolton

Annie disturbs Frances' week in Bolton—Meeting Mabel—A job for Frances—Annie's day off—Messages in Guernsey

A week in Bolton

On Monday, July 21, Frances and the children boarded a bus for Bolton for what was becoming a familiar journey. As planned, they had tea with Gran and Grampy and caught up with everyone's news.

Rose had registered for school that day and was happy to see her two cousins when she arrived home, and they were soon playing dressing up. The Channel Islands Organisation had a meeting planned about schools one evening later that week. Bill and Geoff arrived and swapped news, ready to eat and go out for the evening.

"We like to go out early after tea," Bill explained to Frances, "so we can get back home before dark. If you come back after dark, you can't see a thing and you trip over everything; but we go and come back by the same route, so we know where the tricky steps are."

"One of the girls we know screamed the other night," Geoff added with a grin. "My friend has a dog that went up and rubbed against her legs and she thought some monster was climbing up her and she really yelled. But you can't see a thing in the blackout."

"Well, that's the way a blackout is supposed to be," Gran remarked.

Once the dishes were done, Frances and the girls moved on to Nellie and Otto's for the night. It had become their Bolton home. Next day, she left the girls there and spent the morning queueing up for ration books for Gran and obtaining a cheese allowance coupon for Geoff at the Town Hall. In the afternoon, she took Sheila with the girls to the market. The war news from the BBC was broadcast there each day.

Annie turned up unexpectedly that evening, saying that if she was accepted as a conductress, she would need an autobike. Would Frances come with her to Manchester the next morning to look for one? Nellie said they would find Annie a place to sleep for the night.

Annie was enthusiastic about her work. "It's just the sort of job I like, and it's classified as war work," she said. "But I have to report to the depot at Loveclough at four-thirty in the morning—that's at the far end of Clowbridge. From there they'll give me a lift in the parcels van to Rawtenstall. That's where I start my shift on the first bus at five o'clock."

"There's a nurse down the road who has an autobike," said Otto. "She said they can do about a hundred and twenty miles to one gallon."

"That's right. One of the bus drivers showed me his auto-bike," Annie said. "I reckon a gallon would last me almost a month."

Nellie told Frances quietly that she would watch over the girls the next day if Frances went to Manchester with Annie.

Annie told Bert about her new job: "If I sell a certain number of tickets, then I should have exactly that much money to hand in at the end of my shift."

Bert nodded.

"If I have given too much change and I'm short of money, the company will deduct that amount from my wages."

Another nod.

"If I have more money in the bag than I should have, the company keeps the money and says nothing about it."

"Oh."

"So, you always have to be very careful about counting the money."

"Yes, I see."

Next morning, Frances went with her to Manchester. The diary says they had lunch together and Annie bought some shirts; no mention of auto-bikes. Annie would have paid for the lunch. Did Annie say that she was worried that Frances was getting too attached to Bolton and her family there? They were back in Bolton in time for Annie to catch the five-thirty back to Burnley.

Finding Marion and a quiet August.

As promised, on the Friday of that week, Frances went with Nellie to collect Marion from near Liverpool, where her school was located. Nancy and Bert were left in charge of Alan and the three younger girls.

"While you and I travel on the buses, we'll be able to have a good chat," Nellie told Frances the night before. "The bus routes keep changing because of the bombings and the repair work, and there's no reliable timetable. It'll take us most of the day."

They left at 9.30 and travelled via Wigan. They were shocked at the piles of rubble around Liverpool's huge port area. They reached Marion's school early in the afternoon and she was happy to return with her two aunts to Bolton. They arrived at 6.30 p.m., ate tea, and it was time for Frances to pack her bags again.

Her diary for Saturday, July 26, states: *Returned to Cotton Row this morning. Had to start cooking dinner. Went to Burnley in the afternoon for rations.* This was the only time, in the diary of 1941, that Frances wrote that she had to do something, as if with a hint of resentment. Recording that she did her job picking up the rations (in Burnley) also states that she fulfilled her duties, a reminder to Annie who had no qualms about reading it.

Annie probably got up late on Saturday after her night shift, and she must have been relieved to see Frances and the girls arriving back, and Frances preparing dinner. Annie was now an official conductress with a smart uniform to wear with her new shirts, and she had discounts for her "family," which would be beneficial for Frances. She had found a second-hand auto-bike locally.

Frances felt better about returning to her life at Cotton Row. Seeing her family helped to keep her spirits up, but it was the bomb damage around Liverpool and Bolton that stuck in her mind. In contrast, the hay had been cut behind Cotton Row and it was as pleasant a country scene as anyone could wish for. The children made houses in it, until they were warned not to interfere with the drying process. She took them up the road to what Annie called "the old Haworth farm," where they enjoyed quiet afternoons and could play in the hay without interference.

Annie slept at the top of the stairs for a while, so as not to wake them all at 3.30 a.m., although Frances heard her leave soon after. With the lamp on her auto-bike dimmed, she had to go slowly. On her day off at the weekend, they looked after the garden and went for walks down Limy Lane to the reservoir, or to Crown Point.

School started around August 11, and there was good news for Lynette: she would be able to attend in the afternoons with other younger children. Soon she talked about her friend Beryl, who was also three, and also young Rena Marshall.

Two days later, Frances started a new First Aid course in Burnley, and the topic was Gas Emergencies. Everyone had now been issued with a gas mask, an ugly contraption with a rubbery smell that the children hated to put on. One afternoon there was a Gas Practice in Burnley and Frances attended with the SJAB personnel. Some tear gas was released in one street and citizens wore gas masks and walked along the street as usual, or cycled, as a demonstration that the masks worked. Police and air-raid wardens ushered people along but they all looked like aliens from Mars. Frances hoped that she wouldn't have to deal with gas.

Without a three-year-old at home in the afternoon, she had more time for the SJAB courses and the garden. Hilda offered to baby-sit the children if Annie was on the evening shift. Frances decided she could now look for work to earn some extra cash.

Meeting Mabel & a talk with Gran

Since they left Hawthorne Road a year ago, Frances hadn't seen Vi or Mabel. Vi kept in touch with letters sent to Gran, which were passed around, and Frances wrote to her; but Frances had felt abandoned by Mabel in Burnley, and hadn't tried to get in touch.

Perhaps it was Gran who arranged for Frances and Mabel to meet, just after Mabel's birthday. She would have been thirty-three on August 10. The diary states:

Lynette went to school this afternoon while I went to Burnley. Met Mabel and Pat in Marks and Spencer's. Weather brighter with showers.

One might hope to read: "children enjoyed seeing each other again;" or: "will see each other in Bolton", rather than an unimportant comment about the weather. Pat would have been disappointed not to see the girls. Does the weather symbolise something? Happy to make peace with each other? A few tears? Frances was aware that her diary might be read by Annie or someone else, and developed her own style of cryptic memoirs. At least she and Mabel had seen each other.

Ten days later, on Sunday, August 24, two familiar figures got off the bus at Cotton Row in the middle of the morning.

"Mum! Here's Gran and Grampy!"

Frances went to the door and welcomed them in, and tea was made.

"We thought you were coming to Bolton last Saturday for the Channel Islanders' Rally," said Gran.

"The weather was so cold and wet that I didn't want to go anywhere," said Frances. "The rain was lashing down here." She had an uncomfortable feeling that her mother wanted to ask her about the meeting with Mabel.

"They broadcast it on the radio next day. Did you hear it?"

"We listened to it on Sunday night. And I also heard the Justice du Parcq in London, asking people to donate money for evacuees. He's from Jersey, isn't he? We could do with some help to pay for shoes and clothing for the winter."

"Yes, the Justice is from Jersey," her mother replied. "I hope they get some good donations. There's a lot of women in Bolton needing help."

"I'm knitting vests for Janice again," said Frances. "One of the First Aid ladies found me some thick cotton to knit with."

Annie came downstairs quietly.

"I wondered where you were," said Grampy. "You look half asleep."

"I'm catching up with my sleep," she said. "A cup of tea will see me right."

"And how's your job going?" asked Grampy. "Do you sing some of your songs on the buses?"

Annie laughed. "No, but I'm enjoying it," she said. "It's a lot better than stitching haversacks and tarpaulins in that factory."

"And do you wear a uniform?"

"Yes," Frances answered, "and she looks very smart in it."

"Do you get a discount if you use the Express buses, like if you came to Bolton?" Grampy continued.

"Yes, and for Hilda and Frances and the children. We all get a discount."

"Well, that's worth something," said Grampy.

"Have you been issued with gas masks?" Gran asked.

Frances nodded. "And the girls had their gas practice at school."

"Rose and Graham had a practice at school too. Since we're supposed to carry them with us, we brought one in the bag with the onions."

Frances smiled. "Maybe that will improve the rubbery smell. Anyway, the weather's warming up nicely. Let's have an early dinner and go for a walk."

It was unusually warm, and after putting a meal together they all went for a long walk around the Bonk. Gran had a quiet word with Frances about her meeting with Mabel. Her impression was that Frances' attitude had softened a little and let the matter drop.

A job for Frances

Frances had mentioned to Annie that she wanted to find a job for a few hours a week once Lynette started school. She needed more spending money, especially if her family came to visit. Annie was pleased and saw it as another strand to bind Frances to Cotton Row.

Annie was good friends with the Riley daughters, two young women who went to Crawshawbooth Chapel. The Riley family owned a large sheep farm south of Clowbridge. Annie learned that Mrs Riley needed some help to clean their large house in Rawtenstall. She arranged to take Frances and the girls to meet Mrs Riley when she had a day off work. Frances remembered that they had picnicked with Nellie's family at Riley Brook in the summer. It was part of the Bonk.

On Thursday, August 31, the diary records that they had tea with Mrs Riley, that the children were very good, and that they all had to run through the rain to catch the nine o'clock bus home. Perhaps Annie watched over the children and chatted with the daughters while Frances tried her hand at cleaning. Over tea, Frances learned that the two Riley daughters were keen gardeners, vegetarians, and seemed to be well educated.

Earning undeclared cash was against the law, but most evacuee mothers had to earn money somehow, declared or not. One afternoon of house cleaning per week, would provide Frances with a little extra cash that she needed. She kept quiet about her job and only once does she write in her diary "worked in afternoon," enough for a reader to see but not enough to report her to the authorities.

Annie's day off

On Sunday, September 7, Annie had a day off and she planned to take Frances and the children to Blackpool, taking advantage of her family discount on bus fares. The children had been excited about going to the seaside. Annie had taught them how to sing "Oh, I do like to be beside the seaside," and they had gone to bed early; but when she came home late on Saturday night, she had to tell Frances that there were no more tickets available.

"They've cut down on the service because petrol's in short supply," she said.

"Well, let's go to Bolton instead."

They had looked forward to a day out and they all had an open invitation to stay with Otto and Nellie. Frances thought it would be an opportunity for her and the girls to stay on for a couple of days because Arthur's brother Herbie would be on leave from the navy and might be there with his wife.

They took rations with them and were welcomed at Otto's. Bert was away at school so his bed was available. Sheila and Janice "camped" happily on a mattress, and everyone seemed to squeeze in.

"Otto went with Bert to Oldham a week ago," Nellie told Frances. "He made sure Bert knows how to find his way around Manchester bus station to get to Oldham and back. Bert feels he can come home at Christmas by himself."

Annie left on Monday morning. Frances stayed on for two more days and spent time with Gran, mending and talking. Her father joined them one afternoon to go for a blackberry picnic out in the country at Horwich.

Herbie and his wife Doris came mid-week, and Frances was able to see them before she returned to Cotton Row that afternoon with the girls. Otto said that he and Nellie would bring their visitors to Cotton Row the next weekend, and they turned up as promised. Needless to say, Annie was pleased to see Herbie in naval uniform, complete with gold braid, entering her house; and there was time for talking and a walk after dinner before she left for her shift.

After the children were in bed, Frances thought over the day. Every time she looked at Otto or Herbie, she saw visual reminders of Arthur, like Otto 's visit in July. Otto had recalled their dangerous times serving as lifeboat crew; Nellie remembered watching the 1935 regatta.

"I wasn't there for that one," Herbie said.

"Well, you missed a good one," Otto replied. "You know, Nell and I lived on the left side of *Le Pré*, and Ma and Pa lived on the right side."

"Sheila was just one year old," Nellie added.

"That's right. Bert was only six. Anyway, it was a good thing we had Pa's workshop and plenty of space. We had to turn my boat—*The Mayflower*—into a pirate ship. We prepared a mast and rigging and flags. We had to set up a plank like a springboard, so that the pirates could make one of their victims walk the plank, like real pirates do, and fall into the harbour."

"I bet you weren't the one to walk the plank," said Herbie.

"You're right. It was my boat, so I was the captain. Arthur walked the plank. Well, he kind of danced down it. He enjoyed doing that."

"We'd made Chinese lanterns that had candles in them, hung all the way up to the top of the little mast," said Nellie. "We took the children over the boat to see it the day before, but they weren't allowed to be on board for the show."

"Walter and Charlie helped us. Walter was a pirate too," said Otto. "We had swords, cutlasses and muskets. There was a parade and a fight with the pirates in the afternoon, and another in the evening, and Arthur walked the plank both times. After dark all the boats paraded around with their lanterns or other lights."

"A good job Art was a good swimmer!"

Nellie was glad to see Frances smiling as they all remembered the regatta. The two women had watched it together from the shore in the afternoon, Frances with baby Janice on her knees and Nellie with one-year-old Sheila. It was a happy memory.

Messages In Guernsey

In Guernsey that evening, Arthur and Emily were chatting quietly over a cup of something hot, which was very weak tea, and almost their last. They had been cheered by the arrival of Red Cross messages, replies to those they had sent last winter. The messages lay on the table in front of them.

"Fancy you getting one from Janice as well," said Emily. "I bet she misses you."

Arthur smiled. "Makes me feel rich, having two messages."

"Counting the one from Otto for Ma and Pa, and mine from Louise, that makes four we've got. At least I know Louise is alive and well with her school."

"Mine's from the Burnley Red Cross office, wherever Burnley is." Arthur said. "They have a vegetable garden, that's good. Maybe it's in the country. Janice is doing well at school. Played in snow. I hope they've found something warm to wear. They left here in June with their summer clothes."

" I'll be in town tomorrow morning and if Charlie's in the market, I'll ask if they've heard anything from Marion."

Ma and Pa were in bed already, as daylight faded. Electricity was cut off every evening and there was no point in fumbling around and falling over in the dark. Candles were rationed to two per household per week.

Eric was seventy-nine now, and was still upset following the confiscation of his boat, *The Dream*. She had been one of the first boats with a motor and had provided them with a good living. Every fisherman knew his boat's registration number—GU 91—and he saw her number in his dreams. Ma had sold his fish twice a week in the market when Emily and Elsie were old enough to look after the younger children.

Someone had told him that *The Dream* was in Alderney. He grappled with the problem silently: how would he ever get her back, and in what shape would she be, after this damned war ended? The only decent catch they had this year was in a dinghy in the harbour, when mackerel had been swimming right up to the inner walls and all you needed was a line with five or ten hooks. At least they had eaten well for a week.

Ma had been glad to go up and get under the covers. She looked thin, frequently putting part of her bread ration on to Arthur or Eric's plate and saying she had little appetite; but Emily knew that her mother found the bread hard to digest, and was as hungry as the rest of them. Ma had perked up after tasting a bit of Dorothy's tomato jam on a morsel of bread earlier in the summer; but you needed a pound of sugar to three pounds of tomatoes to make the jam. When Pa and Arthur came home with buckets of mackerel in July, Emily traded some fish for sugar. She made some jam and kept a special jar for Ma, giving her two spoons of it a day like medicine.

"Did you hear the RAF planes passing over again last night?" Emily asked.

Arthur nodded. "Yes. Do they scare you?"

"No. I like to hear their engines actually, now I know how they sound."

"I expect they're off to St. Nazaire as usual to bomb the U-boats."

"Damn the U-boats. So many ships lost. I think about Herbie and wonder where his ship is."

"So do I. Or young Lionel Frampton—my nephew on the Torode side. He's in the merchant navy, probably somewhere in the Atlantic."

They wished each other a good night. Emily poured her mother a cup of the hot liquid, and took it upstairs, leaving Arthur to lock up.

He made sure he left his ID card and lorry driver's permit by his breakfast plate. He was becoming familiar with the German words on them. He listened carefully to German conversations around him to try and understand as much as he could, while keeping quiet about it. He had to report to his employer, Leale Ltd, as usual in the morning; but his job as a driver would probably be moving more islanders out of their houses so that German troops could move in. It was over a year now since Emily had been forced to move, and he and Walter had both moved since then. It was hard to know where anybody lived these days as evictions continued.

17: Sept 28–Nov 15, 1941—Deportations

*Annie's Holiday week—A bomb scare—Birthday Surprise—
Hitler targets English-born islanders—A visit to Vi*

Annie's holiday week

At the end of September, Annie had a week's holiday. She was determined to make full use of her discounts on bus fares. She also had the promise of accommodation in Bolton with Otto and Nellie, and that was central to her plans. By now she felt that she might have won the battle to keep Frances and the children billeted at Cotton Row. Going away for a week's holiday, while staying with Otto and Nellie, was something that would benefit them all. Frances packed bags and rations.

Lancashire folk always headed to the coast for their holidays: to Blackpool, Southport, and Morecambe. These three cities catered to thousands of holiday makers all through the summer, before the war. There was a direct service to all three from Bolton, and now that it was autumn, there should be more space on the buses. Annie planned to take day trips from Bolton, treating Nellie and Gran to one of them.

On Sunday, September 28, the four left Cotton Row and were at Otto's before dark. Janice and Sheila were delighted to see each other as usual. Next morning, Annie and her *family* left early on the Express for Morecambe. The shops were shut for a holiday, so they had lunch in a hotel. Even though it was showery at first, they enjoyed being by the sea. Frances stood and sniffed its familiar smell, closing her eyes and letting herself think of the pebbles, the seaweed, the blue-green of Fermain Bay. The weather cleared, and they walked through Happy Mount Park and then along the promenade.

"This is where I'd like to live, if I could," Annie said.

"Didn't you say that your sister Carrie lives here in Morecambe?" Frances asked. "Isn't she the one who came to say hello with Dora a few weeks ago?" The question slipped out before she remembered that Carrie had been cool and distant rather than warm and chatty, unlike the other friendly Haworth sisters.

"Yes, but…our Carrie and I don't get on that well," Annie said. "She's older than me. She married when I was younger. They're quite well off."

Her reply didn't encourage Frances to ask any more questions, but Annie continued, "Carrie had a good singing voice, too."

Frances wondered if there had been some kind of competition between the two sisters regarding their voices. Carrie had given her the impression of being smartly dressed, a little more attractive, and of living a more elegant life than the Cotton Row sisters.

They looked across the wide expanse of Morecambe Bay.

"Yes, I'd like to live here in the future. It's warmer, and the Lake District's over there." She pointed across the Bay to what might have been mountains on the other side. "It's beautiful around the lakes."

Frances thought about the conversation on the way home. She knew that Annie's mother had struggled to bring up her children, with little support from either of her two husbands. It seemed that one had died, and one had left her. Perhaps Carrie was a half-sister. If her mother had been a single parent part of the time, it must have been difficult to bring up children with a job at the mill. Each child must have had only a minimum of schooling before they had to work. She realized that Annie's job on the buses was giving her a chance to show that she was capable of doing better.

On Tuesday, Nellie looked after the girls while Annie and Frances went to Manchester on a shopping expedition. Annie was looking for warm boots to wear on the buses over the winter and bought a pair of *Ferry Pilot* flying boots. They had arranged to drop in at Grampy's on the way back for a cup of tea, and he turned up early and joined them.

"Well, aren't you going to show us your boots?" he asked Annie.

She put them on. They were high and lined with something that looked furry.

"I thought you were working on the buses, not flying a plane," he said.

"Nay, I've had enough of cold feet," she said. "But if I had to fly a plane, I would."

"I bet you would," he grinned.

On Wednesday, they took an Express bus to Southport. It was really warm; they sat on the beach and the children played in the sand. They found Hesketh Park and saw the floral clock being dismantled. Vegetables would be planted there next year.

The following day, they went to visit Annie's younger brother John and his family.... *took Pat with us*, Frances wrote in her diary that day. Perhaps the rift with Mabel was healing, after all, with Gran's efforts. The children were happy to be together again.

John worked on a farm where blackberries were a summer specialty, and his wife, who was pregnant, had made blackberry tarts for everyone. Their young daughter Margaret shyly joined the children.

For their final day out on Friday, they treated Gran and Nellie to a trip to Blackpool. Again, it was warm: the children paddled on the beach and enjoyed watching over Alan, who would be one year old the next day. There were fewer amusements open than during the summer, but it was pleasant to take a day's holiday, to smell the sea, and to forget the war.

"Well, how did you like your week off?" Otto asked Annie that evening. She was finishing the dishes while Nellie and Frances settled the children for the night.

"It were beautiful," she said simply. "And I thank you for having me here. You've been very good to put me up. "

"That's all right. We really enjoyed coming to Cotton Row and getting away from Bolton. Nellie's always afraid that there'll be more bombing raids."

"It was a nice visit, Otto, and I hope you'll come next summer. Tom—me brother—enjoyed talking with you. Now, I wanted to ask you something. Would it have been better for you to have stayed in Guernsey, if they weren't fighting there? Or are you better off here?"

"Annie, I'm glad we came to England, but we could be bombed here, anyway. It's a big war. I'm trying to find a job where we're not in a big industrial town, though."

"That's what I keep telling Frances. She's better off in a little place like Cotton Row than a town like Bolton."

"I suppose she is," said Otto. He knew Annie wanted to keep Frances and the girls in Cotton Row and didn't want to add another word.

Next morning, Frances and Annie searched the shops for clothing in Bolton before it was time to take the bus back to Burnley. Janice and Sheila sadly said goodbye to each other. The bus wasn't on time, didn't have enough room, and they had to wait for another one. It was almost dark when they got to Cotton Row. It also seemed to be much colder and Frances had to remind herself that it was already October 4 and winter was coming:

...managed to get to Cotton Row at dark. It was so cold up there, we sat by the fire with two coats on all evening. What a difference in temperature.

They finished Annie's holiday week with a visit to the Co-op variety show in Burnley on Sunday. Entrance was free for evacuee families, and Annie always included herself as an evacuee. It was a good family show, and the children enjoyed it.

A bomb scare

After such a giddy holiday week, they returned to normal life. Frances made sure that the children caught up with schoolwork, but her focus was now on winter clothing. The cold was upon them so suddenly and the girls were a size or two bigger than last year. She received a blue winter coat from the WVS, and transformed it into a warm dress for Janice, adding some trimmings from a blouse. She re-fashioned a large, hand-knitted sweater. Mrs Trickett from the First Aid classes supplied her with wool to knit some more underwear for Janice.

At St. James School there were plans for the harvest festival, and on Friday, October 10, the children decorated the church classroom. Pots of Michaelmas daisies and goldenrod were added on Saturday, and small amounts of apples and pears and vegetables were added by those who had a little extra.

There was a family service on Sunday, and this time both girls enjoyed singing with their class. Frances knew most of the congregation by now. Next day, on Monday evening, the baskets of produce would be sold to provide funds for the church.

After the nine o' clock news on Sunday, Frances went to bed. Soon after, the sirens started to wail. Fortunately, they had practiced finding their way downstairs without Annie being there: Janice had her own torch now. They heard planes at a distance, but luckily no bombs. The 'all clear' sounded two hours later and Hilda came from Alice-Ann's to see if they were all right and then departed. Frances settled the children with hot water bottles, made tea, and Annie returned from her shift and was relieved to see that nothing bad had happened at Cotton Row.

"There were incendiary bombs dropped over Bacup," she said. "That's a few miles out of Rawtenstall on the moors."

Next morning, they heard that unfortunately one man was killed. It helped that he was not a local man, and life resumed again.

On Monday evening, the donations of fruit and vegetables at the church were sold. Annie was working, but Frances was able to buy a few apples, carrots and cabbages to add to their store. She settled down to write to Grampy, telling him about the raid and to say that they were all right. Two days later, she received a letter from him saying that they were all well, but there had been a severe bombing in one part of Bolton near a factory, but not the one where Otto worked.

Birthday surprise

Sunday, October 19, was wet and cold. It would be Frances' thirty-fifth birthday the next day, and she felt depressed. She had been preparing a Red Cross message to send to Arthur. She wasn't even hopeful that she would be back in Guernsey for her next birthday. She had tried to make a cake, but even the cake had fallen flat, as though it mirrored her feelings. Late in the afternoon, the weather cleared, and Annie made her come out for a walk with the girls, and that helped a bit.

On her birthday, the children gave her a card that they had made, and a diary. While Lynette was at school in the afternoon, she went to Burnley and sent Red Cross messages and ordered bigger clogs for Janice. Soon after she returned home, there was a knock at the door and it was Louise Jay, Emily's daughter, and suddenly the day became a celebration.

"I was teaching at Amherst School and evacuated with them," Louise explained. "We were taken up to Glasgow, and I stayed there for a while. Then some parents came and took their children, and being the newest member of staff, I wasn't needed any more. I'm now teaching in Doncaster."

"Glasgow! And Doncaster! Were you on the same boat as Nellie and Vauvert School?"

"Yes. I've been writing to Nellie and they gave me your address. And Daisy's address. I had a week's mid-term holiday so I decided to come and find you."

When Annie came home and met Louise, she insisted that she stay with them for the week. As was normal practice, Louise had brought her basic food rations, and contributed to the housekeeping budget. Frances promised to take her to Bolton on Friday to see Otto and Nellie.

It was a morale raiser for Frances. She had always wanted to be a teacher and had a lot of questions to ask. They shared the scraps of Red Cross messages they had received so far, guessing the conditions that Emily and Arthur were experiencing in Guernsey with Pa and Ma.

On the Tuesday morning, they walked to the Goodshaw Chapel area and treated themselves to apple pie at a bakery. After dinner Frances "*worked in afternoon*" according to her diary and Louise explored on her own. The weather was fine that week and they walked every day. One evening, Louise showed them things that she had made from coloured felt, including a beautiful belt with flowers that Janice would always remember.

Frances took Louise and the children to Bolton on Friday, leaving early. They went to Nellie's and left Louise there for the day. Frances and the girls went to see Gran in the afternoon, and then they all met up to catch the four-thirty bus home. Louise felt she was now part of the family web in England, and Frances felt that she had managed to celebrate her birthday after all.

Mid November at *Le Pré*

At *Le Pré* on Saturday, November 15, Pa looked satisfied when he came downstairs for dinner. He had just been checking their store of potatoes.

"We had a good little crop. It'll help us over the winter, whatever our rations are."

"I had to queue up for a new permit for our rations today," said Emily. "We're supposed to get five pounds of potatoes a week each, and they're being really careful that people don't cheat. I think any farmer who's got potatoes to spare can make a fortune selling them on the black market."

"The price will go up all winter," said Ma. "We must make sure we're always watching our own store here. A good thing we have some carrots and cabbages from the garden too. With eggs from the chickens we're not as badly off as some others in the town."

Emily nodded. "There are some men who come into the soup kitchen at Trinity Square that are trying to live by themselves. It's not good to be living alone. Apart from that, two of them really live in England and couldn't return there before the Jerries landed last year. Now they're worried that they could be deported."

"Yes, that notice in *The Press* yesterday has worried a lot of people," Pa remarked. "One of my mates was asked if he knew someone with a boat so that a few men like that could escape; but I can't see it happening."

Emily spoke quietly: "You know, I've always wished that Jimmy was still alive and living with me. It's nine years since he died; but with this threat of deportation—I'm glad he isn't here. He was born in England, and he'd have to register, even if he was living here permanently."

Pa thought: *Yes, and as his wife, I wonder where you'd be*; and kept his mouth shut.

Ma glanced through the window and was glad to change the subject. "Here comes Arthur." She switched on the gas and put the soup pot over it. "Now, why is the gas going to be cut off after nine at night?" she asked. "We can use it at meal times, which is all we need for cooking. It's on from 7.30 in the morning to 2.30 p.m. That's really all we need for cooking."

"I think the Germans are turning the gas on at night to heat their rooms," said Pa.

"Gas fires? I thought those were all sealed up."

"Not where the Germans are living. Not up there in Sausmarez Street and some other places."

Arthur came in, rinsed his hands, and they all sat down to have soup."

"What were you doing today, Arthur?"

"Not much, Pa. We were moving some imported potatoes around; but there's a lot going on in St. Saviour's. They're pouring masses of cement into making something like a big gun emplacement. I've never seen so many cement mixers in my whole life. There's shiploads of cement coming in regularly, I'm told, but Leale's doesn't have anything to do with that kind of military stuff."

"And what are people saying about people born in England having to register?" asked Ma. "Didn't it mean people who still have a residence in England or somewhere else?"

"Charlie told me that it even includes people who only have a residence here. I saw him and Elsie on the way home. Their neighbours were born in England, came over here, and had a little business in town. They don't have a property in England, just a property here; but they have to report to the Greffe[26] by November 15. It doesn't sound very good."

---

26   Registry, Royal Court House.

"Yes, but we've had these kinds of scares so often," Emily said. "There was that awful rumour last month about deporting men over fifteen. We were so scared you might be deported…"

"Oh, Emily…" Ma muttered, frowning.

"Sorry, Ma." Emily patted her mother's hand.

Hitler targets English-born islanders

The Channel Islands were frequently in Hitler's thoughts late in 1941. On August 25, British and Indian forces attacked the south of Iran and took over oilfields and refineries to protect Allied oil supplies. Russia attacked the north of Iran.

Hitler had many German agents working for him in Iran and had planned to seize its railway and its oil.

The old ruler, the Shah, was forced to resign by the British, leaving them free to expel or intern all German agents in Iran. The Allies wanted to repair and extend Iran's railway to send supplies to Russia, which would be a much safer route than the dangerous voyage to Murmansk.

Hitler was furious at this treatment of Germans in Iran. He ordered the deportation of ten Channel Islanders born in England for every one German deported from Iran. There might have been well over five hundred Germans in Iran. Lists of men, women, and children were demanded during September and October and efforts were made to find enough people. There were only about two thousand people born in England in all of the Channel Islands.

Hitler badly wanted his agents in Iran to return to Germany, and there were discussions through Swiss and Turkish diplomats. Could there be an exchange of Germans for British prisoners? But there were not enough British prisoners.

In the Channel Isles, the Kommandant, von Schmettow, did not want to deport islanders. Many of the English-born worked in government or helped to run essential services. He also worried that there might be some kind of rebellion

> by the islanders. Things remained undecided; but the lists of islanders born in England were drawn up for future use.

First snow and a visit to Vi

The first snow of the winter came on the last day of October, a Friday. *Putting on all the clothes we possess,* Frances noted in her diary. Next morning, she did the shopping in Burnley with the children, and as usual looked around the market. Lynette became so cold that she asked to go home, but she also asked for an ice cream.

That night Annie was free, and she went to the Ambulance Social in Burnley. Before she returned the sirens went off, and Frances and the girls scrambled downstairs and sat in the dark under the stairs. Next day they heard that Incendiary bombs had been dropped in the Bacup area again.

On Sunday, Annie and Frances cleaned up the garden at Kit Hoyle's. They had already stored over eighty pounds of potatoes and Annie wanted to make sure they hadn't missed any.

Frances received a letter from Vi in Bradford, inviting her to visit. Fred would be on leave on the eighth of November, and could they please come while he was there? Fred's mother would sleep at a neighbour's house.

The answer was: *Yes, of course.* Frances dressed the children as warmly as she could for the journey. Annie came with them to Burnley to buy through tickets to Bradford, but they had to take local buses via Rawtenstall and a small place called Todmorden. It was a long and cold journey which took three hours.

Fred met them with a big smile, happy to offer them hospitality after the trials of the year before. He kept the children busy in the afternoon while Vi and Frances walked to the nearby shops and talked. *Talked till throat ached*, Frances happily wrote in her diary. They stayed two nights, and she enjoyed being able to bathe the children in a real bath. They stayed mostly indoors because of the cold, but it was a comfortable two days, with the girls eager to play with David, who was now more than one year old.

They talked about their fears of bombing.

"We had a bad night last March, the fourteenth," Vi said. "Just after the BBC evening news, the sirens started, and Fred's mum and David and I were under the stairs for most of the night; and David only seven months old. We heard the bombers flying over, bombing the factories in Leeds, about fifteen miles away. Every fire engine and ambulance was rushing to get there afterwards."

"There are a lot of foundries in Leeds," Fred explained. "Some make airplane parts, some make bombs, and some do plane repairs. The telephone exchange and the gasworks were hit as well. One fellow told me that roof spotters gave enough warning that they were able to put out most of the fires in one huge factory. They reckoned afterwards that over 200 incendiaries had been dropped on it."

"We've been lucky since then," Vi added. "Now Hitler's busy with Russia, I hope it stays quiet. But we have to be prepared."

On Monday, Fred left early in the morning. After dinner, his mother took charge of David while Vi walked with them to the bus station. It was another cold, three hours' return journey, but Frances took comfort from the fact that Cotton Row was a quiet, safe place.

Challenges for everyone

The next week seemed to bring various challenges: on their return they found Hilda fussing over Annie, who was hobbling around. She had fallen on the stairs of the double-decker the previous night, when the driver had to brake suddenly, seeing a sheep ahead in the road. Annie's leg was *"all colours of the rainbow,"* and they persuaded her to see a doctor.

On Tuesday, Frances tackled the washing and finished it by the end of the afternoon. Annie came back from the doctor with a letter giving her two weeks off work. By then, the ache that Frances had felt in her throat at Vi's had become worse and next day she developed a fever. A letter arrived from Joyce that day to say that she would travel to Gran and Grampy's next week and could Frances and the girls come for a day or two.

"Oh, why am I always sick when I want to see Joyce?" Frances moaned.

"You can't go to Bolton with your throat bad again," said Annie. "You'd better see the doctor."

Frances visited Dr Millwood and found him much more pleasant than the evacuee doctor of last winter. However, apart from telling her to avoid milk, the treatment was the same; and she forced herself to paint her throat every hour. She was determined to see Joyce. Annie helped with the housework next morning, and Frances stayed the whole afternoon in bed. Annie decided to make a Christmas cake, and the house smelled deliciously of fruit cake all afternoon.

In the middle of the week, a letter came for Annie and Hilda. Their brother John announced the birth of his second daughter, and could Hilda come over for the weekend as promised. Janice was sent to fetch Hilda and the conversation was all about babies.

"Will you see the baby?" Janice asked.

"Yes, I think so, but I'll be staying with Uncle John and looking after Marjorie."

"Could we come and play with the baby? When we went to Auntie Vi's, we played with David."

"Well, the baby is very small…Mummy and the baby will be in the hospital."

"If you go to the hospital, could you bring us home a baby each?"

"Well, I'll ask for two babies and we'll see."

18: Nov–December 1941 — Pearl Harbour

*Bombs in Bolton—Mirus gun—Arthur receives a letter—
Pearl Harbour—December at Cotton Row*

Bombs in Bolton

With her throat improving each day, Frances prepared to go to Bolton to see Joyce on Friday, November 21. Annie wasn't working that weekend and came with them, which saved money on fares. The four of them went straight to Grampy's and enjoyed tea with Joyce and the others.

They discussed the bombing of October 12, and after tea went to Nellie's for the night. While Sheila and Janice established their shared mattress-camp, and Otto and Annie were deep in conversation, Frances and her sister washed up and exchanged news in the kitchen.

"I think you had some bombing too, didn't you?" Nellie asked quietly. "I wanted to ask you before, but not with the children near."

Frances spoke softly. "We were under the stairs, and the moors were on fire further off. It was frightening, but we didn't have bombs really near to us."

"Well, you were lucky," Nellie replied. "There was a direct hit on a factory here. Eleven people were killed." She shook her head. "Houses were flattened along that street. One huge boiler from the factory was flung right into the street!"

"Oh, Nellie. Did you all go downstairs here?"

"Yes, and the air-raid wardens even checked that we were down there. We stayed quiet for a few hours. And you know, I try to get everyone down there as fast as I can. In this last raid, a metal girder went right through somebody's roof and bedroom, but they were downstairs by then and nobody was hurt. It could have killed them. So it's worth moving as fast as you can."

"And what about Bert? Is he writing to you every week?"

Nellie nodded. "They had some bombs near them. I think he was scared, but at least he's living with a family. It still worries me a lot. And I'm scared it'll be Otto's factory next. Bolton's got a lot of industries and with those high factory chimneys it must be easy for a bomber to find them. I'd like us to move out of the town."

"Where would you go?"

"Otto's in touch with a couple of people he worked for in Guernsey. One of them owned Jethou,[27] and he lives here in England. Otto used to look after the boat service to the island for him. He told Otto that if he ever came to England, he'd find a job for him."

"I see. How has Nancy been doing?"

"She's doing well at school, and she'll take an exam next term, like Bert did last spring. If she passes, she'll be joining the Guernsey Girls' Intermediate School in Rochdale. If her marks are good enough, she could go to the Guernsey Ladies' College, but they've moved to Denbigh in Wales. Rochdale seems better. It's nearer to us here, and an hour's bus ride from Bert's school. It's more on the moors like you are. Don't mention anything to Annie or anybody. All this is just a lot of possibilities at the moment."

"I won't say anything. "

"And while I think about it, I have a bag with two or three winter tops that Sheila's grown out of, and some underwear. They'll fit Janice soon."

"Oh Nellie, bless you. Clothes are the hardest things to find."

Next day, Frances and Annie went to Grampy's to share time with them and Joyce. They looked at the shops and saw some of the bomb damage.

At Otto and Nellie's that evening, they made it seem more like Christmas. Annie went to the chip shop with the children and came back with chips[28] for everyone. While they were out, Otto and Nellie were able to talk with Frances more freely about Annie and life at Cotton Row. They thought she had made a good decision to stay there.

"We're a bit better prepared for winter this year," Frances said. "At least we have extra potatoes and swedes and carrots, jams and a few things I've saved, and I've been sewing warmer clothes; and I know everybody there now."

They had some fizzy drinks and ginger wine and sang carols and enjoyed it. *The children think it's a party*, Frances wrote in her diary. Later, she couldn't sleep, reflecting on her conversation with Nellie. She hoped that if

---

27 A small island east of St. Peter Port, Guernsey.
28 French fries.

they moved, they would still be within reach. Being able to stay with them in Bolton had helped her to settle down at Cotton Row.

On Sunday, they all contributed something to make a good dinner at Grampy's and the girls were thrilled to have a piece of Gran's custard pie. They wished each other a safe Christmas, and the four returned to Cotton Row on the early afternoon bus.

Mirus gun

On November 27, Arthur arrived back at *Le Pré* at twelve as usual. Ma and Emily had dinner ready: beans, potatoes, a few scraps of meat, cabbage and slices of swede, and gravy. They all sat around the table and enjoyed the smell of food and tried to eat slowly.

"Did you hear anything more about a huge gun being landed here, Arthur?" Pa asked. "I was doing the firewood and Jim stopped by and said they'd imported a massive gun."

"We were shifting furniture for the Jerries again this morning, and they were talking a lot. I understood that the French floating crane was used to unload the gun on St. Julian's Pier."

"Near the bottom of St. Julian's Avenue?"

"That's right. Then it was taken on a trailer through St. Martin's to St. Saviour's, where they've been building this big gun battery base. The Jerries call it the Mirus Battery. I understood that it'll have barracks underneath for over 300 men, and the gun control rooms."

"And the shells. They'll take a lot of storage," Pa added.

"One Jerry said the shells weigh 225 kilograms each, and the gun's range is about fifty kilometers."

"About five hundred pounds each and thirty miles," Pa said quietly.

"I made sure I drove back on a route that would give me a chance to see it, and I had to wait at one intersection for it to go by. They had to cut off a few corners of the roads so that the trailer could get through. I thought that the gun I saw in July was huge, but this one was enormous, on a trailer that had twenty-four wheels."

Emily gazed at Arthur. It sounded as though he was understanding a lot more German than she had thought.

"With guns like that, the British navy had better watch out," Pa declared. "It means the Jerries will control access to all the French ports we deal with."

Emily had some other news for Arthur. "You were waiting for the acorn coffee to be ready, Arthur," she said. "I got my share this morning. We tried some and Pa's not too keen, but it's better than no coffee; maybe not as good as what you had in the States."

"It was a bit watery the first time," said Pa. "It has to be strong enough."

"The best coffee in Oregon was when we made it over a campfire after work," said Arthur. "Strong and good. Anyway, I'll try some. You have to roast the acorns first, don't you? How did you do that?"

"Emily and I collected the acorns with the women's Fellowship," Ma said, "and the baker roasted them for everyone in his big oven. Then we shelled and boiled them, and he roasted them again, and ground them. It was plenty of work."

Emily made the coffee stronger and it was a welcome change. They sipped and discussed how to improve it. Then Arthur was quiet and said, "Now, I have something to show you."

He took a folded sheet of paper from his pocket.

"They gave me this letter at Leale's this morning. There'll be no more work next year."

He put the letter on the table, and his father passed it on to Emily.

"You read it, Emily."

Ma and Emily looked at Arthur with concern. "Oh, Arthur," Emily murmured. She flattened the paper. Underneath the official heading of Leale Ltd., Ironmongers & Engineers, she read out loud:

27th December, 1941
Dear Sir,
For reasons which we feel are quite obvious to you, we are reluctantly compelled to reduce our staff.
We are anxious that you should have the opportunity of securing as favourable a position as possible and to enable this, we will continue your employment until January 3rd, 1942, giving you full freedom to leave at any time.
Further, should the wages paid to you in the future be less than you now receive, we will make up the difference over a period to end on March 28th, 1942.

We are sorry to have to take this step and may we add that we have appreciated your services very much and will be pleased to help you in any way to secure employment.
Thanking you.
Yours respectfully,
Signed by the Managing Director.

There was silence.

"So, they are telling you to look for another job right away," said Ma.

"That's what it looks like."

"At least it sounds as though you've got money coming in for a month while you find a job," said Pa. "But could you work as a driver somewhere else?"

"I don't know. The trouble is, back in the summer the Jerries started to requisition all lorries less than five years old, and then the older ones. The driving jobs that I could do are all really Jerry-controlled."

"Charlie was saying the other day that the Jerries pay good wages," said Ma.

"How much are Reichsmarks against the Pound now?" asked Pa.

"It's nine or ten to one Pound," replied Emily. "You know, one way or the other, most people are working for the Jerries now. Keeping the harbour open and the gas and electricity running, and working the farms."

"I was told they were looking for drivers to take the Jerry troops to their gun practices all around the island," said Pa. "That's in case there's an attack by the navy."

"Why would the navy attack us?" asked Emily.

Arthur shrugged. "They always think that the navy might attack, but that would be a military situation that I wouldn't take part in. They have to provide their own drivers for situations like that."

"If only there would be an invasion," said Pa. "You know what I miss most? I miss cooking myself a kipper for breakfast, and I miss my Danish newspaper in the post. The Jerries have overrun Denmark, so you'd think I could still get it through the German post office. We've used all my old newspapers to start the fire so I can't even read an old one."

"The Jerries have got the upper hand, Pa," said Emily. "You'll have to wait for your kippers and your newspaper for a while." She could sympathise with the lack of newspapers, but she was glad she didn't have to smell kippers at breakfast time.

"Speaking of a job for me," Arthur continued, "it'd be better to work at the harbour and unload food from the boats and deliver it. I could do that. Now, I've got the rest of the day off, so I'll bring in some wood and I'll start looking for a job tomorrow."

"I heard that the secretary girls get extra food if they work for the Jerries," said Pa, watching Arthur's face.

Arthur scowled. "The last thing I want is favours from the Jerries."

Pearl Harbour

On December 8, the BBC announced that the Japanese had attacked Pearl Harbour, the large American naval base in Hawaii. Everyone was relieved that this had finally brought the United States into the war, except that now there was war in the Pacific as well. Arthur and the other drivers found the Jerries more nervous. At Cotton Row, Frances made a new map gallery in the kitchen.

> **Allies, Axis, and treaties**
>
> In June 1941, German armies swept east and caught the Soviet, or Red Army, off guard and destroyed most of its air force. Following this, Russia and Britain signed a Treaty of Mutual Aid, although Stalin's rule of terror and Communist principles were the opposite of Britain's ideals. However, neither of them were in a position of strength. War materials were supplied to both Russia and Britain by the United States through Lend-Lease agreements.
>
> After the attack on Pearl Harbour, both Japan and Germany declared war on the United States. *The Grand Alliance* was formed between the United States, Britain, and Russia. They were referred to as the **Allies** as opposed to their enemies: Germany, Italy and Japan, who were known as the **Axis** forces.
>
> The Allies had three main goals: [29]

---

29   Davies, p.1028.

1. Stop Germany from advancing further and supply Russia with war materials.
2. Get rid of German naval U-boats and other vessels. This was referred to as the Battle of the Atlantic.
3. The aerial bombing of Germany, focusing on its industries.

December at Cotton Row

On December 12, Frances and Janice both received a Red Cross Message from Arthur. Knowing that they were thinking of each other was like a special Christmas gift. Making a Christmas card was an immediate response from Janice, and Frances kept it for the day when she would be able to send it.

For Annie, having two children in the house had made Christmas a special event. In November she made the Christmas cake and the pudding. Frances had carefully saved sugar and some dried fruit, so that it was almost as good as pre-war food. The stirring, making a wish, and the licking out of the mixing bowl added pleasure on those two afternoons.

In the middle of December there was a turkey dinner for members of the Nursing Association, which included volunteers like Frances, and their families. It was given at Crawshawbooth. Not wanting to miss anything, Annie made sure she worked the early shift so that she could attend with Frances and the girls. It was pouring with rain, and Frances was glad to have Annie with a second umbrella, as they had to walk part of the way. It was worth the effort: there was turkey, sausages, stuffing, potatoes, carrots and gravy; and apple pie and custard, cider, and coffee: *3/- head. Good do* (Three shillings per head, a good get-together) says the diary.

As the weather grew colder, Annie had a few mishaps while riding her auto-bike from Loveclough. One night she ran into a sheep on the road, and she skidded on ice one morning. She was a valued employee, and her evening shift was changed to a daytime shift for the winter so that she could travel to work on the 5 a.m. bus from Burnley, which stopped across the road.

One Saturday, Frances was overjoyed to find coloured paper in Burnley market. "I'll show you how to make paper chains after dinner," she told the girls. Janice helped to make a flour-and-water paste. Frances cut strips of coloured paper, which were looped and pasted together to make paper chains They enthusiastically decorated the living room until they ran out of paste and paper. Lynette managed to make a few with some help, and decorated the blue pram as well.

At St. James, Annie was helping to organise the Christmas show. As a finale, all the children would be on stage, the smallest ones in front with Annie. Everyone would sing "There'll always be an England," and would have a small Union Jack flag to wave. She taught the children to bow to the audience after the clapping started.

As the show ended, Lynette stood by Annie, in a short skirt and bright top. The singing was done with enthusiasm, and the audience joined in. Lynette wasn't too sure about making a bow. She waved her flag and turned to face Annie so that she could imitate her movements and get it right. Annie turned her round twice, but she again turned to Annie to watch her. The audience laughed and cheered as they had a view of her pink underwear, and she stole the show without knowing it. The evening ended with a lot of laughter.

Frances had saved what she could for Christmas stockings for the girls. She had been able to buy a chocolate bar or some sweets occasionally. She put a few raisins in a twist of paper, and an apple, in the toe of the Christmas stocking, which was just an ordinary stocking. A few pencils, some sheets of paper, a tiny book, a small toy, some mittens, and a pair of knitted socks would fill the rest. Annie also found a few items to add. She located a doll's house, but someone wanted twenty-five shillings for it! Frances decided that they could do without it.

On Christmas Eve, the girls placed an empty stocking on top of the blankets at the bottom of their beds, which were set next to each other. On the 25th, the diary notes: *Children woke at 8.15, delighted with Father Christmas' generosity. They have been lucky.*

Christmas Day was mild and sunny. Annie was off duty and Hilda, joined them for a walk. They enjoyed a quiet day.

A party for New Year's Eve.

Annie and Hilda went to Burnley on Boxing Day, and Frances and the children were surprised by visitors of their own, when Otto and Bert arrived unexpectedly. Frances put the kettle on, and Otto leaned against the kitchen door. "We won't stay for more than half an hour," he told her. "We're on the way to see someone I know in Burnley, but we wanted to say hello. I wondered what it looked like here in winter. I see you've got some snow on the hills already."

"Yes, we had a bit last night," said Frances. "I'm glad you had time to stop." She gave him a tray of cups to take into the living room and followed with the teapot. Bert was standing by the fire.

"Now Bert, how was your term at Oldham?" she asked.

"All right, I suppose," he said quietly. "But the bombing was bad. One of my friends was in a house where two people were killed."

"Oh my… That sounds frightening. Was it part of the October twelve bomb raid?"

"Yes. I was late getting to school the next morning. We didn't sleep much. I walked around to look at some of the damage. But other boys were late too, and nobody minded."

"Was your street damaged?"

"No, we were all right. There's a big cotton mill at one end, but it wasn't hit."

"And did you have any problems coming to Bolton by yourself last week?"

"No. Manchester bus station is pretty big, but Dad and I looked around it in September. It took me most of three hours on the bus, though."

They sat at the table. The girls had some pale tea, but were not allowed cake. They would have their share after dinner.

"What will you do for New Year's Eve?" asked Otto. In the past, he and Arthur and the Enevoldsen crowd always used to get together for a family party.

"It'll be quiet," said Frances. "Not like it used to be in Guernsey. Annie works the evening shift."

"Oh, does she? Well, if you and the children want to come to Bolton, it would be nice to be together. It'll be a squeeze for bed space, but we'll manage."

"Oh, Otto! That would be lovely. Janice, did you hear that?"

Janice beamed. "And Sheila and me, could we camp on a mattress again?"

"Oh yes," Otto laughed. "You'll be sharing a mattress with Sheila again!"

Frances completed a toy she was making for Alan and packed their bags. On the 31st, Annie accompanied them to Rawtenstall to buy family tickets and saw them off. At least it wasn't snowing, buses were on time, and the skies were quiet. The children were delighted to be together again. They sang carols and songs after supper, camped on mattresses, and it was a great morale booster for everyone.

Arthur, Janice, and Frances with Lynette, 1938

September 1940: a walk around the reservoir. Janice, Peter, Frances, Lynette. Cotton Row is on the far side of the reservoir, above Frances' hat.

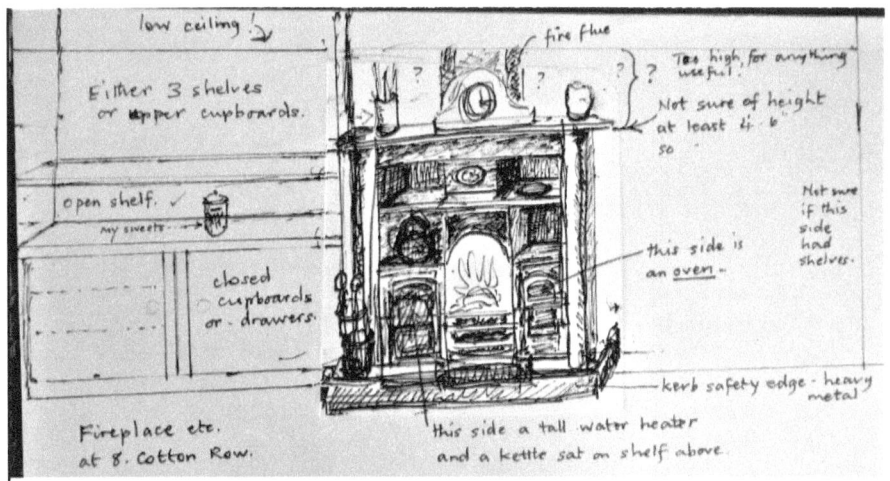

Sketch of fireplace at 8, Cotton Row (by Janice Parkington.)

Rose, Grampy, Gran, Graham, 1940

Sept 1940 Lynette with blue pram

Pa and Ma: Eric Enevoldsen & Emilie le Page, 1939

Louise and her mother, Emily, 1939.

January 1941: Snow on the Manchester Road near Cotton Row
(Source unknown)

June 1941: Lynette, Joyce, Ken, Janice. Cotton Row chimneys and reservoir beyond.

Annie as conductress, July 1941.

A regular visitor at Cotton Row: Daisy Carter serving in the WAAF

July 1941 at Riley's Brook. Above: Tom Haworth, Nellie, Alan, Otto. Below: Janice, Sheila, Nancy, Lynette, Bert.

TELEGRAMS: "LEALE 12 GUERNSEY"
TELEPHONE 17

LEALE LTD
IRONMONGERS
&
ENGINEERS.

ALSO AT ST SAMPSON'S BRIDGE.
TELEPHONE 4002.

7 Bordage,
Guernsey.

27th November 1941

Mr. A. Envoldsen,

Dear Sir,

    For reasons which we feel are quite obvious to you, we are reluctantly compelled to reduce our staff.

    We are anxious that you should have the opportunity of securing as favourable a position as possible and to enable this we will continue your employment until January 3rd 1942, giving you full freedom to leave at any time. Further, should the wages paid you in future employment be less than you now receive, we will make up the difference over a period to end on March 28th 1942.

    We are sorry to have to take this step and may we add that we have appreciated your services very much and will be pleased to help you in any way to secure employment.

    Thanking you,

    We are,

    Yours respectfully,
    for LEALE LIMITED.

    MANAGING DIRECTOR.

Letter to Arthur from his employer, Nov 27, 1941.

Janice, Lynette with Dinah on Wiles Lane. 1942 January

January 20, 1942

Day trip to Morecambe: Janice, Frances, Annie, Lynette. July 1942.

1943 Lynette and Janice in front of Cotton Row. No 8 on right side.

Photo of Janice, Frances and Lynette taken in Bolton in 1943. It was sent to Arthur via Laufen deportee camp in Germany.

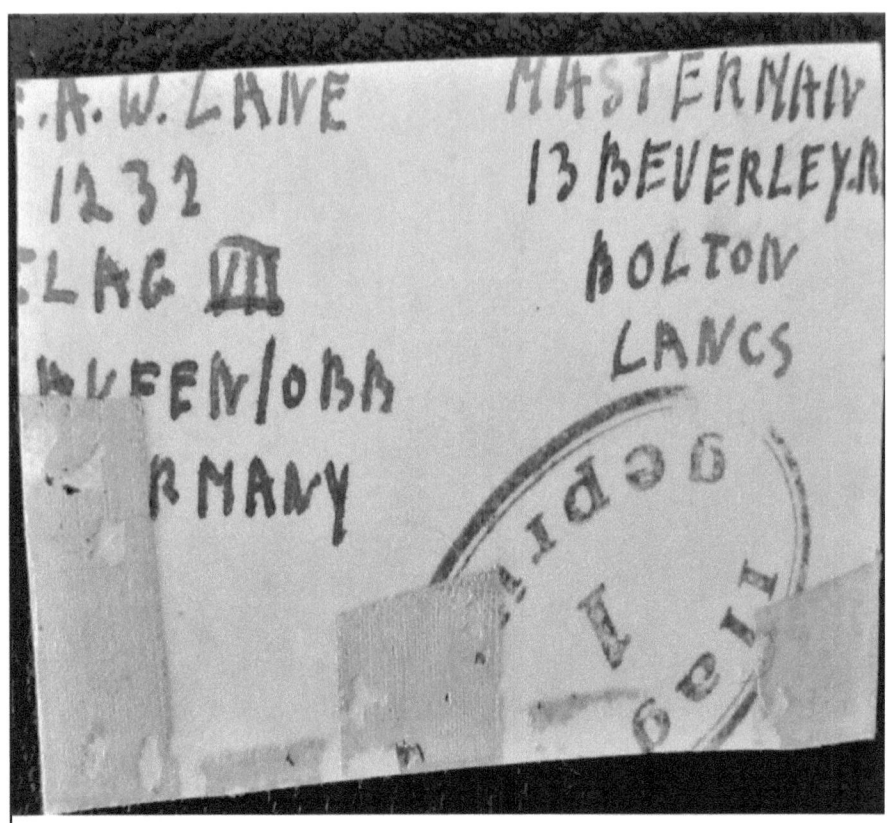

Back of one of two photos received by Arthur. It bears the German Ilag address of Guernsey deportee, Mr. Lane. Mabel Masterman's address in Bolton is shown.

Pa's rented house, *le Pré*, in 1945.
Note the entrance to a tunnel drilled below it.

Source of photo: B.Enevoldsen — Colour added by: D. le Prevost

Pa is at bottom left, with beard.

He is waiting to board the first boat to Alderney—late in 1945—to see if he can find his boat there.

(Source unknown)

19: January–March 1942—Snowstorm

All about the weather & forecasts—Pancakes at Le Pré—
Churchill's speech Feb 15—March visitors

All about the weather

The first two months of 1942 were just as miserable as the previous year: the UK meteorological office has weather records for Bradford, just 20 miles away (30 km) from Cotton Row. In January and February 1942, the average maximum daily temperature in Bradford was less than 37 Fahrenheit / 3 degrees Celsius[30]; nights were always below freezing; and humidity made the cold feel raw and penetrating. Houses were not insulated and warmth came only from coal-burning fires.

> On January 19, 1942, **a great snowstorm** affected much of Britain with much dislocation of life. February 1942 was notably cold—one of the ten coldest Februarys…The severity of these winters caused much hardship[31]…

At least Frances was better prepared for the winter, and this year the girls even enjoyed the snow a little. After the big storm, they went out with Dinah, taking shovels and a sledge that Annie had found for them. Frances took two photos. One shows Annie with Lynette and Dinah, three black figures in a landscape of white, with a huge pile of snow behind them. Across the bottom Frances wrote: *snow up to 30 feet deep.*

The other photo shows Janice pulling Lynette on the sledge in the lane, with Dinah close by. The spades lie by a snow pile that would become a castle. Playing outside was important when there was little sunshine: less than twenty hours of sun in the whole month of January.

Frances had knitted the girls' woolly hats and mended socks and stockings. In the photos, Janice has a deep fur collar, which came from a lady's

---

30   https://www.metoffice.gov.uk/research/climate/maps-and-data/historic-
31   https://premium.weatherweb.net/weather-in-history-1900 to 1949.

discarded coat, pulled up high up around her ears. It helped, but she looks cold, shoulders hunched up, her left hand covered by a thin glove, holding the string attached to the sledge. Lynette is wearing oversized puffy mittens. Janice was probably wearing rubber welly boots with thick socks and stockings. Going to school meant walking in a trench through the snow along the road to the school. Better winter boots were unobtainable, and everyone suffered from chilblains.

Nobody knew the extent of the January storm. Two buses had run into drifts because there had been no warning. Local men used shovels to rescue anyone stuck on the road while they waited for help from Burnley.

> **Weather Forecasts in a War?**
>
> Bad weather took everyone by surprise. Public weather forecasts had been banned as soon as the war began. Britain's weather stations, on islands and ships out in the north Atlantic, supplied data which allowed forecasts to be made for several days as the weather patterns moved eastwards. In wartime, this gave Britain some advantage in planning war strategies. Cloud and fog meant delays in military operations. Clear weather could be an advantage to either side. It was important to keep this information from the enemy; so it wasn't broadcast or printed.
>
> Germany's source of weather information from the west came from Greenland, which was too far away. The Germans tried to take over isolated weather stations, and sometimes had to use U-boats to gather weather statistics. Later in 1941, when the German Enigma Code was decoded by the Allies, Germany's weather information from central Europe became available to them and was very helpful in planning bombing raids over Germany.

It was hard to keep warm in bed: one night Lynette curled up, tummy down in a kind of fetal position, with her arms tucked in underneath her, trying to hold her body's heat together. She fell asleep. In the morning, she found that she couldn't unbend. Janice thought her sister was pretending to be hurt and went downstairs for breakfast. Frances went upstairs after a while and found she had to lift a curled-up child off the floor and carry her downstairs. She found a short walking stick somewhere, and it took till midafternoon for Lynette to straighten up. The grownups made sure that she was warm enough in bed after that.

Annie picked up news from travellers when the buses started running again and the local paper reported what it could. In one village in a similar location to Clowbridge, nobody showed up at an important parish council meeting because of the snowfall, and a formal request for a snowplough was made. *The Express* reported drily:...*the County Divisional Surveyor was agreeable to Worsthorne having a snowplough if one could be obtained...*[32]

There were some accidents, as *The Express* reported:

... The witness noticed a car coming in the opposite direction, on its own side of the road, which was blocked on each side by snow, thus narrowing its width. The lorry, which passed him, and the car, each tried to miss the other, but both went the same way...[33]

Pancakes at *Le Pré*

On February 10, Arthur was back home soon after 4 p.m. Under his jacket he was holding a bag.

"You're early, Art," Emily remarked. She was getting ready to warm up beans and vegetables in a bit of broth, which would be their main food for tea. Dried beans were one of their staple foods now.

"I've got some flour. We were unloading a cargo boat from France this afternoon. So, I did the usual thing."

He had snagged a sack of flour with his knife when he placed it in the corner of the lorry he drove. By the time he unloaded and knocked it around a few times, a pile of flour had escaped from the sack. The German guards on watch liked to keep warm inside the storage area rather than watch the islanders unload sacks in a chilly wind, and the drivers benefited from it.

Some time ago, Emily had sewn a cloth bag carefully and now she peered inside. "It's wheat flour?" she asked, hopefully. Arthur's job, driving for the Germans, was proving to have one small benefit.

---

32 Burnley Express, Sat, March 07, 1942.
33 Burnley Express, Wed, 25 Feb, 1942.

"Yep. Well, it's supposed to be wheat flour."

Pa looked up from the table, where he was reading the paper. "Is that what you've been unloading all day?"

"No, it was oats for their horses this morning." Arthur turned himself round by the fire to warm up. "Those animals are better looked after than we are."

Emily picked out something from the flour and then reached for a sieve and a bowl and poured it through. "It looks good," she said. It didn't look as gritty as the last lot Arthur had brought home. "There's almost three cups. I could make pancakes! We had one egg today and I have one from yesterday. It was so cold that the hens didn't go outside much, but we may get one more tomorrow."

"Pancakes tonight?"

"Unless you want to wait till tomorrow."

Ma was bundled up in a blanket in her chair near the fire. "Oh, let's eat well tonight," she said, "and then we might sleep well. Have we got any milk left, Emily?"

"Oh. Not much. Just enough for breakfast."

"Well, we can have bramble tea for breakfast and use the milk in the pancakes. You'll have to add water as well. And there's still a few apples if you want to have some in the pancakes," she said. "I'll chop them up for you."

"Sounds good," said Arthur. Raisin pancakes used to be his favourite weekend breakfast, but apples had replaced them. "How's the firewood lasting, Pa?"

"I spent an hour chopping wood from the boat," his father replied, "and there's a pile in the storeroom."

It was Pa's small, old boat, *Elsie*, which was keeping them supplied with firewood.

"I didn't start a fire till dinner time. Ma stayed in bed till then," said Emily. "It's the only way she can keep warm."

"And the chickens?"

"I've covered up the door to the hen house and put some more hay in the boxes. It's all done. You don't need to go out anymore."

"Good. It'll be cold again tonight." Arthur touched the small piece of soap by the sink and rinsed his hands fast under the cold water from the tap. Hot water was a thing of the past and soap was rationed and rarely obtainable.

"We'll be upper class tonight," said Emily cheerfully. "We'll have—what shall I call it—bean and vegetable goulash to start with, and pancakes *à la pomme* with some beetroot syrup for dessert."

Ma laughed. It was good to hear her laugh.

"By the way, Arthur," Emily continued, "someone in the market said that some German bodies had washed up on a beach, and people haven't been allowed to go there to get limpets and vraic[34] lately. Did you hear anything?"

"Well, somebody from the Jersey boat told me there were two German boats sunk back in January, and a lot of bodies washed up down there. He likes to pass on their news. I don't talk much with the two Guernsey lorry drivers yet. They're probably all right, but you never know who's an informer."

"Well, at least it was Germans who died. Not like the Dutch nationals when that boat in the harbour here was bombed last month." She almost said, *It's awful the way that the Dutch and the Russians are forced to work in dangerous places for the Germans;* but this was what Arthur did now.

"The RAF made huge holes in the bows of two of those ships," said Arthur, "so at least that delayed the Jerries' construction work till the harbour was clear again."

"And you got two days of work boarding up the windows that were blown out in town," Pa reminded him.

Emily put plates on the table. "I wonder if we'll see American planes flying over, now that they're in the war," she mused. "I wonder if they'll sound the same as the RAF planes."

Ma said nothing. Like the others, she worried that bombers might swoop over the harbour when Arthur was working there.

Pa broke the silence. "Arthur, I want you and me to bring down the single bed and put it here, along this wall," he said. "Can we do that before tea?"

"Why do you want to bring a bed down here?"

"There's too much pilfering going on. Everybody's short of food and we

---

34   Seaweed, used as a fertiliser.

must look after our store. I want to sleep down here at night and in the daytime Ma can have a sleep on it. There was a man here today looking for food. And a couple of Jerry soldiers were asking for potatoes last week. It's a good thing we have ours upstairs in the spare room."

"That's true," said Emily. "Dorothy said the Jerries asked her neighbours for eggs and apples, and one day they walked in when nobody was around. Her friend had made a parsnip and carrot pudding and left it on the kitchen table near the door, and it just disappeared, bowl and all."

"There's a lot of these Spanish workers living up the road in Hauteville, and they come down Havelet quite often," said Ma. "They're supposed to have their own rations. I think the Jerries are the bad ones."

"Dorothy said you have to tell the Jerries, 'Nix, nix,' or something," Emily continued.

"That's right," said Arthur. "Nix means you have nothing. And you need to tell them you'll report them to the Kommandant. Just repeat, Kommandant. That scares some of them. And keep a stick under the bed."

"I've got a couple of good sticks down here already," Pa said, pointing to one corner, and said something to himself in Danish.

Arthur had been watching his mother to see what her reaction was to his father's idea about the bed. She said nothing. She did look frail, but then they had all lost weight and it had been a cold month. He wondered how she would keep warm at night if Pa slept downstairs. Maybe she could sleep with Emily or come down and squeeze in with Pa.

"I think Churchill's supposed to speak on Sunday morning on the BBC," Pa said. "We should listen, I suppose."

"Yes, at nine o'clock I believe," said Emily. "Let's hope he remembers to say something about us."

"Okay, Pa," said Arthur. "Let's get the bed down and then we can enjoy our little feast."

Churchill's speech Sunday, February 15

At Cotton Row that Sunday morning, Annie was listening to the radio, but Frances missed most of the broadcast. She was busy making soup and helping Janice to plan a doll's tea party in the kitchen.

"What did he have to say?" she asked Annie afterwards.

"It's not good, and he gave it to us straight. The Japs have taken Singapore and I think we're losing a lot in the Pacific. He didn't mention Guernsey."

Next day, Annie brought a copy of *The Telegraph* home with her. "Here, Frances," she said, as she came in the door, "somebody left this on the bus this afternoon. It has most of Churchill's speech on the front page."

"Oh, thanks Annie. I'll read it through after tea."

"I said I'd take it next door after tea, before it gets too cold. They missed the broadcast for some reason."

Frances took a quick look at it. It wasn't good news that Churchill had given his audience last night. The Japanese had shown themselves to be real warlords and had taken Singapore, Malaya, and Burma. Oil sources, which supplied the RAF and the USAF in the southwest Pacific, had been mostly destroyed. Now Australia and New Zealand were very uneasy. Britain had lost control of the Mediterranean and ships couldn't use the Suez Canal route. They had to make the longer journey around the Cape.

However, Churchill continued, Russia had held steady, and America had joined the war with us, and Britain would support her allies as best she could.

"We must display calm and poise and renew our strength," he had concluded. Frances felt she'd been doing exactly that. The only bit of good news that she could find on the front page was under the headline: "The RAAF in Notable Victory in Western Desert." That meant the Australians. She read that right through, just to keep herself hopeful, although she wasn't sure where the Western Desert was. It was a world war all right, now that America and Japan were in it. She could have done without Churchill's speech. She folded the paper and placed it on the table for Annie to deliver next door.

March visitors

The weather improved at Cotton Row in March and Annie and Frances started to work on their new garden plot at weekends. Hilda joined in.

Potato pie suppers started up again at various chapels, but were often reduced to *Broth Parties* because of the potato rationing. Annie almost persuaded Frances to attend a Jacob's Join, where everyone brought a dish of food, but rations made it too difficult to manage. She did go to a Beetle Drive, where only tea was supplied. Shaking dice and filling in the beetle's legs and feelers wasn't demanding, and Janice could also take part.

One Sunday morning there were loud calls from the girls when they saw Gran and Grampy crossing the road from the Burnley bus, collars pulled up and scarves tucked in. It was chilly and cloudy again. Once inside, Gran looked Frances up and down. "Well, you look in better shape than you were last year," she said. "I think the children look better, too. And they've grown a lot."

"We've brought you onions like I said in my letter," said Grampy, and handed over a heavy package.

"Just what I needed," said Frances. "And I have eggs for you. I'll put these in the kitchen and make the tea."

Grampy watched from the kitchen door. "Did your store of potatoes last through the winter all right?" he asked.

"Yes. We brought all the potatoes and root vegetables in the house in December. We had carrots, swedes, those white turnips you suggested, and we didn't lose anything. It made a big difference to our meals."

Gran came for the cups. "I've never used so many vegetables as I did this winter," she said, "and with so little meat I used dried beans and lentils in stews a lot. The boys are really fed up with bean stews."

"A good thing we're working in the gardens," Grampy said. "Otherwise we wouldn't have had so many vegetables. Now that the Americans are in the war, I hope they can get rid of some of those U-boats. We've lost too many ships and too much food into the Atlantic."

"And then there's the damage to the ports as well," said Gran. "They were still bombing Liverpool in January. Now, Frances, you can make the tea weak if you like. That's what we do. Who knows if we'll be getting tea in the future."

Frances was glad to reduce the amount. "I drink it weak," she said, "but Annie likes her tea strong." She stirred the pot. "By the way, did you listen to Churchill's speech last month? I would rather be ignorant about what's going on than hear so much bad news."

"The Japs are a well-trained force," said her father. "Yet you know, in the Great War they were on our side. The Germans had some land and ports on the Chinese coast and the Japs took it all from them."

"Yes," Gran nodded, "and I remember we even had a photo in the newspaper of Japanese Red Cross nurses sent to Southampton to help look after wounded soldiers in the Great War."

"That's incredible," said Frances. "It was more of a world war than I had thought."

"There's a lot of people worried that their men might have been taken prisoner in Singapore," Grampy said. "We had thousands of troops around there. Anyway, tell me about your new garden. I'd like to have a look at it."

"We've got a bigger plot. Mr Marshall—he looks after the reservoir—he promised us a piece of land up behind us in the corner of the field, so we've started working on it. It was used as a garden before. We'll go and see it after dinner. Annie's at Alice-Ann's, but she'll be here soon."

"And could you grow something else, like strawberries? Peas? Leeks?"

"We talked about strawberries. We're short of fruit and sweet things. I want to make a rice pudding for a certain birthday…" she pointed to Lynette who was sitting on the stairs with a doll. "I saved the rice from last year. but I can't get a tin of condensed or evaporated milk, and we're only allowed a gill[35] of milk a day for each of us."

"I know, it's the same for us," said Gran. "And now soap is on ration."

"That doesn't bother me," said Grampy. Gran gave him a withering look.

Annie returned and they all went to see the new garden. Janice found a few harebells to give to Gran, and there was a final cup of tea and a bit of singing before the visitors left. Gran and Grampy could see that Frances had come a long way since last year.

---

35   A gill is ¼ pint or about 4 oz.

20: March–May 1942 — Goodbye to Nellie

*Shocks in Guernsey—Quick visit to Nellie—Police on trial—Digging for Victory—
First Aid point in Clowbridge—Churchill's speech*

Shocks in Guernsey

On Saturday, March 6, dinner at *Le Pré* was the same as usual: dried beans cooked in salt water, flavoured with a few herbs that Ma and Emily had carefully saved from last summer, with chopped swede and carrots added in. Emily put dishes on the table.

"We're only allowed two pounds of swedes and parsnips a week each," she complained to her mother. "Finding a cabbage is hard enough, and there's nothing else. Thank goodness we had our own little store. At least we've got this far."

"The Jerries don't know anything about growing," Ma replied, "and I think a lot of growers resented their interference. I hope they work it out better for next year. If this war isn't over by then, we won't have much to eat unless we can grow it ourselves."

Pa and Arthur came in. Pa was waving the newspaper. "Listen to this," he said. "Those rumours I heard yesterday from Jim were right. Five policemen were arrested, and then another three, and the chief of police was in jail for the night. All for stealing food and liquor. But from our shops as well—from Guernsey peoples' shops, not just the OT stores!"

"Our own policemen?" Ma repeated, her mouth open.

"How could they? Is it really true?" Emily sounded doubtful.

"It says the Jerries watched them at night for a couple of months," Pa continued. One of the police had hidden tins of tomatoes and German butter up his chimney, enough to last a long time. Or sell on the black market."

"What do you mean by the OT Stores?" asked Ma. "Is that where you buy our food, Emily?"

"No, Ma. It's the stores that the Germans keep separate for their workers, the OT workers. They're the ones who do the digging and build the walls."

"They'll be building those walls for a while," Arthur stated. I was told that the walls across the west coast and L'Ancresse beach, will be about ten feet high. Hitler doesn't want any invasion forces to land easily. Apart from that, there are the 250 strongpoints to be built around the island, and it all takes concrete."

"That Dutch ship was carrying concrete, wasn't it? —The one that was bombed in the harbour in January?" asked Pa, sitting at the table.

"Yes, it was concrete. That bombing delayed things a bit. They're building that little railway to help carry all their building materials to L'Ancresse and then down to the west coast."

Ma stared at the newspaper and shook her head. "Well, what a morning it's been for news," she said.

> The first of four Mirus Battery guns was in place and ready to be tested on April 13, 1942. It would be so powerful a noise that in two large areas, people and their animals were ordered to move out.[36] The blast lifted greenhouses that were close by, and moved them sideways; the glass was shattered and fell to the ground.

Quick visit to Nellie

Frances received a letter from Nellie at the end of March, saying that Otto had found a new job. They would be moving from Bolton before the end of April. She hoped Frances could find time to come with the girls before they had to leave. Nancy and Bert would be at home during Easter week but would leave on Sunday, April 12. After that, she would have two free beds.

Frances wondered where they would be going. She wrote back saying she planned to come with the children on April 13. She planned meals, packed rations, bought eggs for Nellie, and they left on the morning bus.

As soon as they arrived, the girls disappeared to play with Sheila and Alan, and the sisters were glad to have a private chat.

"I'm really glad you could come," Nellie said over their first cup of tea. "Otto just got permission to change his job, and we must be out of here before the end of April. I had to sort Nancy and Bert's things for the summer

---

36   https://island-fortress.com/2022/10/01/batterie-mirus-the-big-guns/

term and I must pack. There wouldn't have been time to come and see you."

"You said in your letter you would move soon, but where?"

"I didn't dare give any details in the letter. You know how things are in a war. Otto got in touch with someone he worked for in Guernsey, and he's got a job in Devon. He'll be working on minesweepers."

"In Devon! By the sea! Oh Nellie…but you'll be a long, long way away…" Frances was happy for her sister but also disappointed at the same time.

"You know I don't want to be further from you, Frances. But you know how worried I get with Otto working at the ammunition factory here. Sometimes German bombers don't get rid of all their bombs over Manchester, and they drop them over Bolton…I know there are less air raids now that Hitler's busy fighting the Russians, but who knows what's ahead? Sometimes I envy you being in Cotton Row and away from these bombing routes."

They were both silent.

"Well, if you have a chance to get away, you must take it," Frances said quietly. "It'll be warmer in Devon, Nell, maybe more like Guernsey weather. No snow!"

Nellie gave a quick smile. "I don't mind that part of it."

"Now, where's Nancy? Did she pass her exam? And will she and Bert come down to Devon and go to school there?"

"We've let them decide, and they both want to stay where they are for the time being. Nancy passed her exam. We all went to Rochdale with her one weekend and met the family she's living with, and some of the teachers. Then Otto went with her yesterday to start the term."

"And the whole Intermediate School for Girls is there?"

"Yes, your old school. She's with Guernsey girls and Guernsey teachers. We got the feeling that the teachers keep an eye on the girls like parents would. But I'll miss her at home. Sheila and Alan will miss her, too."

"And what about Bert?"

"Well, you know he had a bad experience with a bomb dropping not far away; and then he wasn't too happy at his billet. So, they arranged for a new billet and Otto went to Oldham with him and met the new people. They're a couple, and the father runs a tobacconist shop, and there's another Guernsey boy staying with them. I think he's settling down better this time."

"And will they come to you for their holidays?"

Nellie nodded. "Bert's pretty good at using the buses, and Nancy's just an hour's bus ride from him. The couple that Bert's staying with, promised to put them both on the train to Devon when their summer holidays start. They seem to be a better class of people than the ones he was with before."

"I'm glad they're not too far from each other. The war's giving our children a lot of challenges."

Otto returned from work, and they all had tea. There was a little piece of cake for everyone, left over from Sheila's eighth birthday celebration. That evening, Sheila and Janice both had a bed, but they were side by side and there was a lot of chatter and giggling. The grownups didn't tell them to be quiet. They were also talking.

In the morning, Frances helped Nellie with some packing and then took Sheila and the girls to see Gran and Grampy. On Tuesday, April 15, they wished Lynette a happy fourth birthday at breakfast, said goodbye to each other sadly, and Frances and the girls headed back to Cotton Row.

Police on trial

Around April 25, some details of the future police trial had been announced in the *Press*, and it was the main topic of discussion in most island homes.

"Just imagine, eighteen policemen," said Ma. "They say it's two thirds of our police."

"And four civilians," Emily added.

"Those must have been the people they were selling food to," said Pa. "And liquor. One of them had a hotel. He must have profited quite a bit."

"And there's people like us being honest, trying to live off our rations," said Emily.

"If they just stole from those five stores belonging to the Jerries, it wouldn't seem so bad," said Arthur. "But stealing from our own shops and from the butcher, that's disgusting. We hardly get any meat for ourselves."

"And some of them stole from the brewery and Bucktrout's cigarette company," said Ma. "Those are Guernsey businesses."

"I wonder if those policemen were beaten up to have them confess," said Emily. "Someone said they looked pretty bruised soon after they were caught."

"Well, the enquiry at the Royal Court will be held by the Bailiff," said Pa. "Let's wait and see what that tells us."

Digging for Victory; First Aid Point in Clowbridge

Frances had plenty to do when she came home from saying goodbye to Nellie and Otto. Lynette's birthday was that same day, next day she worked at Riley's, and it was time to plant the new garden. She wrote away for pamphlets about strawberries from the Ministry of Agriculture. Most people outside Burnley seemed to be focused on gardening and there were *Dig for Victory* posters everywhere.

One evening a week, she attended her Home Nursing course. She was told that a First Aid Point was to be established in Clowbridge and she would be expected to turn up there and work if there were casualties from bombing. She might have to be in charge of it. Part of her course included bandaging, and she had to practice.

"After tea I want you to let me bandage your arm," she said to Janice the next day.

"It doesn't hurt. Why do you want to bandage it?"

"I have to practice bandaging." Frances quickly developed her strategy. "You can see how I do it, and then you can practice on your dolls."

Janice was suddenly co-operative, but Lynette found it hard to sit still and be bandaged. Annie found an old sheet and Frances cut a few strips to make bandages for the dolls.

Later in April, she heard on the BBC news that Exeter and Bath had been badly bombed, and she worried about Nellie. It was said that this was Hitler's revenge for Britain's bombing of the historical city of Lubeck in North Germany. Soon after that, York and Canterbury were bombed. The Americans were now joining with the RAF in bombing raids over Germany. In her father's letter a week later, she learned that Nellie and her family had arrived in Totnes safely, and the Exeter bombing was twenty miles away. All was well. Nellie had already registered Sheila in school.

Frances managed a visit to Scott Park one mild Saturday afternoon. The girls were happy to see familiar faces and it was good to hear Guernsey accents. Gladys laughed when Frances took her knitting out. "Being stripey seems to be the evacuee war fashion," she said. "We're all knitting stripey jumpers."

Frances smiled. "I was looking at those *Make Do and Mend* pamphlets," she said. "I think we could have written them ourselves. We're all making new clothes out of old ones and knitting stripes."

"Will your girls be taking part in the May Queen celebrations that you were telling me about last year?"

"Janice will be one of the dancers and they'll start in the village. I'll watch them with Lynette when they come to Cotton Row next day. She's too young to join in yet."

"I was reading my copy of *The Channel Islands Review*. Are you still getting yours?"

"Yes," said Frances, "but I heard that they're short of paper for printing."

"Well, they discussed it in Parliament last month. Someone said they'll allow it to continue publishing, maybe with smaller print or something. That's because 15,000 Guernsey and Jersey people joined the army. Fifteen thousand! So that includes your brother-in-law, Vi's husband."

"Yes, Fred. My goodness, that's a lot of people who joined up. But I know five of them."

"I know a few as well. They also said that we have at least 30,000 evacuee readers, so a lot of us managed to get away from the islands before the Germans flew in."

"Thirty thousand. The islands must be half empty. I heard that those later boats were pretty crowded and dirty. We were lucky to be on the regular mailboat."

Churchill's speech, May 10

On Sunday night, Churchill spoke again on the wireless. This time Frances managed to listen to all of it, and Hilda listened with them. It was a long speech. He said they had come a long way from their state of unpreparedness two years ago, when he became Prime Minister. Now they had Russia on their side and Hitler had made two mistakes: his June 1941 attack on Russia, whose inhabitants would fight to the end; and not being prepared for the Russian winter, which had killed thousands of his soldiers already. Now he had a battle front in Russia that was over two thousand miles long.

Meanwhile, the United States had entered the war as a formidable ally. Bombing in Germany was continuing, and the city populations could always leave their cities and shelter in the country areas if they wished to avoid it. Hitler was now protesting against this kind of bombing, which he had already inflicted on Rotterdam and British cities. Churchill stated that bombing capacity was now greater and more accurate, and defences were doing better.

Churchill then mentioned "a serious matter" to his audience—that Germany might use poison gas against Russia. Britain was prepared and would react as if its own people were affected. In the meantime, deliveries of arms and supplies to Russia were vital, and merchant sailors and the navy were doing their utmost to bring supplies north to Russian ports within the Arctic circle.

Britain had lost access its line of communication through the Mediterranean and ships now had to sail around the Cape of Good Hope instead of using Suez. Britain's base in Egypt and access to the Suez Canal had to be defended. Malta, Britain's one remaining naval port and air base in the Mediterranean, had heroically survived two years of bombing attacks and attempts to blockade its supplies.

Churchill mentioned "two islands" in the news that week, and Frances listened carefully. First, the Japanese tried to take over Madagascar's main port, which might block routes to Australia and the east from this large island; but a British force had been able to land and secure the harbour. Secondly, the Japanese had sustained huge losses in the Coral Sea and were no match for the United States. The huge island continent of Australia had been well defended, thanks to our Allies. He saw Australia as an island! At this point Frances knew that Guernsey couldn't compete.

"Therefore," Churchill concluded, "tonight I give you a message of good cheer. You deserve it and the facts endorse it. But be it good cheer or be it bad cheer will make no difference to us. We shall drive on to the end and do our duty, win or die; God helping us, we can do no other."

"Well, that was quite a mouthful," said Annie. "The war's really all over the world, isn't it? I haven't even heard of half those places."

"I can see why the Channel Islands are never mentioned. When he said 'islands,' I was hopeful at first."

"He said people in Germany could always run out of the towns and live in the country to avoid bombing," Hilda said. "I remember your mother said she didn't like bombing innocent people. But look at what he did to

London."

"I'm glad he said our defences were getting better," Frances commented. "What I don't like is the idea of poison gas. We've only had one practice about gas with the Red Cross."

"As long as Hitler's busy with the Russians, we can be thankful," Hilda said. Let's just do all that we can with gardening and everything to keep ourselves going."

On May 30 it would be Janice's birthday, and in the spirit of the times she was acting as nurse with her dolls. Frances secretly made her a nurse's apron and cap, using the old white sheet. She stitched a red cross on the apron and made a matching piece of headwear. She cut bandages, added safety pins, and the gift was a great success.

The trouble was that Lynette wanted the same thing. Two days later, a second apron was completed, and all was well. The big benefit to Frances was that both girls were more co-operative about being bandaged, although the adults now had to let the children practice on them sometimes.

21: June–July 1942 — Police trial

*Royal Court trial—Wirelesses taken—Convoys in danger—Annie's holiday week—
Gloomy news from Africa—Late Summer*

Royal Court trial

In June it was warmer, and one afternoon Frances studied her nursing notes outside for a while. She heard a cuckoo singing and thought of the blackbirds at Woodlands. Would Nellie have blackbirds in Devon?

June was a strange month, so beautiful and yet so terrible. Her sister Edie had died five years ago in June in childbirth, after which Gran and Grampy had taken charge of Rose and Graham. Two years ago, they had received the Evacuation notice in *The Press* on June 19. Last year had been different, when she was looking forward to Joyce and Ken's visit, and then that lovely week with Nellie and Otto at Cotton Row. Now, without their hospitality in Bolton, she couldn't get away from Cotton Row.

However, Lynette was now four, and Janice seven. They were familiar with the bus journey to Bolton, and a day's visit seemed possible. A few hours of chatting with her parents was worth the effort.

She returned to her nursing notes. This week they would discuss burns and shock. Yesterday they heard of the fire-bombing of Hamburg. The RAF had devastated over 600 acres of the city. If Germany sought revenge by more bombings in England, Frances might have to deal with casualties in the village, including burns. What worried her more was Churchill's mention of gas at the end of his speech in May. That and chemical burns hadn't been dealt with yet. She had better be prepared for practical work as well as an exam.

Wirelesses taken

At *Le Pré*, June 8 was a beautiful summer morning. Emily came in from her work in the garden to prepare dinner. Ma was indoors already.

"I've turned on the gas to heat the soup, Emily," Ma called out. She was looking at their copy of *The Star* from June 2, which had been laying on the table for a few days. "You know, it's hard to believe that our own policemen could steal food from our stores." She shook her head. "No wonder the Bailiff gave them a talking to after their trial."

She read from the paper: *Clothed in your uniform of Policemen, you have abused your privileges, such as being... out after curfew, and have pillaged our property, stolen, thieved... I am filled with shame. It is revolting to see how you have abused your position.*

"I know, Ma. Anyway, they had their trial at the Royal Court. If the Bailiff said that, then they must be guilty."

"I wonder what's going to happen to them. They all have families. And there are the four other men as well."

Pa came in. "Today's paper is here already. Just read this notice." Pa had folded back the front page and showed them an official notice printed in the English section.

Emily read it out loud:

Notice. By superior orders, the wireless receiving sets of the civil population of the Channel Islands are to be requisitioned and placed under the custody of the Feldkommandantur. Sets used by subjects of the Reich and of countries allied to Germany are excepted. Contravention of this order will be punished by imprisonment up to six weeks and a fine of 30,000 RM: 60,000 shillings and 30 pence.[37]

"Oh, not again... That's ridiculous..." she started. "Why are they doing this again?"

"Well, didn't the BBC say we were going to be attacked soon?" said Ma. "And weren't they telling us to help the Allies if they landed here?"

"I don't think anybody thought they'd bother to land here—except the Jerries, of course. But this says superior orders. That sounds as though it comes from their headquarters in Paris or Berlin."

Ma was looking out of the window. "Arthur's coming up the path. I wonder if he's heard about this."

Over bean soup, vegetables and bread, they shared what they knew.

"The BBC did ask us to help Allied soldiers if there was an invasion," Arthur commented. "So, it's not surprising they don't want us to have

---

37   Carey, p 85

wirelesses. But nothing's happened."

"Remember a week ago, when that British destroyer was seen, and the Jerries were running all over the place?" Pa said. "They seemed to think it was an invasion starting."

"Yeah, they were driving the Jerries all around the island in buses to their flak gun positions," said Arthur, "or they were getting ready to evacuate. Who knows? They used up a lot of petrol for nothing. I didn't have any work driving for a couple of days after that."

"You seem to have settled down to driving for the Jerries after all," Ma observed.

"As long as I'm dealing in food and supplies for everybody, it's ok. I need to work and earn my living. I've got a good driving record."

"Do they ever yell at you like they yell at those prisoners, or are they polite?" Emily asked.

"They tell us what's needed and leave us to do the job, mostly. Except one was upset the other day. He'd lost his parents in Cologne and wanted the war to end, or so I understood."

"It almost makes you feel sympathetic."

Pa had been thinking. "Well, I wonder if Churchill sent that destroyer around here just as a trick, to give them a scare, so that they don't send these troops to fight the Russians. Keeping ten thousand troops on this island may be good for Britain. And if you remember, Molotov—the Russian foreign minister—was in London in May. I bet he was pushing Churchill to give Hitler something to worry about on this side of Europe and take the pressure off Russia…"

"You're right, Pa," said Emily. "And the BBC might have made that announcement to make the Jerries think an invasion was being planned."

Arthur nodded. "Keeping them busy here is better than killing our soldiers or the Russians somewhere else, I suppose. They're certainly busy making gun strong points and hacking out tunnels all over the place."

"Well, let's listen to all the news we can get for the next day or two," said Ma. "We have to give in the wirelesses by Wednesday night."

"You can make crystal sets and listen to the radio that way," said Arthur. "They explained how to do it on the BBC. Walter was showing me…"

"But that would be forbidden," Ma interrupted. "If you do that, don't let me know about it."

Arthur grinned and sipped his bramble tea.

Next day, Ma was the first to get to *The Press* and found another Notice: *Regarding the collection of radio sets throughout the Island, readers will understand that the calling in is not in any way a punishment imposed on the civilian population, but for purely military reasons.*[38]

"It must have been an order from Germany," said Emily. "The Kommandant is almost apologizing. Let's hope we'll get our wirelesses back after a couple of months, like we did two years ago."

Convoys in danger

> The USA sent shiploads of supplies to Russia according to their **Lend-Lease agreement**. They shipped everything from food and tractors to tanks and planes, and the quantity increased a great deal after Pearl Harbour. Lend-Lease also supplied Britain with 10% of its equipment, and supported the Allies in the war in the Pacific.
>
> The Royal Navy tried to protect convoys travelling past the coast of Norway to Murmansk and Archangel in Russia; but U-boats and German bombers were based on Norway's coast and were ready to attack the convoys.

One Sunday evening, after the children were in bed, Frances started a letter to her father. She wrote about her plan to come early one day with the girls and stay just for the day. As she finished writing the envelope, Annie returned from a visit to Tom and Mary.

"When's your dad coming to visit us again?" Annie asked. "I'd like to know what he thinks of our new garden now we can see the strawberries are doing all right."

Frances put down her pen. "I've just written to them. He said in his last letter that he wanted to come, but he's had to work a couple of times on weekends. Then they cut the bus service at weekends because petrol's hard to get, so I don't think he'll visit us for a while. I'd like to try going with the children, just for the day, perhaps when they start their holidays."

---

38   Carey, p 85.

"You should go during the week when you can rely on the service. If I can, I'll come with you to the bus station and get you a family return ticket. No good spending more than you have to."

"Thanks. That's a good help, Annie. How are Tom and Mary?"

"They're all right, except Tom was talking about a pal of his from Burnley. His pal's son is working on one of those ships that'll be taking supplies up past Norway to Russia. We were looking at the map. It's right up north into the Arctic."

Annie was full of Tom's worried conversation and walked over to the map gallery. Frances joined her. "I think you've got a map of it somewhere," Annie continued. "Here it is, Norway." She traced her fingers up the Norwegian coastline and into the Arctic. "He showed me where they have to go. Here it is…Mur something. Murmansk…and Archangel. Fancy, a name like that."

Frances nodded. "Yes, I see it. That's what Churchill was talking about. That's what Lionel could be doing too."

In July, Tom's friend received bad news about the convoy that his son was sailing with: On June 22, Convoy PQ17, comprising 33 merchant ships, left Iceland for Archangel. They were attacked on July 4. Only ten or eleven of them managed to reach Archangel or Murmansk.[39]

> **German U-boats**, or undersea boats, destroyed about three thousand Allied ships in World War Two in what was called the Battle of the Atlantic. Britain depended on food and war materials shipped from Canada, the USA and other countries, but British airplanes could not provide air cover in the mid-Atlantic, where supply ships were most at risk of being torpedoed. The supply ships were grouped in convoys with escorts of naval ships which gave some protection.
>
> Germany used ports like St. Nazaire to accommodate its U-boats. The Germans experimented with torpedoes that used magnetism and acoustics to destroy Allied shipping; U-boats would hunt in wolf packs to locate and sink a ship.

---

39   www.historic-.com/HistoryUK/HistoryofBrita/World-War-2

> The British developed radar and sonar to locate U-boats, and made radar available on aircraft.
>
> In 1942, after the USA joined in the war, the amount of shipping to England increased, and American ships patrolled the Atlantic, adding new challenges to the U-boats' survival. The discovery of the German radio codes called Enigma in 1942, and the work of codebreakers, helped to locate and destroy U-boats. By 1944, supplies were reaching England with more regularity.

Strawberry harvest

Once the strawberries started to ripen, Frances and Annie were busy picking and selling them to neighbours, and Hilda helped a bit. If the girls were at home, they played nearby. Janice disliked approaching the strawberry patch because there were frogs in it, and one of the boys at school had put a frog down her back.

Frances liked to hull the strawberries or prepare garden produce while she listened to a new BBC programme after dinner. It was called "Desert Island Discs," in which a guest chose eight pieces of music, and a new world of music opened up.

In the middle of June, she received her father's weekly letter and was surprised to find it included a note from her mother as well. As briefly as possible, her mother said that in July, Frances and the children could come to stay with them for a few days when Graham would be away with the scouts. Rose would sleep at a friend's house. If they travelled during the week, the bus service should be normal. Frances was happy.

Annie's holiday week

Early in July, Annie had a week's holiday. She hoped that they could go twice to Morecambe on Express day trips that week, but petrol was now restricted to official users: regular service buses, ambulances, and farmers. A notice in the Burnley Express stated that the bus company "... *regrets it will be unable this year to operate extra buses for the conveyance of passengers from Burnley and district to holiday resorts as in the past.*"[40]

---

40   Burnley Express July 1942.

However, Annie was persistent and the four of them used the regular buses to get to Morecambe for a day's outing, with Annie using her family discount. They had to change buses twice, and it took a while to get there, but paddling and playing on the sand for a few hours, and walking along the Prom made a special outing. One photograph attests to this precious visit.

The girls had a minor adventure with Annie during this week. It was never described fully to Frances. Annie had promised to take them to the Co-op variety show while Frances was working at the Rileys one afternoon. She described it later in a letter to Lynette:

When I worked on the buses, I used to take you and Jan(ice) to the theatre, or to a show in Burnley. We were waiting for the bus, when this big wagon stopped, and asked if I could get him some water for his engine. So, I went and got it. He then said, "Where are you going?" I said, "Burnley." He said, "Ok, get in."

So, we all got in front and when he just got past the Waggoners Hill, you know it was a very steep hill after that, he said, "Oh God, both my foot brake and hand brake won't work!"

I kept saying, run in(to) that wall on this side. and I could see the traffic lights as we were getting near to the Manchester Road.

So, I pushed you and Jan at the back of me and turned the steering wheel towards a wall in front of a garage. It took all the wall down, but it stopped us.

He said, "Thank goodness I picked you up that knew this road. I'm not really allowed to carry anyone." I said, "Right, we're off. I leave you to sort it out."

I don't think you knew what happened and we caught a bus and carried on to the show.

The girls weren't at all frightened. They had learned that when they were with Annie things usually turned out all right.

A trip to Bolton

In the middle of July, Frances took the girls to Bolton as arranged with her mother. They managed to get tickets for an early Express bus on a Tuesday, and by late morning the girls were playing hopscotch with Rose in the street, and Frances was sipping tea outside with her mother.

Gran wanted to know about her job, and about a gas mask practice at school. They talked about Vi, who was due to give birth to her second child later that month. Gran kept letters she received from the family in her kitchen drawer.

"That drawer's precious," she said. "I have all the Red Cross messages and letters there. You can read them all when you go in, but make sure you put them back."

Grampy came in from work early and was happy to see the strawberries that Frances had brought. "It looks as though your garden's been a success," he said.

"Annie was asking when you were coming to Cotton Row again."

"I'd like to come," he said, "but we've been busy with the vegetables and I want to make sure they're looked after properly. We're still losing a lot of food across the Atlantic. We have to depend a lot on our own production now."

"I think everybody outside of Burnley has a garden—we're all growing potatoes and vegetables."

"That may be the only thing that'll save us. I was hoping we'd win our Suez route back by now. We still have Malta, but Rommel seems to be ready to take over Egypt and the canal. Did you hear that he took Tobruk again a couple of weeks ago? While Churchill was in Washington? Now he's heading straight to take Suez. I don't know if the Americans can help us there, besides what they're doing in the Pacific."

"I was glad to hear the Americans beat the Japs in the Coral Sea," Frances said. "I had to look it up, and it's right next to Australia!"

"Yes. And those Australians are good fighters, they say. They're fighting in Africa with us. Probably they're more used to the heat than we are."

"We'll have to wait it out here whatever happens," said Gran, looking up at him. "At least you're doing what you're good at, even if you want to get back to your greenhouses. And as long as the Russians are keeping Hitler busy and I don't hear bombers at night, I can manage living here, too."

Next day Frances took the girls to see Grampy's vegetable plots in the huge cemetery. They said hello to Geoff and Bill, and Frances did her usual walk through the rose gardens. Clambering around the cemetery's monuments made things more interesting for the girls, but it wasn't allowed for long. Later, they played with Rose in Grampy's Morrison shelter in the living room: it had a metal ceiling to shelter the family during a bomb attack, and with blankets and cushions it was just right to play house with their dolls. However, Frances could see that although Rose did her best, it was clear that they missed playing with Sheila and Alan.

Late summer

On Friday evening they were back in Cotton Row. Frances shopped for rations, caught up with the garden, and made some jam with sugar she had saved or exchanged. She took the girls on walks along Limey Lane by the reservoir, and up the Burnley Road to the old Haworth Farm or Waggoners Farm further on, or to the Bonk.

One day she sat outside the front door, knitting. The girls had a tea party for their bandaged dolls nearby. Soldiers in a convoy of military lorries going north along the Manchester Road called and waved to them, and they waved back.

"Watch out, lady! You've dropped a stitch!" one of them yelled. Frances looked up and laughed. The last of the convoy disappeared, and the girls stopped waving.

"Good heavens, I did drop a stitch!" Frances exclaimed.

Lynette was curious. "How could he see you'd dropped a stitch?" She wondered about it for a long time.

The war seemed to stay away from them. Vi wrote to say that her second child was a girl, Margaret. The girls were told that yes, they would all go to see Margaret and David when the buses were running regularly.

The last summer event was the Rawtenstall Busmen's Show. Annie had made a lot of friends among the conductors, drivers, and mechanics, and she showed off her wartime family to them. Frances noticed that she had a special friend, a driver who she worked with. Annie said that she would like to be able to drive a car, and after the war she would learn. "That's if I haven't found somebody to teach me by then," she concluded.

22: August 1942. Island on Alert—Dieppe

*Prison sentences—Island on alert—G.U.N.S. newsletter—Dieppe—
A good deed on a birthday*

Prison sentences

On the morning of August 19, everything was quiet at *Le Pré*; but the night had been disturbed with the noise of planes flying over. Pa woke, wondering if the RAF were destroying the thirty odd barges that had returned to France during the summer. He moved to the window and watched the sky in the east light up with flashes. Something was happening over the French coast. In the morning, Arthur went to work as usual, ready to pick up news about the night attack.

Around mid-morning Ma was reading the newspaper, sitting outside, with a pile of mending sitting on a chair beside her. Emily was picking the last of their beans when she saw her mother approaching, carrying the *Press*.

"Emily, you wanted to know the sentences that the police were given."

"Yes, did they get a prison sentence or a fine...?"

"It depends which man you're referring to. Some got about four months and the worst cases have got four years, all of them in French prisons."

"Hmm. I suppose, they deserved it. I was thinking, they aren't the only black-market traders getting rich. Everybody's trying to profit somehow."

"Some people are greedy and willing to take risks. As long as we have a garden and keep the chickens, I hope we can last out till the war ends."

"I hope so, Ma. Anyway, I'm glad that the Jerries allowed Mr Sherwill to go back to his job as Procureur. That was a bit of good news."

"Well, he's a Guernseyman and a lawyer, and that's his official position. He fought in the Great War, too. He's a good man."

"Wasn't he supposed to be Bailiff when the old one died a few years ago?"

"Yes. The old Bailiff died suddenly. I think it was 1935. The Procureur takes over the Bailiff's job, but Sherwill had only just started being Procureur. He hadn't enough experience. The next in command is the Comptrolleur—the Receiver General..."

Emily finished the sentence: "... and that was Victor Carey, so that's why he's Bailiff now."

"That's right," said Ma. "I'm glad the Jerries showed a little bit of wisdom putting Sherwill back where he should be. I think there'd be an uproar if they tried to make someone else Procureur. It just wouldn't be right."

"I wonder how long they'll make us wait before we get our wirelesses back. I miss the BBC news and everything."

"Arthur hasn't heard any hints about us getting them back, has he? We'll have to be patient."

Island on alert

Ma went back to her chair and her mending, and Emily continued to pick beans, but there was more movement of Jerry traffic up and down Havelet. Today wasn't as quiet as usual, and she wondered why.

There was the crunch of bicycle wheels on gravel and she looked up. It was Arthur, wheeling his bike up from Havelet Road, but it was only midmorning. He leaned the bike against the house wall and said something to Ma; then went up the slope to where his father was working and they came down together, each with an armful of wood. Nobody shouted any news these days, and it looked as though Arthur had something interesting to say. Emily gathered up her beans and joined them in the house.

"What's happened, Arthur? Why are you back so early?" she asked.

"There were barricades around the harbour when I went to work, and I had a job to get through and report. They told me there was no work today. The three of us who drive all turned up, and they told us to go back home. Some Jerries are in camouflage and some with Red Cross armbands and they're as jumpy as anything."

"It's Wednesday, so I don't pick up our bread ration till tomorrow," said Emily, "but I wanted to go to the market today to buy some French plums that came in yesterday."

"There were planes flying over during the night and then another early this morning," Pa said. "Something happened on the French coast last night. Did anyone see any British ships? I saw nothing from here."

"I didn't see anything. But there were lorries with machine guns on them along the Front[41] and at two crossroads inland. I circled around through

---

41   The *Front* was the common name for the road along the harbour, next to the Town

the lanes on my bike before I came back, and I stopped at the bike shop. He said leaflets had been dropped saying that if planes fly over, we should take cover. I saw a couple of Jerries watching, hiding in the hedges, with greenery on their heads, and then I saw another machine gun on a lorry. I'm not going out again. It looks as though they're expecting an attack and every one of them's nervous and carrying a rifle."

"Well, you can help me get some more wood in," said Pa. "We'll be needing it soon enough." He turned to Emily. "And don't you go anywhere until we're sure things are safe, Emily."

Emily frowned. "Do you think the Germans really think that the navy's going to come here and invade us?"

"The navy's got better things to do, I'm sure," said Ma.

"Exactly," said Pa, "but the Jerries have expected an attack all summer. Didn't Arthur say there are a lot of steel anti-tank girders buried in the sand on the west coast at Vazon Bay? Let's just stay at home and wait. Somebody will let us know."

Emily thought, *how careful we are now. We don't even mention our friends' names anymore. It's always, somebody.* There was her own friend Dorothy, who she now referred to as somebody because she passed news on to her. Another *somebody* was a good contact for Arthur, and she was sure she knew who that was, but they never mentioned his name. There were informers who were paid by the Germans to snitch on their neighbours, and it was far better not to know anyone's name in case you repeated it and the *somebody* got into trouble.

G.U.N.S. newsletter

Next day when Arthur came home for tea, he was careful to check outside before he joined the others in the kitchen. Once they were all seated, he announced, "I have a newsletter that someone's printing. It's a summary of the BBC news." He pushed away from the table and slid out a paper from under an inner sole in his shoe. The others watched in silence.

Pa looked around. "Was there anyone outside when you came?"

"No, I checked. It seems there was some kind of invasion after all."

Pa got up and stood outside the door for a minute, and returned.

Arthur was holding a sheet of paper with print on one side. A few *somebodies* had secretly listened to the BBC news, and had typed and printed a summary. Arthur knew that they called themselves the Guernsey Underground News Service, or GUNS for short, but he didn't mention it. Ma wouldn't have liked to know.[42]

Emily read it out quietly: there had been a British raid on Dieppe, but it didn't sound as though there was any great success; there wasn't much information yet. Two days later, *The Guernsey Press*, on its German language front page, stated that the raid was a fiasco and many Allied troops were killed or taken prisoner. Churchill had made a distraction for his friend Stalin and it had been a total failure.

The islanders had shown amusement at the near hysteria of the Germans, who had obviously been told that an attack on the island was imminent. They realised that many islanders knew about the actual raid before they did, indicating that there were still too many radios about. As punishment, the curfew was to start two hours earlier, at 9 p.m., the following week; and they were warned that access to telephones might be taken away from those who had them.

Dieppe

At Cotton Row, Frances knew something had happened around Dieppe "and a few towns along the coast," as the newspapers put it. Could it have included the islands? As usual, Annie picked up a couple of newspapers left in the bus, and Frances scanned them and cut out the front pages.

Commandos wreck enemy batteries at Dieppe, said the *Daily Sketch*.

She wanted to ask her father what he had heard but wouldn't ask in a letter. Who knows where letters can end up in a war? She quickly wrote to ask them if she could come on Saturday at the end of the month. By then, they should all know a bit more. Frances would be busy enough until then, doing a few extra hours at the Rileys. Her father wrote to say that he and Gran would come to Cotton Row.

On August 23, Annie was looking forward to seeing them again. Grampy had said in his letter that they would try to be on an early bus, unless it was cancelled. The girls were on lookout duty, and as soon as they shouted,

---

42   GUNS was run by former journalist Charles Machon with help of Frank Falla and three others. It was very secret. A 700-word précis of today's news was issued daily. In Feb 1944 one paper fell into hands of *Paddy*, an informer. The five were arrested and Machon and one other died in German prisons.

Frances lit the gas under the kettle and Annie went to the door. The chatter began. Frances noticed newspapers in the bag her father was carrying.

"So, what do you think Dieppe was all about?"

"Look at these," her father said, pulling out the newspapers. "I don't think it had anything to do with the islands. It was too far away from Guernsey, and more like a one-day excursion."

"But why would they take tanks and leave them wrecked on the shore, just for one day? And quite a few boats?"

"I wonder if they just wanted to get Hitler's attention away from Russia for a bit, and make him think it was a major attack, to give the Russians a bit of breathing space. You know, Molotov came to see Churchill in May, and Churchill went to Washington after that. I think they must have been planning something to help the Russians."

Frances looked at the newspapers. "We couldn't find any mention of the islands in the papers," said Gran.

"It sounds to me as though something didn't go right," Grampy declared. "Maybe too many men were lost, and some were Canadians and Americans. Some of these papers make things sound better than they probably were."

"It says, 'it was a vital experience in the landings,'" said Gran, pointing to one newspaper. "I suppose that means they learned where they made mistakes."

"Perhaps it wasn't successful. It's a bit late to try anything more this year, though," said Frances.

"It is too late. Let's hope they'll do it next spring. I'd like to get back into my greenhouses by late next year," her father said.

They had dinner and inspected the new garden. Back indoors, Gran patiently allowed her fingers to be bandaged by two small nurses while a last cup of tea was made, and the visitors left early.

A good deed on a birthday

August 28 was Arthur's 40th birthday. It would go by without a letter or a card from Frances or the children, the third year in a row. Janice made a card anyway, and she helped Frances to send a Red Cross message well before the day.

In spite of the rations, Arthur hoped Emily had managed to make something different for tea. He wanted to forget about his day's work. He had driven sacks of provisions to the tunnel system that was being built under St. Saviour's church. The OT workers, many now from Russia, were doing the heavy labour of drilling into the granite, dragging and loading the stone, breathing the dust after the underground explosions. Every day, some died of starvation, exhaustion, whipping and cruelty; or they might be shipped back to France to be forced into other work. If the body of an Allied soldier was washed up, the Jerries would give the man a respectable funeral; but the OT workers were treated as less than human and just disappeared.

He had driven slowly past a group of them that afternoon. They were emaciated and seemed exhausted. He had eaten a couple of sandwiches at midday because he couldn't get home for dinner. His last sandwich was by him on the seat of the cab. He lowered his window and flipped it out. One of the workers bent forward to grab it and waved his hand; so at least Arthur had done a little good and his own hunger didn't feel as bad. He would finish work at 3 p.m. today. Work hours were becoming shorter as lack of meat and milk affected the energy of all workers.

"Neither Pa nor I could find any fish for Arthur's birthday tea," Emily complained to her mother. "This Dieppe business seems to have stopped all fishing for now. There's a lot of French Camembert in the market though, so that's what we've got. Art likes strong Cheddar, so he'll just have to put up with it."

"If he's hungry he'll enjoy it," Ma said. "I was glad we had some cooking oil with our rations this week. We've been waiting for that for a while."

"Yes, and matches. We were down to our last few."

"We're going to have two desserts to celebrate your birthday," Emily told Arthur, as they sat down. That would cheer him, while they had their first course of beans, vegetables and Camembert.

Arthur was polite about the first dessert. "That was a bit like strawberry jelly," he said quietly. "Thanks Em. It's a long time since I ate jelly."

Emily had made the jelly using carageen, a dried seaweed, which she could now buy from Stonelake, the chemist; but it was sweetened with saccharin and didn't taste quite right. Ma and Pa dutifully ate it, but they knew what was on hand for the second dessert. They watched Arthur's eyes brighten as he saw Emily pouring pancake batter into the frying pan. He got up and watched the pancake cooking, just to be sure.

Ma placed a bowl of plum sauce on the table to spoon over the pancakes.

Emily had made it with French plums and a little of their hoarded sugar. The second dessert was eaten as slowly as they could.

To crown it all, Emily had bought half a pound of black-market tea, which had cost £4, the value of almost two weeks' wages! A good cup of tea was a luxury and completed the meal in style. Ma would dry the tea leaves later for use again the next day.

23: Sept–Dec 1942: An Accident and Monty's Victory

Deportations—Strange bus service—The Accident—Calamity at Le Pré—
Good news from Africa—November break

Deportations

On Tuesday, September 15, Pa met the paperboy on the road just before dinner time. He turned the page of *The Press* to read the English headlines. He stopped briefly to stare at something and then walked briskly to the house.

"Ma! Emily! They've just issued an evacuation order."
The three of them crowded around the table and read the Order.

> … *the following British subjects will be evacuated and transferred to Germany.*
>   A. *Persons who have their permanent residence not on the Channel Islands, for instance those who have been caught here by the outbreak of war.*
>   B. *All those men not born on the island and 16 to 70 years of age, together with their families.*
> *Detailed Instructions will be given.*
> *Der FeldKommandantur, Knackfuss.*

Emily was shocked. " Sixteen to seventy years of age…." she whispered, and sat down. "Jimmy would have been sixty-seven…" She sat down.
Ma put her hands on Emily's shoulders and stated what they were all thinking: "Thank goodness your husband's in a better place, Emily."
Pa was silent. Emily would have had to leave with Jimmy. And what did "and their families" mean?
"They made lists of everybody. Don't you remember how worried we were, that Arthur might be evacuated with other men?" said Ma. "But none of us were born in England, so I hope we'll be all right."
That afternoon Arthur wasn't working. After dinner and a rest, they finished digging up the potatoes, cleaned them up, and carried them to the entrance of the house before tea. Indoors, Ma was preparing the soup.

201

"We'll take them upstairs after tea," Pa told her. "They'll need to dry a bit, but I daren't leave them in the shed."

"No, you'd better not," Ma said. There are some old sacks upstairs that you can spread them out on. It'll be good to have them safe indoors. Emily said nobody dares leave potatoes or onions lying about any more."

"I had to drive past Charlie's the other day," Arthur said, "and he was near the road, so I stopped for a minute. He said a lot of potatoes were destroyed in fields where the Jerries were doing army exercises—marching up and down over a potato field in one place and driving with one of those old French tanks over another one. You'd think they'd know better than that. They grow a lot of potatoes in Germany."

"Did Charlie have much to sell?" asked Pa.

"Not a lot. Cabbage, carrots, swedes. The usual."

Next day Emily called from the door as she came in with the bread ration: "Sorry I'm a bit late, Ma. I just met somebody who'd come in to town on one of the new buses."

"You mean those charcoal-driven buses?" Arthur asked.

"Yes. One woman said it worked all right to come to town from the west coast—from Cobo. But my friend who works at the hospital said the bus from the hospital back to town never turned up yesterday evening, and she had to walk home."

"And Jim said the Jerries commandeered a bus the other day," Pa added. "It was late in the afternoon, and they made the driver go to the cinema." Pa sat down. "Did you hear anything more about the deportations, Emily? I heard that they may send up to two thousand people away."

"From what I heard, a lot of people had a medical exam and the ones who were sick, or pregnant, were exempted; but even older people will be deported. Some people in important positions were exempted, and so were a few farmers, but my friend said we'll lose two or three doctors. It's such a rush. They have to leave next week."

"I think about four hundred have already gone from Jersey," said Arthur. "But I heard that they're not too sure about getting a couple of boats to pick them up in Guernsey. And the weather's been a bit rough lately."

"I heard there were even a few marriages so that some young people could stay together," Ma added. "What a way to start married life. And just because of an order from Hitler that doesn't help his side or ours."

Pa concentrated on pulling his piece of bread apart. He wondered what they had put in it this time—more bean flour and bran, perhaps. Soaking it in the soup helped a bit. "Will you be working on Monday, Arthur?" he asked. "I want to get some limpets and winkles since they're allowing us to go on the beach again."

"Not on Monday. They're requisitioning more houses, maybe houses from the people deported, because some of them have nice places. I think they want to billet their troops closer together, so it's easier to move them in a hurry—in case we're really invaded or some damn thing. So, there's furniture to be moved."

"I thought they preferred people to leave their furniture in the house," said Ma.

"Only if it's really nice stuff."

"Hmm," Ma grunted. She prodded a small piece of bread around her bowl of soup and put the rest back on the breadboard, meaning someone else could have it. Emily halved it and gave the men a lump each.

The Accident

On Tuesday, September 22, Annie left Cotton Row on her auto-bike in the afternoon, as usual. She left the bike at a garage in Loveclough, and the parcels van took her to the depot in Rawtenstall. When her shift finished after midnight, she was driven back to Loveclough. All lights were dimmed as usual. With no warning, an oncoming speeding vehicle crashed straight into the van, and she was thrown through the windscreen.

Her own description of what followed comes from letters to Lynette some years later:

They carried me into a house and rang for the doctor. He came with another doctor, and I was told later that six of them held me down as a doctor put 7 stitches in my head until the ambulance came. And [I was] unconscious for days in the casualty ward.

She was kept in the Emergency room at the hospital and after a few days, Frances and Annie's sister, Dora, said they would bring her home. Annie kept repeating a telephone number, which turned out to belong to Fred who drove the ambulance. He was called and took her home in the ambulance.

Frances and Auntie Dora brought me home, said if I had to die, I might as well die at home. That's when your mum helped me such a lot, put a paper on the door, No Knocking and No Visitors.

For three days at Cotton Row, she was unconscious. As she stirred: *Your Mum... had to sort of sit on me to quieten me down when I was coming round...*

After endless days of being very quiet, the girls were allowed to go inside the curtains around the single bed that she lay on. Annie's talking voice was a little huskier and she couldn't sit up. Each of them took turns to hold her hand as she lay flat on the bed, in the dark. She asked them to sing the song she had taught them: "You are my sunshine..." It seemed to give her the hope she needed. She could only speak a few words. They came downstairs in silence. This wasn't the Auntie Annie they were accustomed to.

Calamity at *Le Pré*

In August, Pa and his household had noticed German officers making a survey on the hill below their rented property, as Ma had noticed earlier in the summer. Later in September, in the middle of the morning, a group of them and a few OT workers appeared on the road below the house. Half an hour later there was some kind of small explosion, and a cloud of dust and debris hovered over the road. It scared them all. Emily calmed her mother, who had caught a cold and was resting indoors.

Pa went down to the road and asked what was going on and Emily went outside. He came back looking shaken.

"What's going on, Pa?"

"They're using dynamite to excavate a tunnel that will go under the house. They have a surveyor and engineer and did a trial explosion. Another damned tunnel! Emily, we're going to have to move."

"Move!" Emily was in shock. To move all that they possessed in this old family home... And to move Ma, who was becoming more and more frail...

Pa looked up at the house with his workshop on the hill behind, and was silent. Emily put her hand on his arm. Her father was in shock.

"Emily, Ma and I have lived here almost all our married life."

"I know, Pa. You moved here the year after I was born, didn't you? In 1892?"

"That's right. We lived in the Bouet for a while, and you were born in

December, and we started renting here the year after. The Bouet was on the north side of the harbour and my moorings are on the south side, so I wanted to be nearer. After you, every child was born in this house."

She nodded. "Then we all grew up and left, and Otto rented half of it for a while."

They were quiet.

"But why do they need a tunnel here, Pa? Did they explain?"

"They say it'd be a safe place to store food, but I bet it would be for ammunition—a safe place near the harbour. Perhaps they'll link it with Fort George up the road as a defensive position."

Emily had tears in her eyes. "We'll work together on this, Pa. I've got Edelweiss Lodge across the road and we'll move in there, if we're allowed. But we're going to have to be careful with Ma."

Watching over Annie

Frances followed the doctor's advice to the letter and watched over Annie carefully. Hilda, Dora, Alice-Ann, and Mary helped with the nursing and only family visitors were allowed. It tied Frances to a narrower routine, but she was pleased that her nursing training helped her to cope. Noise and light bothered Annie most and semi-darkness and minimal noise was the rule. The volume of the wireless was turned down, and the children tried to be quiet. The neighbours helped wherever they could.

Annie had become the person to whom Frances would happily entrust her children if she was seriously hurt or in danger of losing her own life. Annie had taken care of her and the children, and now Frances would look after her to the best of her ability.

Frances managed to buy extra vegetables for the winter at the harvest festival. A proposed visit to Vi in Bradford was cancelled and Eric, Daisy, and Louise were advised not to visit Cotton Row. Kit dug up the potatoes and Hilda helped with the rest of the garden's harvest.

It was the end of Annie being a conductress, and it was also the end of her ability to sing. Her strong contralto voice disappeared.

Settling in at Edelweiss

In Guernsey on November 2, Emily was quite heartened when German summer time ended and, at last, she could make breakfast with some daylight coming through the windows—her own windows! It seemed to be a rare good act of fate that James had been both a good husband and a good manager. After he died, she had become the owner of their two houses, and it left her more secure than most women she knew. Their move to Edelweiss, so near to *Le Pré*, meant that Ma and Pa were still near their home territory.

She was trying to establish habits that would bring some calm into their lives after the urgency of moving. They had been helped by all the family, moving beds and furniture, clothes, and their precious stored potatoes and the chicken house. Cracks had started to appear in two of *Le Pré*'s lower walls, witnessing the explosions that neared its foundations. Pa had moved what was most valuable from his shed, and continued to bring to Edelweiss anything they could use for winter fires.

However, Emily's satisfaction was short-lived. She managed to corner both Arthur and Pa outside the house later one afternoon.

"A German officer was here just an hour ago, and he said we can only stay here till the end of March next year," she informed them. "I spoke to him outside, and I haven't told Ma. Can we keep it from her until we have to move again?"

"Why do they want us to move?" Arthur queried.

"He said it's too near Havelet Bay. There are guns above us near Fort George as well. Maybe we'll be in the line of fire."

"I think they're making another tunnel near where the bathing pools are, just south of Havelet Bay," Arthur said. He wondered if Edelweiss would be damaged by gunfire, but didn't mention it.

"Well, excavating another tunnel would explain those explosive noises that we've been hearing," Pa said. "They must have plans to store a lot of ammunition around here."

"Oh, if only we had our wirelesses back," Emily said. "It would drown out the explosions and it would cheer up Ma, and me too. I thought they would have given them back to us by now."

"There's always my turntable and records," Arthur said.

"Arthur, if you play: *I scream, you scream, we all scream for ice cream*, anymore, I'll give away your turntable."

Arthur drew comfort from the Red Cross message he had received from Frances and Janice this week. It wished him a happy birthday, now long past, but brightened up a dull November day.

That night the underground news service heard about Allied bombing raids on cities like Essen and Hamburg; everyone hoped the Guernsey deportees weren't located near them, and felt thankful that they could sleep in peace on the island.

Good news from Africa

On November 6 they were all heartened by the BBC news which had filtered around the island in double-quick time: Monty's victory over Rommel at El Alamein.

Emily went to the market to buy limpets, which somebody brought to the fish market once a week. She heard a man whistling a cheerful tune loudly, which was unheard of these days. A couple of islanders passed her and smiled broadly.

As she entered the big building, the chattering of voices sounded like a children's Christmas party. Charlie and Elsie were both at their stall in the vegetable section, beaming at her and ready for a quiet but joyful conversation about Monty's success. They didn't have much to sell, but it was as though the sun was shining on them all for the first time in months.

Charlie asked about Ma, and Emily was sad that she couldn't give them better news than before. "She stays in bed to rest; but she's weak, and her cough isn't getting better. If only we had better food! Pa's watching her while I'm out."

Arthur came home at noon bringing the news sheet prepared by GUNS and Pa sat by Ma's bed and read it out: *German army is in full retreat... Defeat in Egypt at hands of 8th Army under Gen Bernard Montgomery. ... capture of over 9,000 prisoners... 8th army has been dug in there between the Mediterranean and salt marshes since first battle in July.... Since Oct 23 Allies have been inching forward... The beginning of the end for Hitler.*[43]

They repeated snippets of the news to each other, marvelling at the Allied success, and Emily swiftly delivered the newsletter to her trusted someone up the road, and returned.

"This news about Montgomery is going to annoy the Kommandant," her mother said, in her pale voice, "but they can't take our wirelesses away this

---

43   News.bbc.co.uk/ Nov 4 1942

time, seeing that we haven't got any."

"Well Ma, it's not our fault that Rommel lost the battle, is it?" Emily gently argued.

"If they're annoyed about anything, it's probably because of that commando attack on Sark last month," Pa remarked. "They lost a few men there. Jim said about eight Jerries were captured. Although why Churchill would send commandos here again, I really don't know. We had enough problems the last time."

Arthur nodded. "One of the drivers was talking about those eight Jerries. Maybe it's like you said: Churchill just wants to keep the Jerries busy here instead of fighting us somewhere else."

"Let's forget about that and have a good cup of tea and toast Montgomery with it and wish him well," said Emily.

The tea was good, and the spark of hope that Monty's victory had awoken in each of them felt even better. Emily was glad to see that her mother seemed cheered by the news and ate a little better.

November break

At Cotton Row in mid-November, there was a sprinkling of snow on the hills in the morning. Frances made sure the girls had enough layers of clothing as they dressed. It was a special day.

"Winter's almost here again, and it'll be cold outside waiting for buses," she told them quietly, and they murmured back. They had got used to lowering their voices to keep the house quiet for Annie.

Hilda and Alice-Ann had told Frances that they would look after Annie, if she wanted to visit her parents for a weekend before winter started. For Frances, it would be like a late birthday present and a Christmas gift rolled into one. They left on Friday morning, suitably bundled up.

Gran was relieved to see them arrive early, and Grampy took the afternoon off work.

"It sounds as though you've taken good care of Annie," Grampy said, after Frances had finished her summary of the accident and the nursing. "I hope all her family appreciate it."

"Well, she's been good to me and the children, Dad. We're almost like family now. And if something happened to her, I don't know where that would leave me as an evacuee."

"It's a good thing you did your nursing training. That must have helped," said Gran.

"It did. I'd just come back from my course on the evening before she had the accident. A week later she was brought home, and Hilda stayed with her and the children so I could continue my course. We were doing head injuries and concussions, so I didn't want to miss it. She has stitches right across her forehead."

"Her family's been helping enough?"

"We've split taking care of her between us all, and thank goodness Lynette's in school in the afternoons. That's helped a lot. I was able to continue with my cleaning work after the first two weeks."

Gran was satisfied. "We had a letter from Nellie last week. They had a message from Arthur's mother saying they are all well and have plenty of mackerel. It's in the drawer. You can read it later."

"That must have been sent in July then," said Frances. "The mackerel always chase the small fish around the harbour in July. Arthur usually comes home with a couple of buckets full. I wouldn't mind a fresh mackerel."

"And what about Monty's victory at El Alamein?" Her mother said. "Wasn't that good news?"

"That's been a hard battle to win," her father said. "They were talking about the first battle of El Alamein a couple of months ago, and Rommel was winning all summer. I never thought we'd beat him."

"Yes, I just cut out the map of it," said Frances. "Now Rommel's cornered between the Americans and Monty, isn't he?"

"Let's hope it's the end of him," said Gran. She was worried that Frank or Fred might be fighting there. Thank God no telegrams had come to anyone in their big family up to now.

Grampy knew that and changed the topic. "I've a paper here for you, Frances," he said. "Just this last week we were mentioned in Parliament…."

"In the House of Lords," Gran interrupted.

"That's right. Some Archbishop asked if the they had information on how the islands are doing for food, and for coal and paraffin."

"And they didn't seem to know much," said Gran.

"Not much at all," Grampy repeated, pulling a paper out of the drawer. "They had—how did he put it?—scanty information. And then he said there was rationing like we have, or a bit worse, but it didn't…er…Here it is: *It didn't impair the general health of the inhabitants."*

"Gladys—my friend in Burnley—said everyone mentions gardening in their messages," said Frances. "I suppose everybody's growing vegetables like we are, but who knows if they have enough? I suppose they're all on rations."

"They must be importing food from France, surely," said Gran. "Your father used to buy apricots and lemons and all kinds of things in Granville and St. Malo."

"Oh, another thing," Grampy added. "They deported British residents to Germany, about eight hundred from both islands. Now, those people are receiving Red Cross food parcels there—in Germany! So, if it was really needed, the Red Cross should be able to deliver parcels to Guernsey as well, I would think."

Graham came in from school and Bill and Geoff from work, bringing onions. There was general chatter, tea was eaten and Frances washed up.

"Did you hear the church bells ring to celebrate Monty's victory at El Alamein, Frances?" Bill asked.

"Not locally, but I heard them on the wireless," she replied. "It was wonderful. I just needed some good news."

"Did you girls hear the bells on the wireless?" Gran asked the girls.

Janice nodded. "Yes, but not too loud because of Auntie Annie."

"If they can push those German armies out of North Africa and the Russians can keep Hitler busy, that's fine with me," said Grampy.

"Well, the Americans are in Morocco," said Geoff. "I wouldn't mind going there."

"Just be happy you're doing war work here. Morocco's a nasty, hot place to die in."

It rained hard all evening. Geoff stayed in and played ludo with Janice, and Lynette watched. It was nice to be in a house where people talked loudly if they wanted to, and they didn't have to tiptoe around all the time.

Annie was slowly, slowly mending. End of term celebrations at St. James School came and went, and Christmas 1942 was quiet.

24: Jan-April 1943: Losing Ma and Moving again

Reading the Burnley Express—Casablanca Talks—Tensions & sadness in Guernsey—Annie's insurance claim—Moving to the Fort Road

Reading the Burnley Express

Noise and bright light were still problems for Annie, and she asked Frances to read parts of *The Burnley Express* to her every day. The paper was now published only once a week because of a shortage of newsprint.

"Start with the *Deaths and Marriages*," Annie would say. "I want to know what's been happening to people." She would be lying flat on her back with her eyes closed, headaches never far away. She made comments about the people she knew.

Frances learned a lot about Loveclough and Burnley during these short sessions. An obituary might state that the deceased had worked in a certain mill or colliery, sometimes for a period of forty years. A young serviceman might have been a weaver or a coal loader before joining up, leaving school at twelve or fourteen years old. Joining the army must have been an exciting thing to do. At one point an elderly mill owner died, and the whole factory personnel lined up in tribute as the funeral procession went slowly by.

After a few obituaries, Frances read items about concerts, suppers, or sales events. They were organised by local chapels, churches, and the WVS to raise funds. They always featured a local singer and musicians. Annie knew many of the singers. The Riley girls seemed to be involved in various groups.

Annie was also interested in Frances' life before her marriage, when she was in charge of Collins' sweet shop in St. Peter Port. How did she keep track of the stock? How did she make decisions as to what to buy, and what quantity? How much profit could you make on each item? Frances explained her work as manager, bookkeeper, window-dresser and buyer, her trip to Paris, when she discovered delicious candied chestnuts or *marrons glacés*.

"Why did you go to Paris?" Annie asked.

"I wanted to see how how they decorated their shop windows—how they do window-dressing. I learned how to arrange the chocolates on trays and in boxes, with ribbons and flowers to decorate…I had a lot of ideas after that.

"Did you go by yourself?"

"No, there was a group of us girls. We looked at the dresses, the bridges, the people…It was wonderful."

"And did your fancy window dressing help you sell more?"

"It did, especially among the wealthier clientele. Even the Bailiff's wife used to like to come in the shop to choose her gifts personally."

"Hmmm."

It was obviously difficult to float above a mill worker's life in Clowbridge. However, Dora had somehow trained to be a milliner and dressmaker, and eventually had her own shop and married the manager of Landless Mill. She always looked elegant in her quiet way. Did she have more schooling or training than Annie had? Had Annie not had the same chances?

The village was mostly a close-knit workers' society, friendly and helpful, but lacked the stimulus and encouragement of Guernsey's community of growers, fishermen, farmers, and summer visitors. Frances was comfortable at Cotton Row now, with her small government allowance and a few hours of work, but she hoped she would be back in Guernsey next year.

In January, Tom continued to pass his national newspaper to them. Late in the month, the news that German armies had been defeated at Stalingrad was a major boost. They found another item which was kept secret from reporters for a while: a conference between Roosevelt and Churchill in Casablanca, to decide how the war would continue.

> **The Casablanca Talks**[44]
>
> Early in 1943, the three Allied leaders wanted to discuss their strategy for the rest of the war. Stalin was unable to attend because German forces were surrounding Leningrad and threatening Moscow, while near Stalingrad Russians were encircling the German armies. Elsewhere along the Russian front, German armies were bogged down. Stalin wanted the Allies to invade France to draw some of the

---

44   fdr.blogs.archives.gov/2017/01/10/the-casablanca-conference-unconditional-surrender/

German strength away from Russia. The Red Army was suffering tremendous casualties.

In 1942, the British had convinced the Americans to attack North Africa first. Having been successful there, with Monty's recent victory, they now wanted to invade Sicily, take control of the Mediterranean, and push up into Italy. If they could control Rome's airport, they would be able to send bombers to destroy enemy aircraft factories in east Germany. Some of the Americans wanted to focus on the war in the Pacific. There was also the question of the German U-boat attacks in the Atlantic, which were cutting off supplies to Britain and the Soviet Union.

Churchill and Roosevelt agreed to meet in Casablanca. This was kept secret because the city was within range of German bombers. It was too dangerous to attempt to cross the Atlantic by ship, so Roosevelt became the first US President to fly. From Florida he flew to Trinidad, and then to Brazil. From there he made the 2,100-mile crossing to Gambia, flying below 3,000 feet. It took nineteen hours. From Gambia he flew 1600 miles to Morocco and met with Churchill for ten days. The main results of their ten-day meeting were:

1. US and British forces would open up a new front by moving north from Africa, through Sicily to Italy.
2. They agreed to maintain a policy of "unconditional surrender" towards the Axis powers. There would be no separate negotiations between Britain and Germany or the USA and Germany. This was reassuring for Stalin. There was no great trust between him and his two allies.
3. They would later open up a new front in France and Germany; the USA would continue to supply Britain and Russia, and increase bombing in Germany.

Tensions and sadness in Guernsey

As the new year began, Emily worried more and more about Ma's general weakness and a worsening cough. Elsie, Charlie and Walter and their married partners had visited them over Christmas and the New Year. They tried to be cheerful with her, sharing her photo album: photos of Emily's wedding when the boys were all dressed up, Walter struggling to survive in his first suit, and Arthur with his hair parted severely down the middle and wearing a suit too big for him.

There was a photo of Arthur and Otto standing on their horses' backs in Oregon, and Arthur talked about logging and his very own horse. Charlie's favourite was of him and his wife Elsie, posing in front of their newly purchased greenhouse and smallholding, when they started their business of selling vegetables in the market. Elsie and her husband Edwin had a box camera, and he described how he had taken photos of Ma's recent July birthday beach parties, often with brother Herbie on leave from the navy, and of course all the grandchildren.

Charlie and his wife Elsie brought some precious apples to tempt her appetite. Walter and Nun called in, bringing her some real tea, and they all enjoyed a cup together. Elsie and Edwin Carter brought some black-market milk—the real creamy milk which they never saw any more—and it gave her a tiny boost. They exchanged news from Red Cross messages.

Besides Ma's condition, there was the worry about reprisals for the commando raid on Sark last October: people were receiving letters summoning them to a medical check at the Gaumont Cinema. They all knew where that led to—a second round of deportations. People selected for deportation included anyone with British birth or military connections who had been listed in 1941; and also freemasons, and petty criminals waiting to serve time in the island's prison. The medical was simply to ascertain if the person was fit for travel to Germany.

Emily feared for Arthur in case the Germans widened their target group to include members of the old militia. The others feared for her because she had been the wife of an Englishman. Who knew how they would satisfy Hitler's demand for an adequate number?

By February 10 they all felt relieved because neither Emily nor Arthur had been summoned, despite the rumours. They heard that Mr Sherwill had been selected because he had been in the British army, although he was a Guernsey-born islander. On February 12, 146 people lined up on the White Rock beside a cargo boat which would ship them to France.

At teatime next day, Pa passed on a few details: "Jim said the Red Cross ladies served them all a hot meal before they boarded, and the St. John's Ambulance people gave each one of them a box of food for the journey, the same as when they deported the others last year."

Emily was tucking a blanket around Ma, who would eat her soup in bed. "And did they make sure they all had warm clothes and shoes to wear?" she asked. "Last year, Ma and I were collecting warm jackets for the ones who were deported in October."

"They did. There was a big crowd to wish them well and a bit of singing to cheer them on."

Next day Emily's nursing friend came to visit and had a look at Ma. "Your Mum needs hospital care," she told Emily quietly. "She'll probably be given a little extra milk, as well as getting nursing care."

It seemed to be the best they could do for Ma. The ambulance people came with a horse-drawn vehicle and took her to the Emergency Hospital.

Next day Arthur and Pa went ormering, and Emily worked hard to tenderise the ormers and cook them long enough. She wanted to take a few mouthfuls to Ma in the hospital. The three of them should have felt very satisfied with their meal, but with Ma's chair empty the usual joy wasn't there. Next day they heard that a boy had been killed while ormering. In spite of warning notices, he went too far and stepped on a mine.

Ma had no appetite for ormers or anything. Emily cycled to visit her almost daily, and Pa managed to go or return with Arthur. Ma quietly left them on February 20, a dear mother gone forever.

At least we were with her, and she knew we loved her, Emily reflected, on the last day of February. She was re-reading the Death notice in front of her: "Emilie Louise le Page, dearly beloved wife of Eric Enevoldsen, of 'Edelweiss Lodge', Havelet, aged 79 years and 7 months. Deeply regretted."

She thought back to the funeral service. At 3 p.m. on February 24, 1943, Holy Trinity Church had been over half full with Ma's family and friends who were still on the island. Ma's dedication to this church was recognised, the Dean himself taking the service. Ma had brought all the Enevoldsen children to Sunday School, Pa insisting that they be involved in church activities as they grew up, keeping them off the streets. No drinking or foul language was ever tolerated in his house.

Emily sighed. Those who had evacuated, like Louise, wouldn't even know she had died until they received her Red Cross message, several months from now.

She thought about Pa's history. His own grandfather had been a Deacon in the Danish Church, and had studied religion, including Sanskrit, in the university town near them. His parents had wanted Pa and his brother Frederik to become ministers, but neither had desired it. They wanted to sail and travel, to fish and be mobile.

She glanced at the list of those who had sent wreaths. It was comforting to read. It included the *de Putron* family, from whom Pa had rented *Le Pré* for all of his married life. Then there was the Trinity Women's Fellowship, the group which both Ma and Emily belonged to. They were all at the service. All the Fish Market stallholders currently in the island had turned up, remembering Ma, who used to sell Pa's fish in the market, as soon as Emily and Elsie were big enough to supervise the younger children at home. Twenty-four wreaths attested to her life in the community.

Emily had secured her neighbours' copies of *The Press* so that she could cut out the *Deaths and Funeral* notices. She would save one for Otto and Nellie, who had rented one half of *Le Pré* from Pa as their young family grew. Their children, especially Sheila, would miss their grandmother very much. She would keep a copy for Daisy, who had often spent weekends with Ma at *Le Pré*. Ma had kept her busy making *spills* out of old newspapers, to help light the fire each morning. Another copy was for Louise, and there was one for herself. Arthur and her father already had theirs. She smiled as she re-read the list of donors of wreaths. At the end of it there was: *and an anonymous bunch of flowers*, and she wondered who the donor was.

Annie's insurance claim

By the end of March, Annie seemed to be more like her old self. The white scar across her forehead told the story, but once she gained her strength, she didn't need any sympathy to get on with her life. Frances was relieved.

Annie wanted to deal with the insurance company which offered compensation for the accident, and Frances was very willing to help with paperwork. There were discussions with Tom and Dora after the insurance company offered Annie £500, which was almost enough to buy two of the houses at Cotton Row.

"We think you need a lawyer's advice, Annie," Tom advised, and the lawyer recommended them to a King's Council. Annie's case was accepted, and her doctor agreed to be a medical witness. The hearing would take place in Manchester and Frances would also go to support her case.

"I'm going with Auntie Annie to Manchester," she told the girls one afternoon, "and we'll have to stay over two nights. We have to discuss her accident with the doctor and other people, so Auntie Hilda will be looking after you for two days."

To the girls, that wasn't scary at all, in fact, it might be quite pleasant. They both liked Hilda, who was a quieter and gentler version of Annie.

Annie was awarded a settlement of £1,500, and both she and Frances were more than satisfied. Annie now had a substantial nest egg, just what she needed to go into business. It was like a springboard to a new life. Time would tell if she used it wisely.

Moving to the Fort Road

In Guernsey, in April 1943, the German garrison was on the move. Following the Dieppe raid last summer and the commando raid on Sark in October, the Kommandant had been ordered to billet the garrison in larger groups and in more defensible locations. One obvious site was Fort George, which overlooked St. Peter Port from higher ground south of the town. The slope that *Le Pré* and *Edelweiss* were built on were close to the new tunnels and gun points on the north slope of the fort. It had been built around 1780 but had never been used in a major war.[45]

German soldiers sometimes walked up Havelet Road to reach the Fort's barracks or further ones at Jerbourg, south of Fermain. A couple of them had wandered up the path to *Le Pré* the year before, late one night, and had given them all a scare. The two noisy Germans had been drinking in the town and probably visiting the official German-run brothel. Arthur had re-directed them, mentioning the Kommandant a few times, and they had wandered further up the hill to Hauteville. Soon most of them found a shorter way up to the Fort.

Arthur knew a *somebody* who had seen the transformation of the old fort area. "They're building houses for officers, re-fitting the old barracks, and they're going to have a big mess hall for the troops and a hospital." Only the old cemetery was left intact. The football grounds south of the fort were

---

45 Le Huray, p 84.

used by the German troops during their time off. The Fort Road ran north-south along the western side of the fort area and wasn't far from Arthur's home territory at Fermain.

The German troops were not the only ones moving up to the Fort Road area. Emily was told that her family must now vacate Edelweiss and move to a small house on the Fort Road. Along its west side was a line of private houses, the larger ones now taken over by German officers. South of this, opposite the football fields, was a small house which had been vacant since 1940. Emily, Pa and Arthur were instructed to move into it.

Arthur wasn't too happy. "It'll be a longer bike ride for me to report to work at the harbour," he said, "and especially coming back up the hill on my bike after work." He was feeling the effects of almost three years of poor nutrition, like everyone. Emily had lost over twenty pounds, and Arthur and Pa had no fat on them at all. "I'll have to see if I can report for work somewhere else, maybe at St. Martin's. The Jerries have a parking area for lorries up there."

"It's probably worth asking. They know you're a good driver," his father advised.

"I hope there'll be a bit of a garden for the chickens; and we need to plant potatoes and vegetables as soon as we can," Emily said. "We'll have to be careful, though. We're a bit too near the Fort for comfort. Those soldiers will be all over the place looking for food."

"I think I might know the house," Arthur said, when he looked at the address. "If I'm right, it's quite small, on the corner of the Fort Road and one of the lanes that connects down to Havilland Road and the Damouette Lanes. It has some garden around it, if I remember right."

"Well, that makes it sound more hopeful."

"Emily, let's go up on our bikes through the lanes and have a look. We can avoid the Fort Road. We don't want the Jerries to know we're living there."

They made a reconnaissance of the area on their bikes through the lanes. Luckily, the small house was the one that Arthur had remembered, and it had a garden gate on the lane. They could get in easily with their bikes and they didn't need to use the front entrance from the Fort Road at all. The hedge across the front of the property had almost grown right across the front entrance, and they decided that the chickens could wander there in front as long as Pa was willing to keep an eye on them. A line of pine trees ran along the other side of the Fort Road and beyond that they could hear the Jerries playing football.

"We can let the chickens roam around the front of the house as well as the side," Arthur said. "We have a bit of chicken wire that I can set up to make sure they don't go out at the front."

Emily nodded. "And with the front hedge blocking the entrance, it'll help to keep us out of sight from the Jerries."

Arthur looked back at the entrance from the lane. "What I like, is that we can come in from the lane without the Jerries seeing us," he said, "and I can come up the lane with the lorry I drive and bring our beds. Walter said he'd help me bring them and the furniture we need."

In the garden behind the house, they found a flush toilet that still worked and a shed which had been partly used for a chicken house some years ago. They decided to plant potatoes, beans, parsnips and carrots right away.

"Do you think you can make a place for the chickens to be inside for the night?" Emily asked. "The Jerries are stealing so many of them now. Dorothy said her three chickens just walk in the door before dark and go to their boxes. Most of her neighbours are doing the same. One of them brings in their two pigs."

"I'll bring up our nesting boxes and put them inside." Arthur grinned. "We can call it the chicken hotel. Pa can be the doorman."

Emily smiled. "Pa will need things to do if he can't be watching the boats. He's going to miss looking over at the harbour. Being in charge of the chickens is as valuable as a steady job, though. I can get a pound of flour or half a pound of sugar on the black market[46] for just two eggs."

"Ok. Now we've a place for the chickens, let's go inside and see if there's room for us as well."

The house was small and hadn't been lived in since 1940. On one side of the front door, it was divided between a kitchen at the back and a living room with an open fireplace in the front. A gas fire had been sealed off, as had the hot water geyser near the kitchen. There was a small bedroom on the left of the front door and the side entrance behind it, where a big cupboard might help to create the chicken hotel. There were two small

---

46   Higgs, p.37.

bedrooms upstairs.

Before they moved in, Emily cycled up for two days and did her best to clean things up. Running water was fairly reliable. Soap didn't exist anymore except for an occasional ration of personal soap. You did what you could.

The second day she had a shock when gun practice literally made the earth shake. They were shooting towards Herm from Fort George, at the top of the Val des Terres Road. Edelweiss would be under the line of fire. There had been a warning about it in *The Press*, some people having had to move out of their houses while the practice lasted. She was thankful not to live in a real war zone.

Arthur managed to move their basic furniture on the lorry he drove, with the help of Walter, over two dinner times. They also took some of Pa's furniture to store with Charlie.

It all seems so temporary, Emily thought to herself, going from one place to another and waiting for the war to end. She was sad for her father: he had lost Ma, the house he had lived in for so long with his growing family, and his closeness to the harbour and friends he knew. With daily stories of robberies, he had now got into the habit of keeping a big stick under his bed and another near the door.

Pa would have preferred to stay near the harbour; and if Jim and his wife had invited him to live with them, it would have been tempting. But he, Emily and Arthur shared rations, and needed each other. Pa agreed that he would be keeper of the chickens, seriously on guard when Emily had to go to the market or the new bakery. She picked up their bread rations twice a week and liked to chat; but if Arthur had no work and was at home, Pa rode slowly along with her, and enjoyed getting out.

The bakery clients soon got to know them, and some knew Arthur already. The weekly ration for Emily and Pa was now 3 pounds 12 oz (1.7 kg) each, and 4 pounds 12 oz (2.16 kg) for Arthur. With a ration of only 5 pounds (2.27 kg) of potatoes a week each, a few vegetables, and half a pint of skimmed milk each per day, it simply wasn't enough unless private stores were available. Soon they would be working hard on their garden.

25: May–Sept 1943: Russian Victory; sending photos

*Annie finds a new job—Annice's peas—Spider crabs & Spitfires—
German Defeat at Kharkov—Photos in Bolton*

Annie finds a new job

By early May, Annie seemed to be back to her old self except for a few headaches. She had missed seeing Gran and Grampy and asked Frances to invite them one Sunday. She was first at the door when they arrived.

"Haven't I missed you both!" she exclaimed, and Grampy laughed at her energetic welcome.

Over tea they discussed all the good news of the spring: Hitler's huge losses at Stalingrad, and the Allies' gains versus Rommel in North Africa.

"I hope we've got the Germans on the run in North Africa now," said Gran. "I thought we'd finished with them when Monty beat them at El Alamein last year, but it's taken a long time."

"They're fighting from Morocco to Egypt in North Africa," said Grampy. "It's a vast area, and Rommel's a smart commander. Who knows if that's the end of him? It took the Americans a while to get used to fighting, but with their American equipment, we're better off. Now I'd like them to invade France and clear the way for us to go home!"

Annie really didn't want to think about them going back to Guernsey, not yet. "Come on and let's have a walk up to see the garden," she suggested. "Your Frances is doing the dinner today."

Gran exchanged the news with Frances, who was chopping a Bolton onion to add to the stew.

"I'd like to take the children to see Vi this summer," Frances said. "She can't come here with two young children. The bus trip's too long and the buses weren't running regularly last year. Now Lynette's five and Janice will be eight soon, we can manage much better than when we first arrived."

Janice pricked up her ears. "We're going to Auntie Vi's, Mum?" she asked. "Will we be able to play with the babies?"

"Well, David's nearly three. He'll be walking a bit," her mother replied. "Baby Margaret will be almost one. We'll try to go during your summer holidays."

"If you do, have you got a camera to take a photo?" Gran asked. "Bradford's too far away for your father and me to manage all the buses. I'd like to have a photo of them."

"Annie's got a camera. I'll take it with me. She'll probably finish the film later this summer, so I should have some prints to show you before the winter."

Grampy and Annie came back in, discussing war work.

"And what are you going to do now, Annie? Are you feeling all right to work again?" Gran asked.

"Well, they'll give me a war work job soon. But I'm looking around. I'd like to choose what I do."

"Back on the buses?"

"No. I want to be selling things, making money."

Within a couple of weeks she found what she wanted: a job in the Co-op grocery shop in Clowbridge. Situated next to the Landless Mill where she had previously worked, it was a busy place, and she knew the people. This was her opportunity to learn about the retail trade. A chip shop was almost next door, and apart from a pub further along and Sarellen's, this was the hub of the village. Once she started work there, she was in her element and soon became as popular as she had been on the buses.

Annice's peas

There was always one afternoon a week when the girls looked after themselves after school. Frances would arrive from her afternoon at the Rileys about five o'clock and Annie worked till five at the Co-op. Under Miss Taylor's management, the group of eight or ten children in her class were like a large family. The girls played with tops and whips and skipping ropes during recess; after school on a fine day, the more adventurous ones became the leaders. The boys did their own thing.

On one such afternoon in June, there were about seven girls at a loose end after school, including Janice and Lynette. Someone had an idea: "Let's go and look at the allotments."

They left the school playground, walked along the Burnley Road towards Cotton Row and came to the wide gate set in the wall. Everyone had to climb over it to get into the field. Lynette waited for someone to help her, but the others went ahead chattering loudly and didn't hear her call for help. She decided she had better climb the gate by herself. She didn't know how to straddle the top and fell. They turned when they heard her cry and hurried back.

"There's blood on her head."

"Shh. Don't scare her."

Janice was really concerned. She would get the blame for this.

"Are you all right?" She helped her sister up. Lynette's tears stopped, and off they all went again, but Janice held her sister's hand tightly.

The allotments belonged to the residents of three bungalows which had been built just south of Cotton Row next to Alice-Ann's house, and a fence erected around it. One of the girls knew that peas were ready to be picked and led the way through the gate. Someone yelled out: "Peas!"

Suddenly, they were all picking peas. Lynette had never shelled peas before, but quickly learned. Delicious! That was her first taste of peas straight from a pod picked in a garden, and she decided that it was a nice thing to do. Pea shells were strewn all over the path. After that, everyone wandered off and went home.

Later that afternoon, Frances returned home from the Rileys; then Annie came from work and it was teatime. Then, a knock on the door and conversation. It was bad news from Annice, who lived next door to the allotments and worked one of them. Yes, it was Annice's peas that everyone had raided.

Lynette wrote later:

We were questioned. Yes, we were in Annice's garden with the others. Yes, we ate peas. Yes, we had climbed the gate. Yes, I fell and hurt my head. At that point, Janice was told off.

Mum was pretty severe. She had tried hard to make us be polite and acceptable evacuees. We realised that we had done 'the wrong thing,' and the blackness of Mum's anger was upon us. It seemed that we were now marked for life.

After disinfecting my head, she marched us to Annice's front door, and we had to say we were sorry. It was like being caught up in a Great Terror. I hadn't even known that picking the peas was wrong, but now at the advanced age of five, I knew it very well.

A visit to Vi

It was summer and Frances and Annie added the picking and selling of strawberries to their usual day's work. Frances managed to make some jam with the sugar she had saved. There was better war news, with the Allies landing in Sicily.

The children had the usual summer picnics as the school term ended, and then arrangements were made to visit Vi. The weather was warm, and Frances had someone take a photo of them all when they had a picnic at Shipley, just outside Leeds. She and Vi shared the good parts of the war news as they wondered where Fred and Frank might be fighting.

Back in Cotton Row, Frances was surprised to receive a note from her mother saying that in Bolton, photos of evacuees would be taken free of charge and prints would be sent to Guernsey through the Red Cross, via POW camps in Germany. It was possible to send Arthur a photo of her and the children! She decided to go to Bolton soon.

Spider Crabs and Spitfires

In Guernsey, Pa was looking forward to a pile of spider crabs for tea in mid-June and he knew Emily had gone to the market for some; but Emily didn't bring any home that afternoon.

"What happened?" he asked, really disappointed.

"Well, there were two huge boxes of crabs. But they wanted to take our fish coupons for them. So, we all said, 'No, we'll wait for real fish.' How much fish is there in a spider crab, for heaven's sake? The Germans won't bother with them. We shouldn't have to give up coupons for it. All the women stuck together and didn't buy any."

"And?" Pa was really feeling let down.

"If nobody buys the crabs, they'll be wasted. The stall owner will ask the States to compensate him. I think they'll be forced to sell without taking our coupons. I'll go back tomorrow."

"Well, what's for tea then?"

"I've got bean soup and fresh peas to go in it, and I have some fresh cabbage to chop in. Also, we have 5 pounds of new potatoes each week, instead of 3 pounds of the old potatoes. I'll chop some in. "

"I suppose that'll have to do."

Next morning, Emily cycled back down to town. She had intended to take her bike and look for twigs, pinecones, or anything burnable for the fire. Their ration of coal and wood was insufficient, and they would need to build up their own supply for next winter.

She arrived at the market and waited with other women. A message came that there would be no need for the fish ration cards. Later that day, Pa's household enjoyed a lengthy tea, feasting off a large pile of crabs.

One Thursday in July, Arthur brought a snippet of good news when he sat down to dinner. "We were unloading some boxes of food this morning from the Jersey boat," he started, "and the Jersey fellow who talks to me said that several VP boats were attacked by Spitfires again. They brought sailors to the hospital, so they must have done some damage."

Emily stared at him. "Are VP boats the small ones that escort the German supply ships?"

"Yeah. It's another name for the E-boats, enemy boats. They have anti-aircraft guns on them and depth charges, so they can do a lot of damage."

"I think we see some of those smaller boats in the harbour quite often," said Emily.

"We do," said Pa. "I'm glad the RAF's going after them."

Arthur nodded. "The Jersey fellow also said they'd imported a complete train engine. They had it running on a short piece of railway line in St. Helier.[47] He said it's similar to the railway line like they've built here in Guernsey from the harbour to St. Sampsons."

"What on earth do we need a railway for?" asked Emily.

"It's not for people. It's to transport all that cement and wire and stuff," said Pa. "At least it keeps them busy. Better than fighting the Allies."

"Well, cheers to the Spitfires anyway," said Emily.

> ### German Defeat at Kursk and Kharkov, July and August 1943
> In 1943 Hitler tried to gain control of the eastern front against the Russians. He won Kharkov after three major battles over two years. There was one bulge of territory, or *salient*, which was still under Russian control around the city of Kursk. The salient became known as the Kursk

---

47 St. Helier is the capital and port of Jersey.

> Bulge.[48]
>
> Hitler delayed attacking this area until July, waiting for drier land conditions for his tanks. In the meantime, Russians laid thousands of mines and anti-tank traps in the region. They were also receiving information from British intelligence, who were decoding German commands.
>
> The Soviets won this battle and won back Kharkov, but at great cost. They lost about 800,000 men, four times the German losses. Over 6,000 tanks and two million men were involved.
>
> Germany never regained momentum on the Eastern Front.

Photos in Bolton

Early in August, Frances took the girls to Bolton. Gran had arranged for them to stay for three nights. That would give them time to have a photo taken and developed, and to take it to the Red Cross office to send to Arthur. As soon as they arrived, Gran asked about Violet and the two grandchildren she had never seen. Frances smiled and opened her handbag.

"Here they are, Mum. We finished Annie's film and had the prints made. This one's for you."

"David's big now," Janice said. "He's not a baby anymore."

"I suppose not," said Gran. She scrutinised the photo, asked questions, and was satisfied. "Now, we can have a cup of tea outside and you girls can play in the sun. Rose will be here soon."

That was much better than being in the kitchen; Janice led the way around the small garden, and then Gran found them a piece of chalk and when Rose arrived they played hopscotch on the pavement.

"Now, Mum, tell me about having our photo taken," said Frances. "Will we have a copy? And how will it be sent to Arthur? I'm not even sure what his address is anymore."

"I'll go with you in the morning to the photo place," Gran said. "They'll make a few copies of the photos for you as well as one for Arthur. The Red Cross has a list of the Guernsey men being held in the POW camp in

---

48   History.com/topics/world-war-ii/battle-of-kursk

Laufen. They'll address the photo to one of them, and that man will send it on to Guernsey. It seems there's a regular postal service between Laufen and the islands."

"I see, but I'm still not sure what Arthur's address should be."

"Well, why don't we send it to your sister, Elsie? We receive Red Cross messages from them, so we're sure they're still at their address. She'll pass it on to Arthur. Mabel said she could send one for you as well, addressed to Bob, and he can pass it on to Arthur. That would give you two chances of getting it to him."

"That's good of her. I suppose she's sent a photo of her and Pat to Bob?" Gran nodded.

"Arthur's missing so much of the children growing bigger," Frances said, "and Bob will find that Pat's grown a lot."

"Sending these photos makes me more hopeful about going home," said Gran. "The Allies must be going to land in France soon. Perhaps we can start preparing to return."

They heard Grampy talking to Janice and Rose in the street, and he came up the steps and joined them for a cup of tea outside. He raised his cup. "So we're chasing the Jerries out of Sicily now," he said. "I'll drink to that. I suppose they have to chase them back up into Italy now."

"At least it keeps them away from England," Gran remarked.

"I hope Stalin continues to keep Hitler busy," Grampy added. "It's very pleasant with no bombing here. Anyway, I wanted to ask you, Frances: have you been reading the Red Cross messages in the *Channel Islands Review*?"

"Yes, I read them all," she replied.

"Some of them worry me. There's the message saying that they'd been to the beach using the wagonette, meaning using a horse; because there's no petrol, I suppose."

"Yes," Gran added, "and someone had written to say they're collecting seaweed to make carageen or something, which I think is to make a *blanc mange* pudding. That makes it sound as though they're short of food. Surely, they can import food from France? It's nearer than England, after all."

"All the shipping routes there must be controlled by the Germans," said Grampy, "but it worries me when you read all these hints in the messages."

"I hope Arthur kept the chickens," said Frances. "We always had chickens at home. There's plenty of room for them at his father's house, as well as space to grow potatoes and vegetables."

"I wish we had space for a few chickens," said Gran. "Can you still get extra eggs?"

"It's been harder lately. I think they killed off some chickens because they couldn't get the chicken feed. I tried the dried egg powder we're getting as part of our rations, but I don't like it."

"Use the dried egg for baking," said Gran. "It's good for making a cake."

They moved indoors to get ready for tea and Frances looked at Grampy's maps on the kitchen wall. "At least we've got the Germans out of North Africa and almost out of Sicily," she said. "That should help the food situation."

Her father came over to the maps.

"It will if they can use the Suez Canal again," he said. "You know, if they hadn't saved Malta from the Germans last year, we would never be this far ahead. I think Arthur's brother, Herbie, was there. We'll have to get him to tell us about it sometime, if he can."

"Malta's our big naval base, isn't it?"

"Well, it was. The Germans cut off supplies to the island and must have bombed it to pieces. I heard that a lot of supply ships were lost around there; but they managed to build up enough aircraft and oil in Malta, so that they could throw the Germans out of Africa and Sicily."

"At least they haven't had bombing raids like that in Guernsey," Gran commented. "Thank goodness it's not an important place." She looked up at Frances. "I do worry about your sister Elsie though. I wish she and Art had evacuated."

"It was a hard choice to make," said Frances. "They're a family and decided not to evacuate, and they're growers. They should be all right, Mum. Lionel's heard from them, hasn't he?"

"Yes. Lionel was here for a quick visit about a month ago."

"He told us that the Americans and the navy are now better at locating U-boats," Grampy added. "My guess is that he's in the south Atlantic."

Frances sighed. "I hope it'll all end soon. It's three years we've been living here now. Three years!"

"Well, the last one was almost five years."

"But we were at home in Guernsey, Dad. It didn't bother us that much."

"Oh yes, it did. I was a grower, and I had a family to feed. We had—Elsie, how many children did we have when that war started? About five?"

"We had seven," said Gran. "And two more during the war—Violet and Frank. And food wasn't easy to get unless you grew enough to swap for what you were short of."

"I remember us being short of some things," said Frances. "But the Germans didn't get anywhere near Guernsey in the Great War, did they?"

"The trouble was, we couldn't do the trading we used to do," said Grampy. "I was about twenty-five when that war started. I used to travel on the boats that went to St. Malo and St. Brieuc and Carteret, and I'd come home with apricots and grapes and a bit of brandy and sell it all. During the war, we had to be careful. The boats were used somewhere else to ship soldiers around. So our boats had to sail at night, and not many of them either."

"And did a lot of men sign up for the army?"

"Guernsey had its own regiment, but a lot of them never came back, about a quarter of them."

"A lot of young women went to England to help do war work," said Gran. "I knew a few."

Frances smiled. "You know, I remember you making apricot jam after the war ended. It's Annie's favourite too."

"Well, don't expect to see any French apricots for a long time," said Grampy.

Everyone came in for tea as usual, and after the dishes were done, Rose disappeared to her room with the girls, and the boys all went out. Frances sat down and looked at a sock she was about to mend. "I need some more grey wool for this sock," she said. "It's more holes than sock now."

Gran looked at the sock. "Don't bother with that one anymore. It's had many lives. I'm knitting socks in all my spare time from wool from old jumpers. Stripey socks. And even old jumpers are hard to find."

"By the way, Annie wants you both to come over and see us while the weather's still nice. She's off work all day on Sundays. Let me know and I'll try to have some eggs for you."

"If you could get me just six eggs, then we could all have one for breakfast next day," said Gran. "And if you know anyone with potatoes to sell, buy about fifteen pounds for us. We can carry that back between us, your dad and me. When Bill and Geoff come in from work, they eat a lot."

"I suppose they've gone out to the pictures again tonight," said Grampy.

"Yes, they wanted to see *Edge of Darkness*. It's a war film. They're probably glad to get away from you," said Gran.

Next morning, they had their photos taken by the photographer, the girls wearing their summer dresses. The photographs were ready the following day. Frances sent one copy to Arthur care of her sister Elsie. The Red Cross addressed it to Mr Lambert in Laufen, Germany. A second one was addressed to Arthur care of Mabel's husband, Bob. It was addressed to a Mr Lane in Laufen. Frances hoped that the two prisoners of war would send them on to Guernsey as planned, and that Arthur would know they were thinking about him.

26: August–Dec 1943. Custard tarts for a Birthday

*A birthday song—Louise visits—Food strategies and G.U.N.S. news—
A sight problem—Christmases in 1943*

A birthday song

On the last Saturday afternoon in August, Frances took the girls for a walk around the reservoir while Annie worked in the garden. It was sunny and warm. In the shopping bag there was a ball, a doll, and a bag for Janice to collect things. Frances quietly added a paper bag on the top.

They noticed a bird, Janice found a flower or two, and they arrived at their usual sitting spot by a twisted tree.

"What's in the bag, Mum?" Janice asked.

"Custard tarts."

"Custard tarts! Why didn't we eat them at home?"

"I wanted to tell you about something before we ate them," said Frances, keeping the bag closed firmly. "It's Daddy's birthday today, and I want us all to remember that he's probably thinking of us, wishing we were all together. Perhaps for his next birthday we'll all be at home with him."

"I'll make him a birthday card when we get home. Can we send it to him yet?"

"Not yet, but soon. You can both make one and we'll put them up on the mantlepiece to look at, and I'll keep them to send."

Lynette just watched Frances' hands holding the bag shut. She couldn't join in this conversation about a person she didn't know; but she knew she should listen and be quiet.

"Well, can we sing 'Happy Birthday,' Mum?" Janice asked.

"Yes, that's a nice idea. He's a long way away, but perhaps he'll hear us just a tiny bit. Let's sing and then we can eat our tarts."

Lynette happily nodded at that and joined in, and suddenly it was serious, as though their notes might just carry southwards to their home island…. The tarts were as good as they always were, and Frances hadn't forgotten the spoons.

Annie hadn't been forgotten. Frances had explained the walk to her and had left her a tart at home. Annie knew, also, that a Red Cross message had arrived that week, saying that Arthur's mother had died sometime in February. For Frances, the custard tarts celebration was dedicated to the father she hoped Janice still held in her memory. She would mourn the passing of little Emilie le Page, her gentle mother-in-law, by herself.

Louise visits

Early in October, Frances received a letter from Louise, asking if she could stay with them for a few days, as she had two years ago. Frances was delighted. Again, it was like a precious gift for her birthday. Louise arrived for tea on Monday, October 11.

"Our school has a week's holiday every year at this time," Louise told the girls. "That means that teachers like me can visit their friends. Do you have a week off sometimes?"

They both looked blank, and Frances laughed. "I don't think they'd be happy if school closed for a week," she said.

"I did miss coming to see you last year," said Louise. "I went to see an aunt living in Norfolk, and we did some walks near the sea. I'm glad Annie's recovered. It didn't sound very hopeful a year ago."

"No, it wasn't hopeful; and it was sad because she enjoyed her job on the buses. She was good at dealing with people, even the ones who'd been drinking and catching the last bus home late at night. She was good at counting her tickets and her money; and we always got cheaper fares, and I miss that."

"They have inspectors checking them sometimes, don't they?"

"Yes, and they also have to know what to do if there's an air raid. She had to know the driver, and they both had to work together if a warning sounded."

"Did she work at the mill before?"

Frances nodded. "It didn't pay as much as the bus company."

"Did you hear Churchill's speech a couple of weeks ago—to a women's group—about how women's lives have changed because of the war?"

"No, what did he say?"

"He said that women had a lot more economic freedom. Working in the Land Army, or being a bus conductress like Annie, has allowed us to earn our own money. There's a big demand for equal pay by some women. I wonder if Annie was paid the same as a male conductor?"

"I don't know, but the mill workers don't get much," said Frances. "I think some of the men were glad to be able to join the army and do better, and I don't suppose the women are getting paid the same as the men were."

"Does Annie like working at the Co-op?"

"Yes, and she's learning a lot. I like her working there too. If they manage to get some oranges, we know we'll get our fair share now, and not be last in line."

"At least it seems that supplies are supposed to be coming in more steadily. Do you still work for Mrs Riley?"

"Yes. Things are much easier with Lynette at school in the afternoons, and she'll be going all day next spring. I'll look for a second half day of work after that."

They heard the bus stop outside.

"That's Annie arriving," Frances said, "and before she comes in, I must tell you: don't talk about singing. She lost the use of her singing voice somehow in the accident."

Louise looked shocked but was ready with a smile to greet Annie. She had brought some cheese and apples and a tin of sweetened, condensed milk, which was a rare treat. Frances made a huge rice pudding the next day, and they all celebrated her birthday a week early.

Food strategies and G.U.N.S. news

In mid-October Emily had been thinking about Louise as she made soup for tea. The school usually had a week's break right now, and perhaps she would be visiting Frances or Otto and Nellie. It would be so good to know exactly where they all were. Words like *sad* and *sympathy* had cropped up in the Red Cross messages she had received recently, as the news of Ma's death had reached everyone.

She felt she had got the right amount of sea water in the soup and added macaroni, carrots, swede, and some herbs. Tomorrow she and Arthur would go to collect some limpets and winkles from the shore to eat with their potatoes.

"If I had my boat, we'd be eating fish," said Pa. "We should be on the sea, you and me, Arthur. Everybody needs fish and we could be making some money."

Arthur looked at his father: "Pa, remember that group that escaped in their boat in August? Anyone with a permit to fish has to pay £20 now as security—just to leave the harbour, as well as having a Jerry on board. The Jerries still take a good portion of the catch as well."

"You can't even buy fish in the fish market," Emily said. "I can't get there early enough from up here on the Fort Road. It's already sold or hidden in boxes under the counter when I arrive. Last week, I asked Elsie and Charlie to buy me some fresh fish, since their stall is near the fish market, but the price had already increased again beyond what I told them I'd pay."

"Yep. It's all black market now."

There was silence, but Emily had an ace up her sleeve today: "Wouldn't it be nice to have a good dessert today?"

Pa looked at her and tried not to smile. He knew what was coming. Arthur looked at her but said nothing.

She smiled. "I had a spare egg, so I made a parsnip and carrot pudding. I've still got some parsnips from the pile we bought in June when they were cheap. The baker in town grinds parsnips and carrots now."

She brought it all to the table with a flourish. A small amount of blackberry jam was spread on top. Sugar for the jam had been exchanged for four eggs last month. They ate slowly.

"I hear they're making coffee from all those acorns that people picked up after the gale last month," Arthur said. "Are they going to be selling some soon?"

"Yes, I'll try to get some," Emily said. "That storm brought down the acorns too fast last month. If we hadn't moved this year, I would have been able to gather them again, but I'm too far away now. I heard that they may be giving away some excess carrots and swedes though, so I'll pick up what I can."

Pa nodded and changed the subject. "Any news going around, Arthur?"

"Oh yes, I was forgetting. All clear?"

"Wait," said Emily. She went to the door, did a quick check of the scenery outside, and then firmly closed it. "It's ok."

Arthur produced a small piece of paper from his shoe and Emily took it and read it quietly near her father. It was the BBC news summary from GUNS.

Corsica has been liberated by the Free French. Most Danish Jews have managed to escape to Sweden before the Nazis planned to take them to concentration camps in Germany. In Italy, Naples has freed itself from German rule and the Allies are moving north and have crossed the first German defence line, the Valturno Line…[49]

"Good luck to the Americans," said Pa. "It's taken them quite a while to push into Naples. The Jerries must have been well prepared. I hope Monty's pushing north with them now. He's come a long way."

"I thought the Italians were on our side now," replied Emily. "I don't know why it's taking so long."

"They are. They capitulated in September. But the Jerries are still in Italy. They won't give in."

"I'm glad we didn't have many Jews on the island. Why on earth do they have to be sent away? I was told there were only three women, quiet residents, and they'll be put in prison somewhere."

"I think they had to list them like they had to list the people born in England."

"I hope they've just sent them to a camp like the deportees." Emily folded the sheet of paper and bent down and fiddled with her shoe. "I'm off down the lane before it's dark," she said. She took a small medicine bottle on her way out. If anyone stopped her, she was taking an herbal remedy to Mrs Ogier down the lane.

"Be careful, Em," said Arthur. "They say there's an informer around here somewhere, maybe somebody on our lane. We don't want trouble."

Emily looked at him gravely and left.

Pa turned to Arthur. "Did you hear anything from the Jerries about bombing in Germany?"

"There were a few talking while I was unloading. One said he hoped the war's going to end soon. He'd been on leave and buried someone in his family. I think his town was Munster. He was talking about Hamburg, and he said the city caught fire after it was bombed and people couldn't breathe, and thousands died. It did sound bad. I think the RAF and American planes are bombing Germany a lot."

"You're understanding a lot of the language now."

"Well, I hear enough of it."

---

49   https: www.bbc.com/news/magazine-24427637

By the time Emily returned, Pa had made bramble tea. They sipped it by the fire in the darkness. Emily had a favour to ask. Her shoes were wearing out fast.

"Art, I'm trying to wear Ma's shoes, but they're too small. Do you think you could cut the front so that my toes can stick out?"

He promised to do something next morning. He wanted to try and make new soles for his own working shoes out of a rubber tyre. Shoes were being repaired in town, but leather was mostly unobtainable, and the cardboard they used didn't last long.

A sight problem

In St. James School, the girls passed their medical checkup in November. Lynette's only problem was with reading. Annie sat with her on several evenings, trying to help. Lynette described it later:

Annie was very patient. She sat with me and tried to explain those thin, black squiggles on the white paper. They meant nothing to me and I wondered if there was a meaning to the white shapes which flowed between the groups of black squiggles. It was only after Annie pointed out each shape and repeated the sound of it, that I began to understand the pattern of the black symbols. Perhaps it had been explained on the blackboard at school, but I hadn't been able to see it.

Later, once we had started to read, Miss Taylor made reading into a little competition between Beryl and I. Reading a page within my natural close-up visual range, or with glasses later, I progressed as quickly as Beryl. The word that still bothers me is "once." It was always at the beginning of a story, and should surely start with a W.

It was during a visit to Bolton that Frances first became aware of her daughter's sight problem. They were waiting for a tram to take them back to Gran's house one morning.

"We need the P or the O tram," Frances said. "Look for the letter on the front of the tram."

Lynette knew her alphabet and the letters on the front of the trams were large and easy to see, but several trams passed and she said she couldn't see the letters although she was looking straight at them. She would soon have her eyes tested and would start to wear glasses.

Paper was hard to get, and books hard to find. Frances found a tiny book in Burnley one day, one of a series about Mary Mouse, by Enid Blyton. It was published in a small 8 x 2-inch format. It was mostly pictures with two lines of story underneath and a whole series was published. Janice enjoyed them, and by 1945 Lynette could also read them. They became part of their wartime treasures and went back to Guernsey when the war was over.

Christmases in 1943

Early in December, there were a few snowflakes in the air around Cotton Row, and Frances was thoughtful as she looked out of the window above the ironing board. She hoped that by this time next year she would be back in Guernsey, enjoying her green valley and listening to blackbirds instead of watching the silent, cold moorland.

She had bumped into Gladys in Burnley the previous afternoon, and they had a quick chat.

"At our house, we all listen to the BBC and enjoy the news, now that it's getting better," Gladys said, "and we hope we'll be back home next year. I'd like to have June back in school in Guernsey by next September."

"I wonder how the children on the island will feel when they hear how our girls talk," Frances replied. "They'll sound like Lancashire children, won't they?"

"They will, and I wonder how our husbands will cope—with us, and the children. The girls are so much older now. June won't know her father and he may not understand what she says."

As Frances ironed, she asked herself, would Arthur recognise the girls? At least he might have had the photos sent from Bolton. But if the war had changed him, would he look the same?

The snowflakes reminded her of Christmas. The girls' memories of it would be the Christmas concert at St. James' school, Christmas stockings opened with her and Annie watching, and playing in the snow. They would talk about the changes that had happened here: Hilda was now married, living up at Lower Nutshaw Farm near The Dell; the May Queen dance, and the trips to the seaside. Dinah was no longer with them after an accident on the road, which had broken Annie's heart.

It would probably be their last Christmas here, and she and Annie would make it as good as they could. They both had a little more cash in their pockets. As usual, the girls had made paper chains to hang around the living room. Cards from Joyce, Vi, Nellie, and Mabel and Pat joined the more local ones. Bing Crosby was singing "I'm dreaming of a White Christmas" almost daily on the radio; they had one Christmas pudding and a small cake already made.

Christmas Day was a quiet success, and the girls found that Father Christmas had not forgotten them. Janice wrote later: *I had some cookery books and tins and a little rolling pin. I was thrilled with them.*

There was a piece of good news for the New Year: the huge German battleship *Scharnhorst* had at last been sunk by the Royal Navy. Its guns had destroyed a lot of Allied ships. Annie's brother Tom was especially glad to hear about that.

In Guernsey, Arthur had a pleasant surprise before Christmas: one of the photos taken in Bolton arrived via Bob Masterman, Mabel's husband. He soon received the second from Elsie Frampton, Frances' sister.

The photos had been cut so that they looked like three individual passport photos. The back of the photos were stamped "*I lag VII Laufen OBB, Germany,*" with the name of the senders, C. Lambert and A.W. Lane.

Someone explained the words: "Lager" meant a camp. "I lag" was the shortened form for "internment camp." Now he knew that two Guernsey residents from Laufen Internment camp in Defence Area 7, had forwarded the photos to him. He wished he could thank them.

27: Jan–April 1944: Allies make progress

*Charybdis tragedy—Bombing Berlin & The Gustav Line—House Rules—
Keeping warm in Guernsey—Soviets move west—Birthday gifts*

Charybdis tragedy

Not much snow fell at Cotton Row during January and February 1944, but it rained frequently and there was little sunshine. Everyone was sick at some point and both girls spent time in bed. Lynette's eyes hurt a lot when the light was switched on, and Annie covered the light bulb with thick pink blotting paper[50] to dim it. When she was well enough to sit up, Frances brought out the Christmas crèche animals and Janice showed her sister how to make a farm in the valleys and hills provided by the eiderdown. That kept her busy for hours.

Later in January, Annie came back from work with a newspaper tucked under her arm. "Frances, I have something for you." She waved the newspaper in the air. "Mary brought this in to the Co-op just before we closed. Tom said it's got something about Guernsey in it."

Frances took the paper and Annie pointed to a small photo near the bottom of the front page.

"Guernsey Honours Fallen Sailors," Frances read out loud. "A British destroyer, the *Charybdis*, was torpedoed near the island last October and some bodies washed ashore. A photo shows a tightly packed crowd of people passing by wreathed caskets last November.[51] November!"

"Somebody must have been there and taken that photo," said Annie, "and then smuggled it to England."

Frances peered at the photo. "I don't see anyone I know, but there was a good crowd there. Perhaps the photo was smuggled out through France."

"It's not what you'd call welcome news," said Annie, "but Tom thought you might want to see it. There's a lot of faces in that photo."

"Yes. That was thoughtful of Tom." Frances peered at the photo again.

---

50   Thick and absorbent paper firmly pressed over words written in ink.
51   Toms, C. p.91.

"At least they were allowed to pay their respects."

The newspaper had other bits of news in it: Hitler had bombed London with three kinds of bombs in order to damage as much as he could, perhaps in revenge for the heavy bombing of Berlin. There was continued fighting on the Russian front; the recent Allied landings at Anzio seemed to be stuck where they were; and please plant more vegetables this year. Nothing new there.

> **Bombing Berlin, and tackling the Gustav Line**
>
> At the start of the war, British bombers were only able to reach Berlin on summer nights in clear weather. The city is 1,000 km from London, and the science of night navigation and precision bombing was in its infancy. In August 1940 Hitler was shocked when he was giving a speech and the RAF managed to drop bombs around Berlin at the same time. The psychological damage was great but there was little material damage.
>
> In January 1943 the Allies carried out at least three heavy bombing raids on Berlin as part of the Battle of Berlin, which started in November 1942 and continued till March 1943. Areas of cities could be destroyed rather than precise targets because of the curvature of the earth and other problems not yet resolved. Damage was similar to the Blitz of London.
>
> In Italy the Allies pushed north towards Rome. A major line of German defence was called the **Gustav Line**. The long battle at **Monte Cassino** started there around January 17. In order to get around the end of the Gustav Line, 40,000 Allied troops were landed on a beach at **Anzio** on January 21.
>
> There was little space to seek protective cover on the beach, and a destroyer and a cruiser, which gave the troops fire cover, were both sunk, as was a well-marked Red Cross ship. Over 65,000 Allied troops lost their lives.[52]

---

52   https://www.britannica.com/event/Battle-of-Anzio

> By the end of the month, with reinforcements, they broke through the Gustav Line, but it took till June to capture Rome.

House Rules

One day when the weather was miserable, Annie decided to give the girls a little treat. She loved those two, and they wouldn't be with her once the war was over. Certainly, Frances was the boss where the girls were concerned. One day, though, the girls learned that Annie could also do 'The Wrong Thing.' This is Lynette's account of what happened that evening:

After tea one day when Mum was in the kitchen, Auntie Annie leaned over the table and said to me and Janice: "You know what happened today? I was selling a lady her ration of sweets[53] and when I tipped up the jar to let the sweets fall into the weighing scale, two of them fell out of the jar and straight down into my pocket."

She was still wearing her white apron with its large pocket across the front. We could see the ends of the wrapped sweets sticking out of it.

"So…" Annie continued, "I said to myself, that will be a nice treat for Janice and Lynette—"

"Annie!" Mum interrupted—she'd been listening. "Just a minute. Are these sweets part of our rations? And did you pay for them?"

Annie was taken aback. "Of course, I paid for them, but—"

"Are they part of our rations? Did you take the coupons?"

"Nay, they'll not be noticed…"

"You must put them back. If the children tell their friends that they had a sweet last night because it accidentally dropped in your pocket at the Co-op, what do you think people will say—about us, and about you?"

"Well, I never thought about it like that. "

"Well, you must."

Annie patted her pocket. "They'll be back in the jar tomorrow morning. I'm always there early."

Mum looked at Janice and me. "And you keep quiet about this."

"Yes, Mum," said Janice.

Mum spoke slowly and clearly: "You never say a word about it to anyone, do

---

53   Candy, toffees.

you hear, both of you?"

She was looking right at me. I nodded silently and managed to squeeze out a feeble "Yes." I just hated it when 'The Wrong Thing' hovered in the air around me; and it looked as though we weren't going to get a sweet after all.

We never spoke about it again. I never dared ask anyone for a sweet, in case that was 'The Wrong Thing' too; but if someone offered one, I always accepted.

There were other rules: the children learned to eat what was put in front of them. You finished what was on your plate, and food was never thrown away—leftovers were eaten the next day. It was also a mistake to think that you could skip the main course to get to the dessert. However, Annie allowed a little leeway to the rules if she and Lynette were by themselves. If Frances found out, she tried to correct things as best she could. Another story from Lynette:

One day, Janice had already eaten and had gone back to school. I had the afternoon at home. Mum had put both our desserts on the table. I stopped eating, eyeing the dessert on the table. I reasoned to myself that if I didn't eat all of the first part of the meal, I'd be able to eat all of the pudding. I knew this was risky, so I just sat quietly and waited for Mum to remove the first part, as Annie might have done. In the end, she took away both the first and the second parts. I wailed as I learned my lesson.

Keeping warm in Guernsey

In Guernsey that winter, it seemed harder than usual to keep warm. Around mid-February, Pa had a nasty cold, and Arthur and Emily squeezed all three beds into the living room to try to keep their body warmth together. It was almost a year ago that they had lost Ma.

Arthur came home just before dark one Saturday after collecting firewood. Pa seemed to be asleep. Emily had lit the fire and sat on the edge of her bed with her knitting. Arthur spoke quietly. "I picked up an armful of branches, and I've put it all in the shed for now. It'll need to dry a bit. I have another lot hidden that I'll bring tomorrow. I see the chickens are in already."

"Yes, I brought them in," Emily replied. "Nobody saw you getting the wood?"

Arthur shook his head. "It's too cold for people to be outside watching. I picked up this lot just inside the limit of the Fort at the south end. It's all overgrown there and people don't go in."

"Mrs Ogier called in, and she said an Allied plane came down somewhere and some Canadians were taken prisoner last week."

"I overheard the Jerries saying something about Canadians, so maybe something did happen. How's Pa been this afternoon?"

"I've kept him under the blankets, and he slept quite a bit. He had some soup about two o'clock and sounded a bit better. It may be just a bad cold. But there's scarlet fever going around. Mrs Ogier gave me some beetroots for one egg, and I've made a beetroot and carrot pudding for tea."

"That sounds good. Any other news?"

"Well, at the bakery they said the Russians are pushing towards Warsaw and a river somewhere. Vist, or something."

Pa had his eyes open and was listening. "Vistula?"

"That's it, that's the name," said Emily, and put down her knitting. "You've got good ears, Pa."

"My father was in Warsaw, just once," said Pa, as he sat up, and took time to cough. "He brought me back a picture of a bridge over the river—the Vistula—and a sailing boat on it. I kept it for a long time. Well, the Russians don't have far to go. It's fairly flat all the way to Berlin."

Soviets move west

During January, the Soviet armies moved steadily west into Poland. There was fighting, looting and rape by soldiers or their thousands of prisoner-followers. One Soviet army headed to Leningrad to break the twenty-eight-month siege by Hitler's armies. Over a million people had died there, mostly from starvation. The siege was broken near the end of the month.

Other Soviet armies moved into Lithuania and the Baltic nations.

The Polish government in exile in England was distraught, knowing that once the Russians arrived in Poland, Stalin would try to claim their country. They issued a Declaration of their authenticity. Stalin ridiculed this and the Polish government turned to Churchill and Roosevelt for support.

"I miss the GUNS newsletter," Emily said. "Do you know what happened to those men who printed it, Art? I was told they even managed to send it to people in Sark."

"The man who took it to Sark was beaten and put in prison," said Arthur, "and the others—four or five of them—were sent to Germany. Someone informed on them, someone they thought they could trust."

"I heard that there's another newsletter that very few people know about. I think you have to be in town to access it though."

Arthur made no comment. "Somebody will be listening to the news somewhere," Pa said. "So we'll hear about it. I hear that a few of the Jerries even leave their radios accessible to the Guernsey people they're billeted with."

Emily knew that one of her brothers used an illegal way of listening to the news, but she wasn't going to mention it. They were quiet for a while.

She broke the silence. "There's another thing I heard at the shop," she said. "Some people are able to make a cake or some fancy buns every so often to entertain each other, and I ask myself, where is the extra flour and sugar and butter coming from? You can't do that on our rations."

"Some people will always have things that we can't get," said Pa. "It's like you trading eggs for sugar, Emily. If you had a farm with a lot of eggs, you'd have more of everything, even with spies and regulations on everything we produce."

"I also heard that some deportees in Laufen have sent tea and chocolate to their relatives here, from their Red Cross parcels, and last week a few deportees were sent back here from Laufen and they brought their Red Cross parcels with them. One had a tin of cheese!"

Arthur looked at her. "A tin of cheese!" They hadn't seen cheese for a while.

"The Laufen men said that the parcels were the only food they had though, except for a little bread. By the way, I'm cooking macaroni for our tea. We had half a pound each this week, so I'll make two meals out of it. I've got an onion, a bit of thyme and butter, and two eggs to mix in."

Arthur was going to say, *We should have one of those tins of cheese to go with it*, but there didn't seem to be any point. "That sounds good," he said instead.

"There were more RAF planes flying over these last few days," said Pa, "and I'm wondering if it's part of the Allies' invasion planning. Perhaps they're flying over to see if there's any new fortifications."

Arthur put a few more sticks on the fire. "The RAF must know about our fortifications like the Mirus Battery. It's well camouflaged, but they fly over often enough to have seen them building it. I bet they noticed a couple of greenhouses slumped down after the Jerries practiced using it."

"I'm glad it's the other side of the island," Emily said. "When they have gun practices you can feel the earth shake here, even with just the regular anti-aircraft guns."

Pa stood up and moved to the fire. "They'll need to know the tides if there's an invasion," he declared. "In Normandy it's like here in Guernsey: thirty-foot tides or more, twice a day. Of course they learned a lot at Dieppe. They'll want some moonlight to help them though. Once it's warmer, we must watch for when the full moon comes round. Things may start to happen."

"Speaking of the full moon, there'll be an ormering tide soon, Pa," Arthur noted, "at the beginning of March."

"In that case, if we get some, I'll call that my birthday celebration for this year."

Birthday gift

Frances wanted to find something special for the girls' birthdays this year. Books and paper were unavailable, but Annie found some paper—Co-op wrapping paper. Frances decided to make a drawing book for Lynette. If it was successful, she would make one for Janice also. She cut fourteen pages, each 11 x 9 inches. How to cover it? Annie somehow got hold of a pre-war sample book of elegant wallpaper. Frances chose a page which had a pattern of blue, gold and orange shapes embossed on its surface. She used knitting needles to bore two holes through the pages and threaded yellow tape through. The spine was neatly sealed off with nine inches of her best first aid tape.

Lynette was delighted, but almost scared to use up a whole page for a picture. After thinking about it for a few days, she drew a picture of the moors behind the house. Two triangular shaped girls hold the ends of a long, curved skipping rope and a third jumps in the middle, with a smile. She labelled it "Skiping." Drawing in school was always on slate tablets, which were wiped off at the end of the day. Having something that didn't get wiped away was really special. Frances showed her the correct spelling, and it was re-titled enthusiastically.

Another drawing was made to celebrate Janice's birthday in May, and the next three pages were recklessly used to draw Annie spring cleaning in October. After that, she decided not to use any more precious pages until her next birthday in 1945.

28: April–June 5, 1944: Invasion jitters

*A hotpot in Bolton—Lionel brings bananas—A birthday—Railings disappear—
Arthur takes Pa for an outing*

A hotpot in Bolton

At the end of April, with the weather warming a little, Frances prepared to visit Gran and Grampy. She loaded a shopping bag with eggs and rations, and they caught the noon Express from Burnley. Gran was pleased to see them and noted that the girls had grown some more and all looked healthy. Frances passed one bag to her.

"Goodness, that was a lot to carry." She turned to the girls. "It's a good thing that you two are getting bigger and can help your mum. Now, I'm making a hotpot for supper. Do you know what that is?"

They nodded.

"I've sliced the potatoes to go on top. You two can wash your hands and place them all around the pot, after I've sliced your parsnips and put them in."

The girls nodded again, feeling honoured to be allowed to do something.

"You know, Frances," Gran continued, "I've put in almost half of our ration of meat for this week, but it isn't much when you look at it."

"We've had our meat ration this week, Mum. Just give us the potatoes and vegetables on our plates and I'll put some of my grated cheese on top for the girls and me."

"That'll help a bit. With three men working, it's hard to feed them. By the way, you girls," she continued, watching their faces, "I'll be making a custard tart as usual tomorrow, so you'll be able to have a piece before you leave on Sunday."

They were full of smiles, and Janice managed, "Oh, good."

Gran turned to Frances. "Do you get a few extras now, seeing that Annie's working at the Co-op?"

"Extra food? No, they just have enough to give everybody their share. There's nothing extra."

"And are you still doing your housework job?"

"Yes. Apart from the money, it does me good to get away from Cotton Row. I always have a cup of tea with the Riley girls when I've finished and we talk about all kinds of things. They've travelled a bit and they're also vegetarian. Now that Lynette's five, she can go to school all day, and she likes that. So I've found a second job, cleaning for a lady near the village, a Mrs Fletcher."

"Good. You could do with some extra money. At least you only have two children to look after."

Frances thought over that remark. Her mother had born twelve children and had lost one. She had always had her husband living with her and had never had to evacuate; but life had been hard and Grampy had joined his pals for a drink on Saturday nights, and there had been some misery because of that. Yes, Frances realised, she was fortunate with only two to cope with, and they were both in school.

Grampy appeared early, and settled at the table with a large pot of tea.

"Have you planted your garden?" he asked Frances.

"Yes, there's been articles in the newspaper for a couple of months, pushing us to prepare. We've planted dwarf French and haricot beans, cabbage, carrots, those little white turnips that you suggested last year, and potatoes of course."

"We're all done too; and we've been trying not to use heating at work at all. There's a real shortage, and they need the energy for the munition factories. We had someone from Huddersfield looking at the gardens and he said they'd stopped heating all public buildings a while ago; and they're sitting on a coalfield!"

"So, what's the war news at work today?" Gran asked.

"Just the same as on the wireless: we aren't getting anywhere from the Anzio landings. They're still stuck on that coast. They should have been in Rome by now. And now we're fighting in Burma as well. We're all over the place as usual."

Frances had already checked his maps on the wall. "I was looking at your map of Anzio and Rome."

"I'm just glad that Bill and Geoff were too young to join up. I wouldn't like them to be stuck there with German bullets flying at them. At least they're doing a good job here producing food, and it's war work, as they say. I wish they'd start invading France and get on with it. If Stalin gets to Berlin first, he's going to gobble up half of Europe before the Allies get there."

"What I don't understand," replied Frances, "is why food's still difficult to get this year. They seem to be sinking a U-boat every day. Yet we're told to grow more vegetables all the time."

"I heard at work," said Grampy, "that we have so many American and Canadian soldiers in England now, that it's harder to feed everybody. They say even beer's in short supply in London. But that's good, because they must be here for the invasion. Once they've gone into France, there'll be more meat to go around."

"They'll still have to take food with them," replied Gran. "By the way, Frances, if you have dried eggs, try making what they call 'cottage cutlets.' You mash potatoes, mix in the dried egg powder, add some fried onion or dried onion, a bit of parsley, make cutlet shapes with it, and fry them. it went down quite well here the other day. "

"I'll try that. At least it sounds tasty."

"I've started to look for suitcases to take our stuff home. I've found one. I'll show you later."

"Oh, I never thought of that," said Frances. She was mending socks by now.

Lionel brings bananas

About a month later, Frances received a note from Gran saying that they would come over with Lionel the next Sunday. Half a chicken was obtained from Kit for dinner and there was a big welcome. Lynette was getting over a cold and watched from the bottom of the stairs.

Lynette wrote later: *After some chatter Lionel came over to Janice and I. He had two bananas in his hand. He had travelled by train from somewhere, and said he had brought a huge bunch of bananas, which he handed out to various children along the way. I didn't know what they were until they told me, but Janice knew. There was some talk about giving me one. I took the banana when it was offered, but was suspicious because everyone was looking at me.*

"Well, eat it," said someone. I felt obliged to put my mouth and teeth on it, but the outside skin didn't feel good, and I frowned and stopped. That caused laughter and I didn't like being made fun of. I burst into tears and ran upstairs.

It would be years before I found a banana to be a desirable fruit.

The Tip

After school one sunny afternoon in May, while Frances was at Mrs Fletcher's, the girls returned from school and decided to walk up to The Dell, which was a natural pond further up Wiles Lane. They had caught tadpoles there each spring with Annie, and there were marsh marigolds growing around it.

After a while, they wandered further up the tiny valley and found a pile of interesting things that had been thrown out. They weren't aware that this was the bottom of The Tip, where once a week a lorry would tip off its load of waste from the dustbins in the area. The tipping off point was way above them, and a slope of debris had accumulated. It was interesting to poke around and see what little treasures had accumulated around the bottom. Lynette discovered a jar of potted meat paste, inserted a finger and decided it tasted good.

"You shouldn't do that," Janice warned, and made her put it down.

Soon after that they heard Frances calling them: "What are you doing up here?"

"We were just looking around…"

Suddenly they knew that she was upset. They had done 'The Wrong Thing' yet again. Luckily, Frances was more concerned with their health and safety. Her own reputation was at stake if her children were hurt while she was out working. The girls were bathed and disinfected according to First Aid manuals, and luckily Lynette wasn't sick and they didn't have to confess about the meat paste. Annie came home later and found the girls very quiet, and already in their pyjamas. She asked only one or two questions and made no comment, although the girls knew she was feeling sympathetic towards them.

A birthday & railings disappear

At the end of May, Frances managed to make a small cake for Janice's birthday, and re-used some candles. An extra treat was a red jelly, fruity and sweet. There were no dolls to buy, but Frances had found a paper doll cut-out book. The doll was made of card stock and the dresses were printed on sturdy paper, with little tags to fold over the doll's silhouette. Lynette had to be quiet and patient while Janice took her time cutting out the dresses, and then she was allowed to play with one.

Early one morning there was noise outside. Men were sawing off the iron railings that surrounded the front garden, dumping them in a lorry. Nobody was telling them not to, as the girls thought they should. The railings were fun: you held them to climb up and walk along the wall. They had nice patterns and you could walk small toys around them and poke things between them. It was part of the children's territory. In less than an hour, the whole row of houses looked forlorn and pillaged.

The wireless was switched on frequently, and the adults seemed to be waiting for something. People were advised not to use trains but to let them be used for war work; and to keep their use of coal or gas to a minimum in order to let this energy boost production of war materials.

The children became used to funny programmes like ITMA (It's That Man Again). Annie loved the Lancashire singer, Gracie Fields. There was a strange four-chord sound, like the beginning of Beethoven's fifth, a dark mystery. Perhaps it signalled a message to someone behind enemy lines. There was Bing Crosby and Sinatra and when they sang, Frances turned up the volume.

Arthur takes Pa for an outing

In May, the Jerries were getting very jumpy. It seemed strange that if an RAF or American plane flew over the island, there was no anti-aircraft fire, and people wondered if they were saving their ammunition for the expected invasion.

On Saturday, May 27, Arthur worked for a few hours, and had to leave his lorry in town. He had an idea: his route would allow him to pick up Pa on the way back to town. Arthur could drop him off near *Le Pré*, and Pa could look around and enjoy the walk down into town and meet Arthur. They could return home on the five o'clock bus that was mostly for Jerry use. Emily was delighted to see her father bristle with interest after his boring days looking after the chickens, and she promised to be watchman instead.

Pa was duly picked up and dropped off, and met Arthur midafternoon in town. They sat on a bench and Pa was full of comments about what he had seen. He would have liked to see the German U-boat in the harbour, but he couldn't get near enough. They waited on a bench to catch the bus home and hoped that it was still running. If not, they would walk. Pa was happy to wait and sniff the harbour breeze.

All of a sudden they heard planes, and soon there were at least a dozen circling around, just south of the town; perhaps twenty of them.

"They're over the Fort," Arthur said, and they heard the anti-aircraft guns loud and clear. One after another, a plane would swoop down and they felt the vibrations of a bomb exploding; the noise of the anti-aircraft guns didn't stop. The roar of the planes, and the guns, the thumps, the explosions and the smoke all came at them.

Pa stated what they were both thinking: "Emily's up there in the house."

The raid stopped.

They both worried about Emily, silently. The bus was their quickest way home. They saw more Jerry vehicles, including several with red crosses on them, heading past them for the Val des Terres, which was the quickest route up to the Fort.

The bus came early. Jerries took up most of the seats, bound for the Fort or their lookout point in Jerbourg, south of Fermain. Pa was allowed a seat near the front and Arthur stood. The bus climbed up through town and up the twists of Colborne Road, and they started to smell smoke. They were stopped by Jerries and all soldiers had to get out and go directly to help at the Fort. A lorry with Red Cross signs on it drove past.

The bus was diverted along Havilland Road, which took Pa and Arthur nearer their house. They got off and headed for their lane. The breeze whipped the smoke and smell of burning around them.

"Well, at least we got a ride further than we thought," said Arthur. "Are you ok, Pa?"

"I'm ok. I'll walk up at my own speed. You go up and see if Emily's all right."

Arthur jogged as fast as he could, thankful that there was no sign of bombing along the lane. Luckily, the west wind was carrying the worst of the black smoke from the Fort area out to sea. He rushed in to the house, calling Emily's name, and heard some kind of noise from the living room. Emily sat there on a chair, a broom in her hand.

"I'm here. I'm all right. But look what happened…Oh Arthur, those bomb blasts were terrible! I was outside at the back by the chickens." She pointed at the floor, covered in glass. "It's a good thing I wasn't in here. The front window must have been blown in."

"Thank goodness you were outside. Don't get up, Em. Just stay where you are."

He looked her over. She wasn't cut or wounded. He took the broom and cleared a way to the stove, lit the gas and put the kettle on, relieved that they still had gas. Now he must check on Pa and the chickens…

Upstairs, the front bedroom window has also been blown in, but they usually kept the curtains drawn up there, and that helped. They cleaned up and managed to put a meal together. Emily found an old sheet, and they stretched it over the hole that used to be a window in the living room. After dark, she went to see Mrs Ogier, and Arthur slipped out to talk with another neighbour. They learned that other houses along the road nearer the Fort had lost their windows and some had roof damage. Some of them housed German officers; but the Fort itself had taken the brunt.

That night they went to bed partly dressed, just in case.

Next day was a day to recover, and Emily did a second cleaning, looking for glass. Arthur went down to *Le Pré* to fetch an old piece of sail which they could use to cover the two window frames. He saw children picking up shrapnel on the roads as souvenirs.

A few planes flew over and it sounded as though another bomb hit the Fort and another was dropped in the harbour.

"They really want to sink that submarine that's been hiding in the harbour," Arthur told Pa and Emily, "and there's still something at the Fort that they're aiming at. Maybe it's the wireless station. I think they have radar equipment there too." [54]

"It's not the invasion yet," Pa declared, "but they must be preparing for it. There won't be a full moon for a couple of days, and the sea's still too rough for an invasion."

Invasion?

A cargo of wheat and coal arrived on Friday, June 2, and Arthur was glad to work that afternoon and all the next day. He noticed a hospital ship had arrived in the harbour, so the bombings must have caused some casualties. Some had said over a hundred were killed at the Fort.

---

54   Sinel June 6: "The BBC announced that a wireless station in the Channel Islands has been destroyed, and this is taken to be the one at Fort George, which was bombed again yesterday."

He was told to drive the wheat to the tunnels at St. Saviours where guards were talking to each other in an agitated way. Every Jerry was holding a rifle and waiting for orders.

On Sunday, June 4, there was another afternoon raid on the Fort, worse than the May 27 raid. Pa and Emily saw American and British bombers, and someone else said they saw at least four bombs dropping on the Fort.

On Monday, June 5, Arthur had another day of work to transport coal. Late that afternoon, he left his assigned lorry at St. Martin's and was on his bike going home when he heard planes overhead again. He got off and stood by a wall, heard an explosion north of him and some anti-aircraft fire, then two more explosions. There were trees overhead, but between the branches he saw what looked like an American plane. He jumped back on his bike and pedalled fast towards a large plume of smoke, knowing it must be near their house.

When he turned on to the Fort Road, he could see that the Fort itself was the source of the smoke and fire. Their house on his left was intact. He turned into the lane and sped in through the gate.

"Pa? Emily?" he yelled, and ran inside.

"Arthur? I'm here…under the table." His father's voice sounded shaky, but he seemed to be in one piece, and Arthur helped him up. The piece of sailcloth covering the window was dangling to one side.

"Sit down, Pa. Where's Emily?"

"She went to exchange eggs for flour. Where did the bombs fall?"

"At the Fort again."

"It's been going on for a while. They machine gunned the Fort football field across the road. The Jerries were playing a game. Screaming, yelling. I thought I'd better take shelter." Above his beard, his face was pale.

"Stay there, Pa." Arthur headed out to look for Emily, but heard her call.

"Are you there? Are you all right?" She came rushing in. One, two, three. Thank God they were still all alive and together.

"Perhaps this is the beginning of the invasion," said Pa, shakily. "Full moon tonight."

29: June 6–Sept 1944: D-Day Invasion

*D-Day moonlit flyover—D-Day at Cotton Row—Explosions in Guernsey—
Glass in the streets—Moving again*

D-Day moonlit flyover

After the attack, and knowing it was a full moon, it didn't surprise Pa and Arthur when they heard waves of aircraft passing overhead around four the next morning. They got up and went outside to look at the sky, and Emily soon joined them. The moon had risen and lit up everything. Arthur remembered the moonlit night before the evacuation, the beginning of this hell, almost four years ago. Perhaps tonight would mark the beginning of the end of it.

Emily was worried. "Will they bomb us, do you think?" she asked, as another wave of aircraft flew over.

"They've got better things to do," said her father, "and we're only on the edge of it. I think there's a lot more over Cherbourg way."

Their view was limited. There were pines along the other side of the Fort Road, and beyond them the bombed football field. No view of the sea.

"I'd like to sneak out on my bike and look towards France from the top of the Val des Terres," said Arthur.

"Don't think about it," said his father. "They'll have sentries everywhere, ready to shoot."

"I know. I'm only thinking out loud. I'll pick up on all the news in the morning."

Emily went indoors and decided that if she heard an explosion, she would dive under the kitchen table like her father had. Then she used some of their precious dry twigs to make a tiny fire and heat water. They had a hot drink to raise their hopes and cheer on the RAF and the Americans and all the Allies. None of them were going to be able to sleep.

Arthur reported for work next morning, hoping to pick up information. The Jerries were all armed and there would be no work for a few days. He saw machine guns on the back of lorries, and everything was camouflaged. It reminded him of the Dieppe scare two years ago. There were large Red

Cross signs in front of two buildings.

One of the other drivers whispered to him that the radio station at the Fort had been hit yesterday—at last—and doctors had been summoned to help with the wounded. In the town, someone confirmed the story and said that more coffins had been requisitioned up at the Fort. With that jewel of information, he returned home.

> **D-Day, June 6, 1944**
>
> The choice of a day for the invasion of Normandy relied very much on the moon. A dark night for Allied bombers to approach the targeted area, with a full moon rising at the right moment to illuminate it, was desirable.
>
> Even more important were the spring tides: there was a difference of 30 to 40 feet between high and low tide levels along the Normandy coast. German defence obstacles placed low on the Normandy shore could only be destroyed at low tide. German defences included huge sharpened logs designed to tear holes in landing craft. Additional dangers were wires strung between them and mines.
>
> The tide rises a foot (30 cm) every ten minutes. In a few hours, the fast-rising tide would allow landing craft to penetrate further and more quickly up the beaches while they were exposed to enemy fire. It needed careful planning.[55]

D-Day at Cotton Row

Everyone seemed to be chattering outside with their neighbours on June 3, after hearing that the Allies had taken Rome, at last! From Rome, Allied planes could reach east Germany, and bomb the factories that made the hated Junkers and Messerschmitts and other bombers.

A couple of days later, all the rumours about invading France came true: D-Day started on June 6. Frances kept the wireless tuned in while she was ironing. There had already been an announcement that paratroopers had arrived in France. By mid-morning she heard a news bulletin from a

---

55   https://www.cbc.ca/news/canada/nova-scotia/d-day-date-june-6-1944-astronomy-allied-invasion-1.5161516

well-known announcer, John Snagge:

D-Day has come. Early this morning the Allies began the assault on the north-west face of Hitler's European Fortress. The first news came just after half past nine, when Supreme Headquarters issued Communiqué No. One... under the command of General Eisenhower, Allied forces... began landing on the north coast of France... the group includes British, Canadian and US Forces....

It was a fine day and after tea, most of Cotton Row's inhabitants were outdoors discussing the day's news. Tom arrived and found Frances.

"Frances, I heard that Eisenhower sent a message to resistance groups telling them to show restraint, but that he'll give them a signal when they can start to help more actively. I wondered if there'd be any resistance in Guernsey."

Frances shook her head. "I don't know. It's a small island. There's nowhere to hide if you went and did some damage to the Germans. It's not like the mountains in France."

Annie joined in. "We haven't heard anything about the Channel Islands so far."

Everyone was talking.

"The BBC's sent some reporters that are travelling with the armies," Tom said. "I don't think they've done that before."

"That's something new. So we'll know exactly where they are and what's going on."

"One of the BBC reporters was on a landing barge that struck a mine and he managed to climb on another barge, but he lost his notes in the water."

"Eisenhower's sent messages to all the other western countries, from Norway to Belgium."

"And Charles de Gaulle is over in France as well. Somebody said he was going to broadcast a message..."

After work next day, Annie came home waving a newspaper. "I've got a paper," she called to Frances, waving a copy of *The Yorkshire Post*. They spread it out on the table.

"*All goes well so far. Beaches held and we move inland,*" Frances read.

"*Channel hail of bombs and shells...*[56] And there's a lovely map of Guernsey and Jersey and the French coast..."

"I bought the paper," said Annie. "We can keep it. You can cut out your map."

The girls helped Annie get tea ready, and left Frances to read every word, but there was nothing about Guernsey.

Explosions in Guernsey

Early on Thursday, June 15, Pa and Arthur slid out of bed fast after they heard an explosion. A second, different type of explosion followed, and another.

"That sounds like a bomb, or ammunition, or maybe both," said Arthur. The sound of planes faded away.

Emily joined them. "I'll go early to pick up the bread," she said. "They always know the news at the bakery."

Arthur went along with her. He had a job to do for someone in exchange for some vegetables. There had been no ships to unload recently, and he was looking for work. They joined a group at the bread depot and learned that there had been another attempt to bomb the German U-boat in St. Peter Port harbour. After the last attack, the Germans had wedged it between two ships and covered it with netting. It had escaped injury again, but the other two ships had caught fire and a crane had fallen on one of them.

Emily took the news back to Pa with their bread ration and Arthur cycled on to earn his basket of vegetables. After that he would spend time on a rocky beach where they were allowed to gather limpets and winkles. They never seemed to receive any meat in their rations now. He had noticed that the horses brought into the island by the Germans all seemed to have disappeared.

Bolton visitors

On the second Sunday after D-Day, June 18, Gran and Grampy visited Cotton Row. Janice was at the window watching. Earlier that morning, she had carefully wetted the front flagstone doorstep, let it get almost dry, and had *stoned* it using the cream-coloured stone that local housewives

---

56   Yorkshire Post, June 07, 1944, p.1.

preferred. That meant edging the big flagstone and its sides with a wide, straight edging, and she added a little pattern along the edges. It had all dried nicely.

Gran understood it all right away.

"Well, what a nice doorstep you've made," she said, and it was admired and stepped over carefully. Janice was pleased.

"In Bolton, they use a whiter stone, but I like this one. Where do you get it from?"

"We get it from the rag and bone man," said Annie.

"Do you stone your doorstep?" Janice asked.

"No, I don't," said Gran. "I don't have time for that." To her, it was a local custom that she had no intention of wasting her time on.

Annie was really pleased to see them again. "It's a long time since I saw you! Come on in. How are all your gardens, Grampy?"

"They're fine," he said. "We wanted to come last weekend, but you couldn't get a ticket for love nor money. Even today it was full, and we were at the bus terminus really early. Take this bag, Annie. We've brought you some onions."

Not to be outdone by Janice's doorstep artistry, Lynette showed Gran the picture she had made in her birthday colouring book. After that, they were all staring at newspapers on the table.

"I brought our copy of the *Daily Express* with the D-Day news," Grampy said. "It has a good map with Guernsey and Jersey on it, but they don't mention us anywhere."

"Look, it's the same map as ours in *The Yorkshire Post*," said Frances. "I looked right through their whole page of news. Every time they have the word Channel, I think it's going to be something about the Channel Islands, but it's not. It's the English Channel looking gray and choppy or how many destroyers are on it."

"There's a lot of fighting in Cherbourg and Caen and every town, from what we hear," said Grampy. "They have a News report at the cinema that Bill and Geoff go to. It'll be hard enough for the Allies to fight their way to Paris by the sound of it. I suppose they'll come back later and kick the Germans out of Guernsey."

"But once the Allies get to Paris," said Frances, "or when they reach Germany, there would be no point in the Germans staying in Guernsey, would there? Wouldn't they just leave the island?"

"Perhaps there's a lot of bombing and fighting in Germany, and Guernsey's more peaceful," said Gran. "I know where I'd prefer to stay."

Annie had managed to get half a chicken from Kit. Frances and Gran looked after dinner while Annie took Grampy to see the garden. Luckily, it was a pleasant summer's day and after dinner they enjoyed a walk near the reservoir and came back for tea before they left. All the conversation was about going back home.

Lynette asked Janice: "Do you remember our garden, and our father?"

She nodded. "Yes, I do…well, a bit. I remember sitting outside the front door with you on a blanket, and he was with us."

Lynette's memory didn't connect with any of that. She turned back to her dolls. They were talking about a world she knew nothing about.

Glass in the Streets

On Monday, June 19, Emily was tidying away the breakfast plates when they heard planes flying over, and there were three loud explosions from the direction of the harbour. Arthur and Pa went outside and saw American planes overhead. The sound of anti-aircraft fire and planes flying over continued, and there was plenty of vehicle activity down the road near the Fort.

Much later, Emily cycled to the bakery and picked up the news. "It was three American planes," she announced, when she got back. "They were trying to hit the submarine that's hiding in the harbour. Evidently the Jerries keep moving it around; but the blast blew out all the windows near the harbour."

"All the windows?" Arthur repeated.

"Even the Town Church windows. They say that there's glass all over the streets. I wonder if the windows at Edelweiss and le Pré were smashed, because someone said that some windows up in Hauteville were blown out."

"Well, in that case I'll go and see if there's some work for me," said Arthur. "I might get a day's wages out of it."

Windows had been blown out all along *The Front*, bordering the harbour. Windows were also smashed on the side of any building facing the harbour for several blocks inland. Arthur worked with hundreds of others for two or three days, sweeping up the glass and boarding up windows. At first he wondered why there were no OT workers on the job, and realised that every one of them had been shipped back to France. One of those boats had sunk. He hoped that the man who had grabbed his sandwich had survived.

> Constant Allied air reconnaissance, and the presence of Royal Navy ships in the area, convinced the Germans that the **Channel Islands would be isolated by the Allies**. They shipped out the OT workers early in June and July, knowing that supplies of food and materials could be blocked.
>
> Hitler himself ordered the concentration camps in Alderney to be closed down and all prisoners to be shipped out "because in no circumstances must they fall into enemy hands." [57]

Moving again

Like many others, Pa's little family would have to move again. All along the Fort Road, houses had been damaged; they had been lucky to get away with only windows broken. They knew that the authorities would allocate them a new place and hoped it would be in St. Peter Port where they would be near food rationing centres, and Pa could arrange to buy some fish from his friends. However, no permits would be issued for fishing at the moment. The rumble of guns from the French mainland explained it all.

Occasionally there was more hopeful news. There was an attempt to assassinate Hitler on July 21, as the Allies fought their way towards Paris, and there were rumours that a revolt against Hüffmeier was in the works. Paris was captured on August 23, but it didn't seem to affect anything in Guernsey. In the meantime, they must prepare to move.

"The war's not over yet. We don't want to move before our potatoes and carrots are ready," Pa said. "I'd rather stay until it's a bit colder in September and make sure we have our own store."

"If we're allocated a house that has a garden, I'll be happy," said Arthur. "We'll need garden space for the chickens. We can't buy food for them."

The chickens were the most important. Each one had a name and came

---

57   Cruickshank p. 222.

into the house at night before dark.

By late September supplies of gas, electricity and cooking fuel were running low, as well as food. The Kommandant now decreased rations for German troops as well as for civilians. He wanted to make sure that he could feed his troops until the new harvest next summer, and requisitioned more eggs, wheat, and potatoes from stocks reserved for the islanders.

Emily, Arthur, and Pa were relocated to Victoria Road in St. Peter Port. It was very near Emily's house in Victoria Terrace, where German officers had been living since 1940. She avoided walking there. Since they were in the town, they hoped they would be sure to have a ration of gas and electricity.

Victoria Road was located on one of the hillside slopes which led down to Trinity Square, where they had said goodbye to Ma eighteen months ago, and Arthur had said goodbye to Frances and the children over four years ago.

They would have to take buckets to the square to bring home salt water for cooking, although someone would deliver salt water for a price. They would pick up their rations at Luffs on Mansell Street, near the square, and their bread at a bakery nearby.

Island bakeries were supplied with increasingly mouldy cereals, including oats and pollard, from damp storage areas. The bakers didn't like the smell of the loaves while they were baking, and more people had digestive problems. One term for this discomfort was the Occupational, and for some it was a permanent discomfort. Others coped with it more easily.

They took with them about 30 pounds of potatoes and 10 pounds of carrots; and sacks of twigs and firewood. Since their new dwelling had no garden, they reluctantly decided to exchange one chicken for potatoes, and to eat two chickens at intervals before they moved. They took the last one with them, intending to feed it if they could, but there was no garden or food and it was eaten soon after.

30: Islanders despair; Oct–December at Cotton Row

*Surrender refused—Who should feed islanders?—Louise visits—
Snow White—Christmas 1944 and V1 rockets*

Surrender refused

On Monday, September 25, Arthur had a day's work loading sacks of cereals from a German storage area and delivering it to one of their canteens. He returned home with a bag of rye flour under his jacket and a leaflet in German dropped by the RAF. He lifted his bike inside the front door and turned into the living area. Pa was looking at the day's paper, which was now reduced to a single sheet three times a week.

"Hello, Pa, Emily. I have something for you."

Emily turned from the sink and saw the bag. "Oh Arthur, that's such a help."

"It's wheat," he said. "And if you're thinking of pancakes…" He took two apples from his pockets.

"We'll have pancakes tomorrow at dinner time," she smiled. "What a lovely change. At least we still have gas at meal times. I just have one egg, but that lovely flour will make up for it. Eggs cost such a lot. Even dried beans have gone up to two and six (2 shillings 6 pence) a pound."

Pa looked up from *The Press*. "Arthur, it says here that they're still looking for men to cut wood, if you want more work."

Arthur nodded.

"Can you get down my box of papers and charts from the attic after tea?" Pa continued. "I want to tidy it up a bit. Oh, and did you hear anything about a boat that came at the weekend? A few people said they saw a ship outside the harbour."

Arthur nodded. "They say there was an American boat with a white flag and somebody came to talk to the Kommandant. Then the boat went away."

"That's what I heard. Did anybody know what it was all about?"

"There's plenty of rumours. Let's hope it was about surrendering and arranging for some food to come in. I think it's all connected with those pamphlets the RAF dropped a couple of weeks ago.[58] I found another one today, a new one."

"The pamphlets in German—telling the Jerries to surrender?" asked Pa.

"Yeah. How did you hear about it?"

"From Patourel—our neighbour down the road," said Pa. "I meet him when I walk every day. He used to do some fishing at one time. Oh, he also said they're looking for a copper to make soup in another communal kitchen that's supposed to open soon. Is there a copper[59] anywhere in this house?"

Emily gave the soup a final stir. "No, there's no copper here, Pa."

"I know some of the Jerries wouldn't mind surrendering," Arthur said. "And they say von Schmettow wouldn't mind surrendering, if he had the ok from Berlin."

"Some of the Jerries look as though they're as hungry as we are," Emily commented. "Anyway, the soup's hot so let's sit down and eat. It's lentils and carrots and potatoes. We're supposed to get a two-ounce meat ration next week, by the way."

By the end of that week, there were rumours that von Schmettow had been to Jersey and the Bailiffs had been asked to a meeting. Everyone knew that arrangements had to be made for food to be imported, but was it up to London or Berlin?

Who should feed islanders?

On October 4, those who had a wireless heard about a statement made by the government in the House of Commons. It answered a question about the Channel Islands: *The Germans in the Channel Islands have been given the chance to surrender but have refused; there is nothing to show that they are not treating the civilians properly*[60].

When Emily heard about it the next day, she was furious, as was everyone she met. "I don't know anyone who isn't angry," she declared as they managed their dismal teatime food. "We're being forced to give the Germans our supplies and the British Parliament seem to think we're being

---

58   Bunting, p.243.

59   A large cooking pot.

60   Hansard.

treated all right! They should be sending us food parcels."

"Yes, but if they send us parcels, who's to say that the Jerries wouldn't grab them all?" said Pa. "They've still got thousands of troops here."

"Those words they spoke in Parliament were so callous," Emily said. "They don't care what's going on here. They need some of us to tell them the truth! They only speak to the Germans and listen to their lies! We can't just live on hope!" She was almost in tears.

Pa was silent, remembering his father's advice to him and his brothers. "Leave Denmark…" If he had stayed in Denmark, would he have more food on his plate today? He wondered what Nils was eating in Oregon.

> On October 6 the Germans attempted to bring in **supplies from St. Malo** by air. One plane crashed and the other dropped its load in the sea.
>
> Two days later another attempt was made, and the planes arrived in Guernsey. Besides food, they were the first planes to bring mail in four months. Some days later, the Allies took St. Malo. There were no more flights.[61]

On October 8, Arthur had a day's work taking cereals from the airport to storage at St. Saviours, and as usual Emily was delighted to receive the makings of pancakes or a pudding in the cloth bag.

On Friday, October 13, Emily returned to the house in mid-morning and found Arthur reading the thin sheet of newspaper.

"Where's Pa?" she asked "I wanted to ask him about getting some fish through one of his pals."

"He's down the street talking with Patourel. They were looking at one of his charts. Emily, there's a notice in the paper, if you can make sense of it." Arthur passed it across the table to her.

It was a notice from the Kommandant regarding supplies:

In view of the diminishing local supplies, the Kommandant had been in touch with the German government or Occupying Power. The latter would be in touch with the Protective Power—the British government—and would leave further action to them. Any action by the Protecting Power would therefore be

---

[61] Cruickshank, p.237.

beyond the control of the Occupying Authorities.

In Jersey, this notice had been published on October 4.

"Well, now we're learning all the legal war terms," said Emily. "Does that mean that the Jerries are leaving it up to the British government to bring food in?"

"I hope it's all about getting us some Red Cross parcels," said Arthur. He couldn't forget Emily mentioning a tin of cheese a few weeks ago. It was like a perpetual vision in his head.

There was a noise at the front door and Pa came in.

"Did you see this notice, Pa?" asked Emily. "It looks as though the Germans aren't taking any responsibility."

"Let's hope Churchill will accept responsibility," said her father. There's plenty of Guernsey men fighting in the army, so they should do something."

Later that month, a barge of potatoes and wheat arrived from Jersey, and Arthur helped to unload it. His Jersey contact let him know that there had been a few attempts by young people to escape to France. One man was shot, a couple were drowned, but some had probably been successful and had taken letters and information about food shortages with them.

Potato pie suppers and after-school challenges

Around Clowbridge, potato pie suppers were being held again. The decreasing numbers of U-boats made food supplies more reliable, and local gardeners had been productive. The Harvest Festival offered more produce, which pleased the vicar.

Janice and her friends received a challenge from the boys after school one afternoon. One boy had obtained a barrel, and each boy was going to climb inside and roll down the short slope behind Annice's bungalow, ending up behind Alice-Ann's house. The first boy climbed inside, let himself roll down the hill, and came out unscathed. The other boys did it and then the girls were challenged. After Janice and the girls had succeeded, Lynette agreed to get in the barrel. She was at the bottom of the hill before she could even shout, and luckily for Janice, she came out unblemished. Neither Frances nor Annie heard about it.

The next challenge was trying to walk down the tops of the walls which ran along Wiles Lane. Nettles grew along the walls on both sides of the road, and jumping along the wall wasn't easy. Lynette tumbled into the nettles and was crying with the resulting prickly, burning pain as Frances got off the bus from the Rileys. Calamine lotion helped to relieve the pain, and Lynette didn't have to be told not to do it again.

Louise visits

Louise came for a few days in October. She brought a tin of condensed milk and Frances had put aside rice to make her usual birthday rice pudding.

"Have you received any Red Cross messages lately?" Louise asked, as the first cup of tea was made.

"No. I was going to ask you if you'd heard from your mother."

"Not recently. Last year I heard from Mum after Grandma died. Then I had one this spring to say they were well and had a small garden. I wrote back to say I'd be visiting young people in the autumn. She'll know I mean you and the girls. Since then, I've had nothing."

"Mabel sent our photos to Arthur via the deportees in Germany, and we had a message at Christmas. Since then, I've heard nothing."

"Actually, I wondered if they've moved. Mum said a *small* garden. It doesn't sound like Grandpa Eric's place."

"Some of the Burnley evacuees have noticed hints that people might have moved; but we haven't heard of any bombing there."

"It's awful just guessing what's happening. I thought that after D-Day, the Allies would have the Germans out of the islands in no time at all; but perhaps we'll have to wait till they take Berlin."

"I know. Stalin's so near to Berlin, and I hoped the Americans would get there first with all their planes."

"Are you still doing the First Aid courses, Auntie?"

"Yes, Louise, and I want to claim half an hour from you to practice bandaging your knee after tea. I'm helping the nurse with demonstrations to teach our class of First Aiders in Clowbridge tomorrow evening."

Janice giggled. "Mum might want to practice on you a lot."

Louise grinned. "You know, I'd like to know how to bandage someone's knee. Perhaps you can bandage my knee as well, after you watch your Mum doing it."

"Oh." That was a new idea. Janice went to find her nurse's apron to be ready.

Frances smiled. "We'll have tea and later I want to show you what I've been making with that new crepe paper."

She had discovered crepe paper in Burnley and was making decorations: bright little owls with watchful eyes perched on a twig; and empty cocoa tins covered with cotton wool and red crepe paper, looking like Father Christmas. They had a lid and could contain home-made sweets and could be sold. Louise liked the idea and wanted to try her hand at it. However, most of that evening was used up by two small nurses who were busily bandaging her elbows and knees.

Snow White

Winter arrived, and everyone was layered with clothes again; chilblains appeared on heels. On Saturday, December 9, there was the annual prize giving and Christmas party, with a potato pie tea; everyone received a small book or token, and the potato pies had extra cheese on them this year.

Since October everyone had been preparing for the Christmas show, produced this year by Annie's friend Elsie Niels, who had a talent for presenting musical evenings. This year they were rehearsing *Snow White and the Seven Dwarfs*. Lynette and Beryl were given the parts of two of the dwarfs, Hans and Max. They had only a dozen words to say, but Annie coached them thoroughly. Janice had a more important part and a special costume.

Lynette wrote later:

The operetta was put on after tea, and there was a special feeling about doing our very best. Perhaps that was pushed by Mum and Auntie Annie, who knew that this was probably the last December that we would celebrate together. I'm glad I never sensed that current of sadness.

Beryl and I wore strange hats and our dressing gowns to play our first major roles, Max and Hans. We did very well—we were told. The whole village came to see it and it seemed to be a memorable success.

Christmas 1944

On Christmas Eve, the girls went to bed after they had carefully placed one of Frances' brown lisle stockings across the bottom of each of their beds, which were side by side.

Lynette wrote later:

Before I slept, I patted the stocking to make sure it was in place. On Christmas morning I woke and gently lifted my legs and was overjoyed to feel the weight of my filled stocking, reassured that Father Christmas had visited. I didn't dare make a noise with the adults sleeping in the same room. When I heard Janice moving quietly, we started to guess what we felt in the stockings in the dark, until Mum woke up and put the light on.

There was a chocolate bar, a Mary Mouse book, a pencil, a small oval dish with some raisins in it, socks, some black liquorice, and an orange right at the bottom.

Downstairs, we were surprised again. On the table was a spread of items: a Post Office play set on my side, with tiny stamps and envelopes; and a colouring book and some colouring pencils....

Janice's description:

...we came downstairs, and the living room table was divided into two halves. In my half was a shop with little sacks of dried peas, rice etc, little scales, and tiny paper bags. It was absolutely wonderful. It must have taken a lot of effort and ingenuity to produce.

One of my friends was given a choice of having a Christmas stocking or 2/6 and she chose the money. It would not have been my choice. Christmas was always magic to us as young children.

Retreating into their bubble of Christmas was a luxury. The life of the village was also pleasant, but the outside world brought news that broke through the aura of Christmas. The Allies were having a hard time fighting through the woods of the Ardennes of Belgium, dying in thousands in the Battle of the Bulge. The Germans didn't seem to know it was time to surrender.

V1 Rockets

The joy of Christmas Day was shattered for everyone as the news of a new bomb attack on Manchester, in the early hours of December 24, was passed around.

The city had been the target of Hitler's new V1 or V2 rockets. They were faster than sound and flew in the stratosphere, so that there was no way to give a warning. There was no engine noise. They seemed to fall silently, but the destruction they caused was equivalent to a 2,000 pound bomb. Several had fallen wide of their targets. One had landed near Chorley, only twenty-five miles from Cotton Row, creating a forty-foot crater and damaging over a hundred houses in the village of Brindle. One fell in Oldham killing twenty-seven people, and another near Bury. Frances breathed a sigh of relief knowing that Cotton Row and Clowbridge had been spared, and also that Bert and Nancy were in Totnes with their parents for their Christmas holidays.

Each rocket carried a 2,000-pound bomb. They had already destroyed targets in London in the days following D-Day; but there had been little "news" of them. Now, all of a sudden, every place was in easy range of these flying killer weapons, and just when the end of the war seemed to be in sight.

31: Guernsey Nov–Dec 1944: Facing Starvation

*Noyon escapes—Bailiffs contact Red Cross—Living on Hope—
Home Secretary speaks—SS Vega arrives*

Noyon escapes

On November 6, Emily came back from town at noon and Pa lit the gas under the soup pot as soon as she appeared. She put down her bag and held her hands near the pot. "It's so cold again out there. I had to wait for the fish lady in the market; but I managed to get a piece of bream for us. It cost a lot, and I only got it because I gave her some apples as well."

Arthur stood near the stove cutting the bread portions. "Bream! Good shopping, Em, whatever it cost. It's always good to have apples on you."

"Or a few cigarettes," Pa added.

"I'll be getting a few more apples where I have to do a job next week," Arthur continued. "They usually pay me with apples or potatoes."

"And guess what I heard?" Emily continued. "Someone escaped! A Captain Noyon."

Pa looked up. "Noyon?"

"They say he took a lot of information. I was told he was at the States meeting on November first and he took notes of what we need. He went fishing with someone and left in the night, two days ago. He's not a member of the States though, is he?"

"Good man," said Arthur, placing the soup bowls on the table. "He's a registered pilot, Em. We all know Noyon. He's not a States member, and he's not on the Controlling Committee either. He'll get to England all right."

Pa nodded. He seemed to be thoughtful. "It was calm two days ago. A good night to leave."

"How did he get enough petrol, though?" Emily queried.

"I think there must have been some careful planning for this to succeed, planning well before that States meeting," said Arthur. He was looking directly at his father.

Pa nodded. "Looks like it. People think Churchill doesn't know what's going on here. Somebody had to do something."

Arthur made no comment. He thought, *I hope the planning was good. I hope Noyon and his mate survive that cold sea and a freezing, damp wind, heading to England. At least there are Allied ships around now, and one of them might pick them up.*

Pa shared out the soup. His thoughts were very similar.

Arthur announced more good news: "Emily, tomorrow there's a barge coming in from Jersey. I've got a day's work unloading. Maybe wheat and potatoes."

"And do you think you might…?"

"Yes, I do think. How many apples are left?"

"Only three, now that the fish woman has the others. Apple pancakes next day?"

"As long as it's wheat, yep," Arthur nodded. He placed their bread ration on the table. Not much, but there were bits of potato, parsnips and beans floating in the soup; and at teatime they would eat bream. Tonight they might be able to sleep without hunger keeping them awake and restless.

Bailiffs contact Red Cross

On Saturday, November 11, there was a notice in *The Press*. Pa read it out to Emily.

The German Authorities have allowed me to send a radio message to the International Red Cross at Geneva stating the present serious shortage of many essentials in the island, and asking for immediate help and a visit from a Red Cross representative without delay.

I am informed that the message was dispatched last Monday morning.

Victor G. Carey

Bailiff.

"Dispatched last Monday. That was November fifth," said Emily. "Surely something must be happening now. Noyon left on the fourth. They must soon know in England and in Geneva what's happening here."

"Patourel said that both of the Bailiffs [62] wanted to ask the Red Cross for help, but the Germans wouldn't let either one of them handle the message, and insisted on sending it for them. Let's hope they really did. Anyway,

---

62 Victor Carey, Bailiff of Guernsey; and Alexander Coutanche, Bailiff of Jersey.

Noyon should be in England by now."

Arthur looked at the notice. "I heard someone from the States say that Coutanche sent his message to the Red Cross about a week ago," he said. "So with our Bailiff's message and Noyon's escape, that's three messages that have gone out."

"You heard that from someone in the States? Who?" asked Emily.

"It was where I got the apples from last week. I did some work for them."

She didn't enquire further. She found her precious scissors, cut out the notice, and leaned it against the box with their Red Cross messages on the mantelpiece.

When Emily returned from the bakery early on November 14, Arthur was trying to mend a shoe and Pa was under a blanket on his chair. Pa didn't like the smell of the bread.

"What are our rations of potatoes now?" he asked. "Are we getting all we're allowed? Seems to me I could eat more of them instead of bread."

"Arthur and I always keep an eye on the weight when we shop for the potato rations," said Emily. "But I find the bread is getting a bit rougher. I don't know what they're mixing in it. Next week we'll be down to five pounds of potatoes a week each.[63] We still get three ounces of butter and sugar a week, and about half a pound of macaroni."

"When we were unloading the boats last month, the Jersey bloke said they hadn't had gas to cook with since early September," Arthur said. "I thought it was just a rumour, but I hear they've been using communal kitchens for quite a while. I think you take your food to have it cooked and then bring it home, or they have your rations and give you a meal once a day."

"Well, we're a bit better off then," said Pa. "We don't need a cold walk to a kitchen and back again with the dinner getting cold. At least we have gas at meal times."

"I've been thinking," said Arthur. "If our gas is cut off, we'll need to cook over the fire. We must get as much wood and kindling stored here as we can."

"The wood is too green," said Pa, "and it's hard to make a fire with that anthracite dust they send us. I get warmer from pumping the bellows than

---

63   Carey, p.186.

I do from the fire. A hundredweight[64] of dust a month doesn't go far, and it needs to be mixed with tar."

"I think I'll go back to *Le Pré* and Edelweiss tomorrow," Arthur said. "I want to see if there's anything we left there that we can chop up and burn. I've fixed up that little cart thing that we found behind the house."

"We already burned *Elsie*," sighed Pa, "but now that I think of it, didn't we have two or three old chairs in the small room upstairs? You'll have to watch out for the Jerries though."

"Yes, I'll watch out. There are those old chairs and even the floorboards. I'll hitch up the cart behind Emily's bike and see if it works."

"Be careful, Art. You know there were cracks in the walls after the explosions for the tunnel. You don't want it collapsing on you."

"I'll be careful. If there's still a bit of garden hose at *Le Pré*, I'll bring it back as well. If I can fill it with sand, I can probably make a tyre out of it for my own bike."

Pa looked at Arthur. "Are they still working on that tunnel under le Pré?"

"I think they stopped excavating, last time I passed by. I'll be careful."

Emily was looking at the floor. "The two women who live further down the hill said their friends were burning the linoleum from their floor. I think it might smell though."

"We'll only do that if we have nothing else to burn," Arthur stated. "There are floorboards upstairs here in the attic that we can burn if we need to."

Living on hope

November 22 was damp and foggy and cold, but a ray of hope warmed Emily's soul when she saw a notice in The Press regarding supplies:

Following up the negotiations brought about by the Occupying Power, as regards the provisioning of the civilian population of the Channel Islands, a supply of medicaments, soap and foodstuff has been promised as a beginning.

It didn't say a lot, but they all read it two or three times, hoping it was real, and Emily cut it out and placed it by the box on the mantlepiece. Hope was almost as good as food.

In November, they were allowed a ration of a gallon of tar per month

---

64   100 lbs.

per household. Mixed with coal dust, it created a longer lasting fire. People were asked not to buy root crops if they already had a good supply for themselves. There were many who had no garden and needed to buy their full quota. Hairdressers were closed to save on electricity.

Working hours would be reduced in December to a 5 ½ hour work day: from 9.30 a.m. to 12 p.m. and to 5 p.m.

In December, the weather was bleak. A few foreigners died from eating flower bulbs, thinking they were onions. Everyone was hungry except German officers. German soldiers moved around at night and robbed gardens, stole chickens, tried to grab cats, dogs, rabbits and goats. They continued to creep into farms and milk cows.

The ration of bread was now only three pounds per week per person. Once they had their bread ration, most people went home and tried to rest and keep warm under a blanket. Streets were quiet. Even the Jerries were suffering from malnutrition and were supposed to rest for two hours every afternoon.

On Tuesday, December 5, Emily braved fog and drizzle to fetch their bread. The loaves were still warm, but the smell wasn't enticing. For each person, she received only a small one-pound loaf and a round bun. Sometimes her head felt it was in a different world and her sense of balance wasn't quite right. Walking back up Victoria Road she had to pause; she wasn't the only one to do so. However, this was her job and she wouldn't miss doing it—it was at the bakery that the news was swapped, and rumours added spice to a miserable existence.

As soon as she was in the house, Pa lit the gas under the pot of soup. "Emily, they were allowing access to the beach today and Arthur went to get some limpets."

"Well, that's good news. Here's the bread. It's cold and my shoes are damp inside. Arthur's already tried to repair these. I think I'll have to wear Mum's old gardening shoes in future."

"We should be making clogs like they're doing in Jersey."

"Did Patourel tell you that? Perhaps they could send us some."

Arthur came in holding a small bag. "Em, I've got limpets, and winkles. Can you make fish cakes with them?"

"Yes, we've got a few parsnips and potatoes. I'll mince them with the potato skins. That'll make a good tea. Arthur, Pa says they make clogs in

Jersey. Do you think your contact on the boat could get me a pair?"

"I can ask him. The only thing I heard was that they need repairing quite often and they don't have enough of the right kind of wood. I think I can fix up Ma's gardening shoes for you, and they'd be better than those clogs."

Emily was disappointed. "I'll make do with the gardening shoes. Now, someone at the bakery said the Jerries are taking peoples' food stores during the day, just walking into their houses. Is that allowed?"

She sat at the table and Pa served the soup.

"That was the new rule that came out a couple of weeks ago," said Arthur. "The Jerries with yellow armbands can come into your house and search for any food you've got hidden. I saw one of them in the country last week when I did that job. It's the farmers they're searching mostly. They're looking for large hidden stores, not the little amounts that we've got."

"I thought they weren't supposed to take our food."

"The Jerries are the Occupiers. They'll take what they want," Pa stated, "and especially if they think Britain's sending us a shipload of food."

Two days later, on December 7, Arthur had a day's work unloading a small shipment of wheat and potatoes from Jersey. As usual, he had to take it to the underground storage tunnels at St. Saviour's; and, as usual, he managed to take something home. That was one more "good day." Next day, there was a notice in the *Evening Press* saying that a Red Cross ship had left Lisbon[65] and was bound for Guernsey with 750 tons of cargo. Emily added that to her mantlepiece collection.

Home Secretary speaks

On Saturday, December 16, there was plenty of chatter at the bakery. Emily came home and found her father and Arthur already in a discussion.

"Emily, did you hear about the Home Secretary's speech? Morrison's speech?" Arthur asked.

"Yes, that's all that they were talking about. Do you think Noyon managed to get to England?"

"Probably. Look, someone wrote it out, but it's hard to read. They didn't have paper. I must give it back."

Emily placed her bag on the table and looked at the handwriting which

---

65   Higgs p.55.

filled the margins of two printed pages torn out of a book. It took a while to read along each side.

In view of the reports received as to the conditions in the Islands, His Majesty's Government have decided that it would be right to supplement the rations of the civil population... by sending supplies of medicines, soap, and food parcels on the basis of those supplied to prisoners of war. The German Government have now agreed... and have granted a safe conduct to the ship which will convey these supplies to the Islands. His Majesty's Government have every reason to believe that she will be ready to sail within the next few days.[66]

"They were saying that those words that are underlined—about "reports"—means that Noyon got through to England," said Arthur, "and that it was confirmed on a broadcast from the BBC."

"Yes, that's what Patourel told me," said Pa. "There was a special message on another radio wavelength, a message they'd agreed to before he left here in November.[67] His friends heard it on December 9 as arranged, so they knew he'd arrived in England."

There was a sort of satisfaction and certainty in her father's tone that made Emily pause. His mention of Patourel made her remember that Pa's chart box was still downstairs, short of a couple of items lent to Patourel. Where had they gone? After the war, she would have questions to ask her father. She didn't need to know the answers right now.

"Well, they heard it on the BBC, from the Home Secretary," said Arthur. "I just hope they get good weather, and the boat gets here fast."

"But we thought the Red Cross ship had left around the seventh or eighth," said Emily. "It was in *The Press*." She took the cutting from the mantlepiece. "Look, I cut it out. And now, it may not even have left yet."

"I want to know how we'll get our food parcels when they arrive," said Pa.

"I suppose we'll pick them up at Luff's where we get our rations," replied Emily. "They have a list of our names."

"We can get them with our bikes," said Arthur, "or with your bike. I've just got one tyre at the moment."

---

66   Hansard HC Deb 12 December 1944 vol406 cc 1055-6.
67   *"Personal message to George. The answer is Yes."*

Emily smiled. "And I heard that they're going to give the children the day off school to go and see the boat."

"They can't let them get close enough," said Arthur. "The whole harbour's mined. There are shells to blow it to pieces."

"But it'll be exciting! Even if they see it at a distance."

"What if the Jerries want to grab the parcels?" asked Pa. "They're the ones with the guns. Who's to stop them?"

"That's what somebody was explaining to us," said Emily. "There's a lady who's in charge of the Red Cross, Mrs Trouteaud. She said the St. John's Ambulance Brigade and our Red Cross people will be in charge. I was told that someone from Geneva will come too and be in charge of unloading the boat."

"Well, if von Schmettow was still the boss, that might work," said Pa, "but they say Hüffmeier's trying to take over and Schmettow is on his way out. I hope the Red Cross will be carrying guns. Hüffmeier's taken every bit of food from us that he can find." He clearly wasn't convinced.

"The Jerries prefer von Schmettow," said Arthur. "I think he was all ready to surrender and get food in for them as well as for us. They call Hüffmeier *The Admiral*, because he's a navy man, the sort that'll never give in."

"Yes. And soldiers don't like to be bossed around by navy men," Pa interjected.

"Exactly. He doesn't care if his men starve as long as they don't surrender. They don't like him. Anyway, Em, I've got something…for Christmas."

"Christmas! Arthur, we aren't going to have a Christmas…" Emily's voice tailed off as Arthur dived around the corner and retrieved something feathery from the next room. "A chicken!"

"Charlie got it for us. If we want to eat anything at Christmas, we need to get it now and keep it in the house. I've got a bit of food for it, but we'll have to look for more."

Emily decided that this time, she wouldn't give the chicken a name.

On December 20, the BBC announced the departure of the Red Cross ship from Lisbon, but many wondered if it was another false hope. By then, the Christmas chicken had been eaten, because they had been warned that the gas would be shut off on December 21. Now they had to cook on their wood fire. They were grateful for a few hours of electric light, although that might soon end.

For Christmas they had potato, cabbage, carrots, and swede[68] cooked with what remained of their chicken soup, heated over the fire. They lived most of the day and night together in the living room, making a fire around noon for a few hours. After that, it was best to be under blankets, but you didn't sleep much when you were hungry.

SS *Vega* arrives

Late in the afternoon of December 27, there was shouting in Victoria Road and Arthur went outside. He heard, "They've seen it! The Red Cross ship…" and other doors opened as a few more people grabbed their coats and came out. From the south coast a ship had been seen: she had the word INTERNATIONAL and two large red crosses on her side. She had been seen around noon.

Emily came out and found herself crying. Arthur couldn't speak. Pa pulled on his coat and walked downhill and met Patourel walking up and they shook hands and went back home again. That evening Arthur went outside and heard cheering from the harbour. The SS *Vega*, a Swedish ship, was now moored outside the harbour for the night. Next morning he cycled a short distance to look at the ship. He wanted to go down nearer the harbour but couldn't afford to use his strength to do so.

The SS *Vega* carried more than 100,000 food parcels, 4,200 invalid diet parcels, and also soap, salt, medical supplies, and cigarettes.[69] Current rations were down to 3 ounces sugar and fat per week, about 8 ounces of macaroni, 3 pounds of bread and 5 pounds of potatoes.

To each, a parcel

On December 31, Arthur and Emily went early to pick up their three parcels from Luff's grocery shop near Trinity Square. People had started to queue up well before daylight. Things were well organised: ration books stamped and parcels signed for. They brought the three parcels home using Emily's bike and the little cart Arthur had repaired, and they both pushed it up Victoria Road. They stopped to rest and managed tearfully but happily to greet people with pushcarts, prams and bikes.

---

68   Rutabaga
69   Cruickshank, p 232.

It was like Christmas; but they were careful, heeding the warnings published in *The Press* the day before, about tasting a little at a time, since their bodies were not used to rich food. They had Canadian parcels and each of them lined up their tins and packages: biscuits, tea, cheese, chocolate, powdered milk, sardines, salmon, butter, corned beef, raisins, prunes, hand soap. They tried tea with powdered milk in it. The parcels were re-packed and each one slept with their parcel within reach.

Colonel Iselin lays down the law

They picked up several stories over the next few days. On December 28, Colonel Iselin, the on-board representative of the Swiss Red Cross, met with Hüffmeier and the German High Command. They had turned out in their best uniforms, all polished up, carrying guns, and had demanded 25% of the parcels. Colonel Iselin, unarmed, had shouted them down. He would not unload one single parcel unless rules were followed: the parcels were for the islanders, and not for the occupying forces.

Hüffmeier knew that if the islanders received the parcels, it might free up a bit more food for the garrison, which he had already put on minimal rations. He knew also that there was talk of insurrection. He decided to go along with Iselin's directions.

The two Bailiffs were present but were not allowed to speak with Colonel Iselin privately. They gave him lists of the islanders' needs and a list from one of the island doctors. Colonel Iselin ordered flour and yeast immediately, saying that the bread was unfit for human consumption.

German troops helped to unload the parcels, which were carefully scrutinised for intelligence or sabotage equipment; but the Guernsey Red Cross and the St. John's Ambulance Brigade (SJAB) were in charge of the handling and distribution. First the parcels were taken to St. George's Hall and stored overnight under SJAB guard. The Germans placed an armed guard outside the building but were not allowed inside. The distribution of the parcels to the grocery centers began very early the following morning, December 31, by horse-drawn vehicles.

32: January–May 1945, at Cotton Row

*Snowstorm—V1 rocket traced—Evacuee petitions—Annie's plans—
American headline—May Queen—Nursing Award*

Snowstorm—V1 rockets traced

January 1945 at Cotton Row was as cold as 1941: the temperature hovered around the freezing point all month,[70] the dampness was bone chilling, and snow fell frequently. Everyone pitied the British and American soldiers fighting the Germans in the snow and mud of the Ardennes. They called it the Battle of the Bulge from the shape that the Ardennes made on the map of eastern Belgium, and Frances could see the bulge on her map. She thought of the five members of her family who were in the armed forces. She thought of Arthur who, according to the latest evacuee news, had very little rationed food.

The V1 rocket that fell near Chorley on Christmas Eve had scared everyone. After Christmas, a farmer discovered that a second one had landed in one of his fields at Oswaldtwistle, which was only five miles from Cotton Row. Frances and Annie listened to the radio to learn the sounds that the rockets made before they plummeted to earth, hoping to be prepared. The children were also made to listen carefully, and instructed to fling themselves under any nearby table or shelter.

If a rocket hit Clowbridge, Frances would be involved in giving first aid, and Annie would watch over the children. They had discussed all possibilities.

After school had started in January, Annie came home from work one day looking very pleased. She told Frances quietly that she would share a secret with her after the girls were in bed. When Frances tiptoed downstairs later, Annie had just rescued something that she had left outside in the dark when she had arrived from work. She held it up.

"A doll's house!" Frances exclaimed, in a loud whisper.

"I was asking around before Christmas," Annie said. "Someone found

---

70 G. Manley: Average temp 0.4C January in England.

somebody else in Bacup who had one. It's not got any furniture, but we can always make a few things. It'll keep the girls busy if we're snowed-up."

"I'll clean it up while they're in school, but we'll have to keep it in the wash-house for a day or two."

Frances looked for match boxes, pieces of fabric and small containers. By the weekend there were enough items to keep the girls busy using their imagination to create furnishings. The Christmas crèche supplied animals and more ideas.

On January 29 and 30, a huge storm swept across Britain and left almost a foot of snow in Lancashire and Yorkshire. Trains were buried in Scotland, and even Cardiff in the west, in Wales, was cut off by snow. The weekend after, every child in the village turned out with a parent dragging a sledge of some kind, eager to whoosh down the hill next to the school before the snow melted.

Annie and Frances both went along at the girls' insistence and pulled the sledge up one side of the slope. Janice sat in front, and Lynette was persuaded to sit behind her and hold on. Down they went with terrifying speed, and what seemed like no control. Lynette managed not to do it again.

Evacuee Petitions

February delighted everyone by being steadily warmer than usual, and Frances decided to attempt a weekend in Bolton. The Allies had managed to push the Germans out of The Bulge and the enemy was retreating into Germany. There was just too much to talk about. As usual, they left on a Friday afternoon. Grampy was already at home from work when they arrived. Tea was brewed, and the girls disappeared to play in the Morrison shelter until Rose arrived.

Gran passed a letter to Frances. "That's from Vi," she said. "It's about one of the evacuee groups. She says that three thousand people signed a petition asking the Home Secretary, to evacuate Guernsey or give the Germans on the island an honourable surrender."[71]

"Three thousand, that's a lot of signatures."

"Yes," Gran nodded. "It was a petition written by the Horsforth Channel

---

71   Bunting, p 242.

Island Society. It's not the group she belongs to. It's another one near Bradford."

"I didn't hear about that one," said Frances, "but I heard about the one signed by nine thousand people from the Sheffield Society that was sent to the Home Secretary—Morrison—in December. I think a letter went to him from our Society in Burnley also."

"Yes, we heard it on the BBC," said Grampy. "And we've sent a petition from Bolton as well. It's been discussed a few times in Parliament."

"We heard, kind of unofficially, that there were people who escaped from both islands—from Jersey as well as Guernsey; and they had all the official information from the States' meetings," said Grampy.

"Churchill must surely know what the situation is, in that case."

"It's about time Churchill remembered we exist," said Gran, "and that our men have joined up to fight as well. We've got your sister Elsie in Guernsey, and Mabel's worried sick about Bob, like your Arthur. She's been trying to send him letters through the Laufen camp in Germany—like she sent the photos for us—but that connection's not been working since D-Day."

"They may not have seed or fertiliser," Grampy added, "but the growers know how to keep seed from their own crop if they need it. The Germans must be interfering. They say that cabbages are the only vegetables left. What I don't understand is, how can the POWs in Germany receive Red Cross food parcels, and Guernsey people are starving and weren't getting any till after Christmas."

"They could have got the Red Cross people in months ago," Gran declared.

"And after the Red Cross finally arrived there," Grampy added, "and delivered the parcels, their report just said that things weren't too…too…"

"Weren't too disquieting," said Gran.

"That's the word. *Disquieting*! The ones who escaped with information from the Bailiffs said they were starving. That's a lot more than disquieting!"

"And there's no gas for cooking. How on earth can you live like that?" Gran continued. "You'd think they might try to evacuate them like someone suggested." She walked over to the breadboard and prepared to slice a loaf.

"In the House of Commons, Lord Portsea suggested they find another ship to take in anthracite and coal and whatever they need," said Grampy. "It sounds like common sense to me, but they just don't take much notice of him. Mind you, he comes up with some foolish ideas at times."

Gran shook out a tablecloth. Frances cleared the table of cups. "I hope they can keep that Red Cross ship going back and forth with supplies."

"One islander escaped," her father continued, "and he wrote a letter to *The Times* in December. He complained of collaborators on the island, and informers and jerrybags[72] and black marketeers. You find out what people are really made of in a war. I bet we'll hear some arguments after we get home."

"It's amazing how well we've all worked together here," said Frances. "I haven't heard of much black marketing going on around our way, and Annie's very careful at the Co-op. But we aren't starving and living with the enemy like they are."

Grampy looked up. "How's Annie doing at the Co-op?"

"She's done well. She's manageress now."

"When it's warmer, we'll come and see you. I'd like to see her in the shop."

"If you walked in one day, she'd be delighted. There's a fish and chip shop next door to it as well, and it's a busy place sometimes."

"Geoff and Bill bought some fish and chips last week," Gran commented, "but they said they didn't like the taste of the fat they were cooked in."

"And they said the beer was watered down," Grampy laughed. "Serves 'em right. They just waste their money sometimes."

Annie's plans

Annie became uneasy as the Allies fought their way into Europe. She knew that Frances was thinking more and more of her return to Guernsey, and Annie didn't want to lose her new family. The girls had become almost her very own children. Frances was like a trusted sister. With her previous experience of running a sweet shop and her educated ways, she would make a smart business partner. They should work together after the war. It was just good common sense. Annie was now manageress at the Co-op, handling both suppliers and customers, and she had her own money to

---

72   Women who made themselves available to the occupying soldiers.

invest.

She had already started going out with one of her bus driver pals, Leamington Aldous, or Leam (pronounced *Lem*) for short. A widower with a son in the army, he was pleasant, reasonable, and willing to help in her plans. He waved to the girls if he saw them walking along the road when he drove past in his bus. Annie needed a partner for life, and she felt he was the right one.

Her Plan A was to buy the Post Office business—which she felt Frances could run—and combine it with the Co-op, which she would continue to manage. She and Leam planned to get married after the war ended and he would work with her. It was a splendid scheme. Arthur could come to England and be part of it all.

However, Frances remained firm in her refusal. Her husband and her home were in Guernsey, and she needed her family. She longed to return to the island's more reasonable climate, and to her view of Fermain Bay. Staying in Lancashire was not a possibility. On some evenings, after the girls had gone to bed, there were sometimes arguments as Annie tried to persuade Frances to change her mind.

In the spring, Annie's Plan B came out of the blue one day. It started with the sound of a motorbike. Annie introduced a friend from her conductress days, Billy D. He was one of the best mechanics at the Rawtenstall Bus Corporation. Smiling and handsome, he arrived on his motorbike more than once. Frances wouldn't go for a ride on it, although she allowed the girls to sit on it once. He disappeared from view after a couple of visits.

Easter Sunday was April 1. There was a family service, including Sunday School in the morning. Everyone discussed the war news: the Allies were crossing the Rhine and Dutch cities were being freed. Newspapers were giving the count of how many prisoners were captured each day.

Lynette took her drawing book to school and devoted one page to an "Easter Test" picture. Again, she drew the line of hills behind Cotton Row with sheep on them and a sun shining above. Later, in June, she wrote "Midsummer Test" on the next page and drew in ink what she saw in the back field: a horse pulling a wagon with a load of hay on it, and three people with two-pronged pitchforks and a large rake, picking up the hay. It was a summary of the local farming technology and represented a stable period in her life that she would value forever.

An American headline

On Friday of the next week Tom dropped in after tea brandishing his newspaper. "I want to keep this copy for a bit, but I said I'd bring it up for you, just to read."

It was the news of Roosevelt's death, on April 12, which had shocked everyone.

"I didn't realise he was so ill," Annie said. "Infantile paralysis! You know, you hear him speak on the wireless but I didn't know he was in a wheelchair most of the time."

"Bless him. I doubt if we'd be winning this war without his Lend-Lease plan and the American armies," Frances commented. "We were lucky that the Japs forced them into the war, weren't we? We weren't doing too well until then."

"Yes, and we were lucky the Russians came in on our side," said Tom, "but it was the Americans who supplied them, and us. Even with all the Commonwealth helping, we would never have done it without them. The trouble is, Stalin's reaching the big cities before we do. The BBC said this morning the Soviets are almost in Vienna now."

"What do you mean, Soviets? Why not call them Russians?" Annie asked.

"I think they're all Communist regions fighting together, under Stalin. Not exactly who you want to have fighting with you though."

"So who takes over from Roosevelt?" Annie asked. "I've been so busy at the Co-op I haven't caught up with it all."

"Truman, the Vice-President. He'll be sworn in next week. I hope he was prepared to take over. They were also starting to discuss a new organisation called *The United Nations*, in San Francisco. It was Roosevelt's idea."

"What a shame he died before Berlin was taken," said Frances. "We're almost there now."

Tom sighed. "Let's just keep our fingers crossed. They're still at war in the Pacific."

May Queen

Frances was glad that the girls' lives followed a steady pattern while the war seemed to be nearing its end. There would be enough irregularities in their lives when the time came to return to Guernsey, and who knew what they would find there? They were big enough now to be more independent, and were sent together to Waggoners Farm each week to bring home a ration of freshly squeezed orange juice in a small bottle. They had a spoonful each day. They also went to Brownie meetings once a week, straight after school, dressed in their uniforms, with some other class mates. While waiting for the bus to bring them back home they had a penny to spend and bought an Oxo cube. No sweets were available without a ration book, and sucking on the beefy flavoured cube was very satisfying when you were hungry.

Lynette came home bursting with news later in April. "Miss Taylor told me that I'm going to be May Queen this year." She took it as a great honour.

"You're only just seven, are you sure?" Frances asked. Janice confirmed it.

"I think I have enough sugar to make a cake," Frances said, and Annie nodded at her. Annie would make sure there was enough.

Frances was glad to take part in the tradition one more time. May 1 was a warm and breezy day, and Lynette wore the precious daisy chain headdress and held the Maypole, while the others danced around. Mothers came out to watch and share the news as the Allies closed in on Berlin.

A week later it was Frances' turn to be honoured: she was awarded a three-year service medal for her nursing activities, and was presented with a decorative wall mirror to take back to Guernsey to thank her for her support.

33: Guernsey Jan–April 1945: Trying to Survive

*Hüffmeier takes over—Managing Food parcels—Finding fuel—No bread—
A light and fluffy two-pound loaf—Laufen camp freed*

Hüffmeier takes over

The German command under von Schmettow had been decent, but in the autumn of 1944 *Vizeadmiral* Hüffmeier was appointed Seekommandant of the Channel Islands. He was known as *The Admiral*. He felt the troops' rations were too high and the attitude to the islanders too generous under von Schmettow. He managed to expel some senior army officers and bring in naval officers whose ships were laid up. There was a permanent feud between him and von Schmettow, who was removed from the scene on 'health grounds' by the end of February 1945.

The Admiral requisitioned more food than was allowed under the rules of the Hague Convention.[73] After Britain had agreed to send Red Cross parcels to the islanders, Hüffmeier decided to seize property—including food—for his military objectives. He continued to requisition stocks of wheat, potatoes, and vegetables from the islanders' stores.

On the Channel Islands the garrison consisted of 3,500 naval personnel and 32,000 soldiers and airmen[74] so that there were plenty of German mouths to feed.

"The Admiral has said he hopes to see us all on our hands and knees through starvation and, as he is the head of civil administration, he is able to do what he likes with us."[75]

---

73   The Hague Conventions defined the rules that must be followed by opposing sides during a war.
74   Cruickshank, p 233.
75   Carey, p 200.

January: managing food parcels

On December 30, 1944, the day before the islanders received their first food parcel, there was a notice in the paper telling everyone to manage the new foods with care. They were not used to the rich fats which they would find in tinned cheese and salmon, or chocolate. There was so little fat in their diet that housewives had found it relatively easy to wash dishes in cold water with no soap.

"We need to divide up the food so that we have a little bit of something nourishing every day," Emily said.

"You do the planning," said Pa, "as long as we all get our share."

They agreed that they would share one tin at a time of the rich proteins, and Emily only opened the tin after they were all together at the table. She made a rough schedule for the next four weeks, hoping that the next parcel would be received at the beginning of February. It was a security for them all, but they were always hungry. Arthur hid the tins that they shared under a floorboard in the attic. If any Germans pushed inside the house, at least those items should be safe.

Each one of them kept the sweeter items, like jam and chocolate, for part of a meal or a snack or when they felt desperate. Having control over that part of their parcel was important, and each had a hiding place for those precious items. The others knew the secret locations and would deflect attention away from them if a Jerry came inside.

Emily returned from picking up their meagre ration of bread one morning. She was wearing two pairs of stockings with holes in them, mended where she could. She had noticed several women's bare legs were almost blue with cold.

"You know, Pa," she said, "The Kommandant hasn't done anything about Jerries milking the cows during the night on some of the farms."[76]

"That's been going on for far too long; and I heard that a couple of children were caught doing it too. This morning Patourel told me that the Jerries were asking for men to go fishing with some of them, to show them the best spots, fishing with a rod and line from the shore. If you have a boat, they'll let you go fishing, but they still want sixty or seventy per cent of the catch! I wouldn't go out in a boat with them or help them on the

---

76   Carey, p 201.

shore either."

"If they'd let the growers be in charge of planning the crops, at least we'd have plenty of vegetables," Emily moaned.

"Patourel's friend lives near one of the growers and he said the Jerries are trying to grow potatoes in their greenhouses to get an early crop, but they didn't look after their seed potatoes and they're all rotten. Stupid people."

"Maybe they stored the potatoes in one of their drippy tunnels. It's tough at the hospital too. There's a woman down the road who's a nurse, and she said they don't have any candles. She has to dip a shoelace in petrol like a candle wick, and set a match to it, to make a light to go around the wards after dark. And if you have to go to hospital now, you have to take your own sheets."

"Well, I'm not planning on being sick."

Emily smiled. "That's good, Pa,"

Finding fuel

Early in January, Arthur and Emily managed to bring home a load of wood from one of the wooden packing cases which had held Red Cross parcels. They now used the little cart behind Emily's bike. One of her tyres had been replaced with the spare one that they had kept hidden. Arthur had repaired one of his tyres with garden hose and one with rope, but it was an effort to ride it.

He had also been busy making a contraption for the fireplace so that they could make one soup meal a day, but feeding the fire under it was a constant task and they were lucky that Pa took over the job of being fire watcher. With a friend's help, Arthur managed to obtain something a little more efficient: a 5-gallon oil drum, which people called a *cooker*, which sat outside the back door in a sheltered corner. It was packed with sawdust, and one flame emerged in the middle. That was a very slow way to cook, but Pa was willing to watch over it, which was better than constantly feeding the fire in the fireplace. Eventually, Emily allowed it to be brought just inside the back door on the coldest days, but she disliked its smoky smell.

She chopped up potatoes, cabbage, parsnips, swedes, and whatever herbs she could find and stirred it into sea water. Their meat ration mostly never appeared, but they carefully rationed themselves with a small piece of cheese or a spoonful of tinned salmon or sardines from the parcels. Occasionally there were limpets. They had squeezed their beds into the living room to concentrate their bodies' warmth.

They all knew the bad news: forty-five islanders died in January, most of them being older and suffering from both malnutrition and cold. German soldiers seemed to be dying as well, according to those who watched the German cemeteries. One elderly couple had been killed and their house robbed for the food in it.[77]

Their comforts were the old Red Cross messages, and the news passed around at the bakery. The photos they'd received late in 1943 were there with the messages, but when Arthur looked at the plump faces of his children, it just reminded him of how pinched and drawn their own were. He had other photos including one of him in his militia uniform taken in the 1920s. Wearing his peaked hat, at attention, he looked fierce and proud. He was an excellent shot. If he was given a rifle today….

They all retreated under their blankets long before the fire went out. They might receive one or two hours of electric light, if it functioned, and then it was time to dream. One night Emily said, "What will you do, the day after the war ends?"

"I'm going to Alderney on the first boat that sails there," Pa replied. "I'll take my papers and show I'm the owner of *The Dream*, and I'll bring her home."

"I'll go home and clean out Woodlands," said Arthur. "But I'll go to Alderney with Pa first."

"And I'll do a big clean-up of my house on Victoria Terrace," said Emily. "We could all live there together, for a while, until things get back to normal. Pa, you can stay with me as long as you like."

There were no replies. Survival didn't seem all that likely.

They delved into their memories while they tried to fall asleep. Pa remembered being shipwrecked on Guernsey's west coast with his brother Frederick. It had eventually led him to meet Emilie. Arthur thought about how hungry he had been at the logging camp in Oregon, and the smell of

---

77   The wealthier families had lived more normally, having large properties where stores could be held in secret, and holding goats and chickens which provided nourishment; but those with smaller gardens fared badly, and the ones who had no gardens at all were in desperate need of medical help. It was estimated that 450 islanders never recovered.

the coffee and sausages that hung around. Emily thought of her visits to Jimmy's family in Devon, and the first time she tried cider. What if they had settled in Devon?

Towards the end of January, Arthur helped a couple of older ladies by sawing up their banisters for them to burn. They gave him some cigarettes and a box of matches.

"They own the house," he told Emily, "and they have no other wood left."

Emily had hoped they would give him some food, not cigarettes. "I hope we'll be able to have a fire for an hour or two every evening," she said.

"At least I managed to get those attic floorboards out of *Le Pré* before Christmas," Arthur replied. "We've got our ration of anthracite dust and if we're short, I'll pull up the attic floorboards here as well."

No bread—time forgotten

The *Vega* arrived late, around February 9th, some problem having delayed it, and that extra week of waiting was grim. Emily diminished their daily helpings from the Red Cross parcels, wondering when they would receive the next batch.

This time, the ship carried food parcels from New Zealand, but there were fewer than before. Some said they were missing about two thousand, and some families with very young children didn't get one for the youngest child. Emily now worried that even cabbages would become scarce. They were the only vegetable for sale. The parcels were supposed to supplement their rations, not replace them.

A few days later, when Arthur came in from doing a short job one afternoon, his father waved *The Press* at him. Emily looked on in silence.

"What's up?"

"It's not good news," said Emily.

A notice from the Bailiff was printed on the English page and Arthur read it out.

> *Our Flour — Important notice to the people of Guernsey.*
>
> *To my deep regret I have to inform you that the supply of flour will be exhausted after next Tuesday's bread issue, but I have received a letter from Colonel Iselin in Lisbon...in which he states that on her next trip, the Vega will bring flour. This has been confirmed...the Vega is expected*

back about the 5th March…arrangements for distribution of parcels on the 15th and on the 1st March. We hope to increase rations as far as our resources allow.[78]

"As far as our resources allow!" Emily exclaimed. "We have plenty of resources, except it's under lock and key in those German tunnels!"

The third parcel was distributed on February 15. They knew that another would come early in March, and Emily planned accordingly. Each person's rations now per week were:

> 4 pounds of root vegetables
> 5 pounds potatoes
> 2 ½ pounds macaroni or flour
> ¼ pint of separated milk.

It seemed like less than half of what they needed. They never saw meat, and without bread they needed extra potatoes. In Jersey, where potatoes were more plentiful, the ration was 10 pounds per week. Emily followed the advice from *The Press* and made four meals a day. Everyone was thinking about the next meal all day long, and four was better than three; except that meals seemed to be getting smaller anyway.

> This was the part of their lives that they wouldn't talk about in the future. They would die and be released from the pain of starvation, or survive and die soon after the war, or survive and be haunted by it forever. Diaries stopped being written around this time as energy failed…memory would try to erase it all or refuse to grant it space…

One day, Arthur felt the end was near for him. He went outside to be in fresh air and sat on the curb stones, feeling his life seeping out of him. The street was silent as usual. His eye fell on a stone in the gutter. Funny, it looked a bit like a parsnip. Something clicked. It *was* a parsnip! Shrivelled and dry and dirty, but a parsnip. It was like a sign that he should keep on struggling to stay alive. He nibbled on it for three days.

"Enjoy the light this evening," Emily said before tea on February 24. "There won't be any electricity tomorrow."

---

[78] Carey, p 200.

"Thank goodness the days are getting a bit longer then," said Pa.

"We have some limpets with the potatoes and cabbage in the soup. I opened one of our tins of butter, so it's got a bit of flavour."

Arthur dreamed of having chickens again. If they had an egg each, and bread, what a feast it would be! A Jerry soldier had asked him today if he could find *ein Katz*, and offered him ten pounds for a good one. He was beginning to feel he could kill and eat a cat himself, to heck with ten pounds. He didn't mention any of that to Emily.

On March 1, summertime started. Everyone received a Red Cross parcel. Little work was being done. Streets were quiet and there was no market; there had been no bread ration for two weeks and no-one could anticipate early potatoes: growers had been reluctant to plant seed potatoes because the Jerries would creep into their greenhouses during the night and dig them up to eat, although guards had slept in some greenhouses to prevent that.

One farmer who lived alone was tied up and robbed of his parcel, his rabbits, and his rations. Communal feeding centres were closing because of a lack of potatoes; yet some people had been dependent on those centres. Worms, birds, seagulls, rats, and limpets had become human food. Some people said that one man died each week of starvation, but others said seven.

A light and fluffy two-pound loaf

On March 5 the SS *Vega* was sighted—at last—in the evening, on a beautifully calm sea, the answer to many prayers. This time it was carrying flour, and two days later everyone received a light and fluffy loaf: "a two-pound loaf of first grade Manitoba white flour,"[79] was repeated over and over again from bakers to clients to families. It was the best day of the year: to handle the loaves, the smell at the bakery, and the light texture which was like magic to most—yet some preferred the grainy bread of previous months. They were still feeling uplifted by it when they were told the next day that the supply of water was reduced to four hours a day and could only be used for drinking. Rainwater must be collected for use in toilets.

Early in March, Arthur managed to collect some ormers, and Pa had

---

79 Carey, p.202.

ormers for his annual birthday dinner. The slow cooker made them wait an extra day before they could eat, but it was worth waiting for; and he had a gift of good news, quietly passed around, that British and American troops had crossed the Rhine into Germany. On his real birthday, March 11, Emily promised that as soon as the war finished, she would make him his favourite cake.

"Emily, a loaf of good bread would be more than enough for my birthdays in future," was his reply.

On that day, Arthur heard that there would be no more potatoes or root vegetables after March 18, but they didn't let the news get to Pa that day.

On March 15 Arthur came in for soup before Pa had returned from a chat with Patourel. He looked more relaxed than usual. "Tomorrow there's a shipment of potatoes coming from Jersey," he told Emily. "I'll have a few hours work."

"Thank goodness," she said. "I don't think Pa heard the news yet, that we were out of potatoes. Will you…?"

He nodded. A few potatoes would probably fall into a corner of his lorry at some point. A good day.

"We're supposed to receive a hundred tons, but we asked for two hundred. Anyway, it'll get us a bit further ahead."

"Look at this little news item in *The Press* today, Art. The SJAB is going to open up the big manor house in Saumerez Park as a residence for elderly people. That might be a good place for Pa to go eventually, although I'd like to look after him myself for a while after the war."

"Sounds like a good idea."

"I must take *The Press* next door at two o'clock, so read it while I warm up the soup. We have about two hours each before we pass it along. Pa will want to read it."

"It's getting to be such a small paper now that it doesn't take much time to read."

One of Arthur's dreams was that he would have a whole, big newspaper to himself, and he would sit and read it after tea, from one end to the other, every day.

On March 24 another parcel was distributed in Guernsey. The Bailiff was urging that more people contribute to Guernsey's Red Cross Fund. About £17,000 had been collected so far, and within a month the amount increased to over £28,000. The survival of 24,000 islanders, depended entirely on the Red Cross shipments of food.

Those who still had a functioning fishing boat were again invited to go out fishing, and given free petrol, as long as 60% of the catch went to the Germans. Few accepted the offer.

On April 6, the *Vega* arrived for the fourth time. By now, both islands had officially run out of root crops. Only those who had larger hidden stores had any left. The Bailiff asked people who had their own stocks of food to forego their food parcel so that it could be given to someone who was desperate.

Laufen camp freed

On April 27, Emily heard that Laufen Camp had been freed. "That's where the deportees were sent, isn't it?" she asked Pa and Arthur.

"Some of them were there, yes, and some were at Biberach," said Pa.

"Let me look at those photos of Frances and the girls," said Arthur. "I think it was someone in Laufen who sent them to me."

Emily passed the box, and he took out the photos and turned them over. "Yes, from F.A.W. Lainé and the other was sent by Lambert, and both from Laufen. When they get back, I must thank them. And now they're free and we're not!"

The following day, someone told Emily that the *Vega* had been sighted again, but it was just a rumour; someone said that the Germans staying at a neighbour's house had been burning all their papers. Someone else said Hüffmeier said he would never surrender, but he had returned from Alderney looking upset. Was there going to be an uprising by the Jerries against him? Rumours were all that life offered.

34: Victory in Europe and Guernsey's Liberation

*Hitler's death and VE Day at Cotton Row—
Liberation in Guernsey and VIPs visit*

VE Day

On May 2, Hitler's suicide was announced on the wireless and everyone left their houses and made sure their neighbours knew. Annie brought *The Daily Mail* home after work. Frances read the headlines out loud: "Hitler dead. News the world's been praying for."

"Just think, he and his girlfriend committed suicide two days ago. I hope whoever takes over is going to surrender now."

"It's some Admiral," said Frances, "Admiral Donitz. Anyway, the Russians are in Berlin, aren't they? Let's hope this is the end."

The newspapers were certain it was the end. A few had headlines saying that total surrender was imminent.

And, at last, the surrender was announced on May 8. Hilda called in that morning and listened to the news with Frances. She looked tired. "I went with Bill and Alice-Ann to Burnley yesterday evening," she explained. "They were already celebrating. The streets were lit up. There were parties in the streets for the children all yesterday afternoon. They couldn't wait. Then we were all singing…"

The children were back at home early, well before dinner time. "It's VE Day. It means *Victory in Europe*," they were told at school, and they were allowed to leave school early if they wanted. People floated around. The factory was closed for the day and not many people were working. Indoors, people were listening to the wireless while the reporters embedded with the advancing army, broadcast their reports. People searched for flags and bunting to hang outside.

Sticks and branches were piled up on one side of Wiles Lane between Annie and Kit Hoyle's houses. A bonfire was lit after dark and everyone in Cotton Row and from the farms up Wiles Lane came out, leaving lights on and no blackout curtains drawn. They had listened to Churchill's speech, and joined in "Land of Hope and Glory" afterwards. Later they listened to the King's speech.

Nobody told the children what to do or what not to do that evening, and they wandered around and threw sticks on the fire. Annie would have led some singing, but that was now in the past and there was nobody with a voice like hers. The girls, with Peter and Margaret Newsham, decided to do what the others were doing: find a potato and put it in the ashes to cook. Each ran home and ransacked the kitchen. The grownups were in a different world.

Later, the children nibbled on half cooked potatoes, and the burnt skin had to be spat out and made your fingers and face black; but that was funny, and they were outside with the light of a bonfire and no more blackouts…There was no bedtime, no rules. Everyone chattered in the darkness…it didn't matter where you went…it was different…

Next day Frances took the girls to Burnley and there were flags and banners everywhere. The children were given cake as they passed a street party and Frances bought ice cream. It was a child's dream.

Good news in Guernsey

On May 2 there was a cheer outside in Victoria Road, and Emily went to see what was happening. "Hitler's dead!" Another rumour? Pa and Patourel met on the street and sat on the kerb and talked a little. Arthur went up the road and saw two Jerry flags flying at half mast, so it must be true! Later, they heard that on German radio it was announced that both Hitler and Goebbels had committed suicide. Surely this must be the end now?

There were several stories about quiet *Hurrahs!* from the Jerries that morning. They had endured enough hunger and wanted to go home.

On May 4, the *Vega* arrived for the fifth time and brought flour and sugar and women's shoes besides parcels. Emily cried and hoped the war was over.

Four days later, on May 8, everyone knew about the surrender. A neighbour knocked on the door and told Emily that they had kept a wireless hidden all this time, and would they like to come and hear Churchill speak on the BBC at 3pm? After his speech, Hüffmeier would allow them to wave flags; but they were not yet liberated.

> **Liberation Day, May 9, 1945.**
> On May 8, Brigadier Snow left Plymouth in HMS *Bulldog* and went to Guernsey with surrender documents for the Germans to sign. The British force met a small German ship four miles from the Hanois lighthouse. Hüffmeier had sent a junior naval officer, in a shabby minesweeper.
> The naval officer said he was there to discuss armistice terms. Snow told him that Hüffmeier must be prepared to accept unconditional surrender. The junior officer returned to the island, making it clear that the British force must withdraw from the meeting point or it might be fired on by shore batteries. The European cease-fire would start only at 00.01 hours on May 9.
> At midnight, Major General Heine was sent by Hüffmeier to meet the British force at this further location. The points of surrender were discussed. Next morning, the two ships sailed to St. Peter Port, guided by a German pilot to avoid minefields. At 7.14 a.m. May 9, 1945, Major Heine signed the surrender documents. Finally, Guernsey was liberated.

On May 9, Arthur and Emily picked up their next Red Cross parcel and ate a little more than usual before they went to join the crowds in the town. The British landing force had landed soon after 8 a.m., but there were few onlookers before 10 a.m. Sweets and cigarettes were passed around by British soldiers, if you could get near enough.

Later, British soldiers marched ashore amidst cheering crowds, and hoisted the Union Jack in front of the Royal Court building. Planes flew in and out all afternoon; the carefully planned delivery of food, medication, clothing, and other necessities started. Both Bailiffs sent a message of loyalty to the king, and he welcomed them back.

Hüffmeier had stockpiled canned food, and when these stores were found by his troops after the surrender, they opened tins. They had not been advised to take very small portions and some died when they ate more than their bodies could cope with.

Hüffmeier had feared mutiny from his starving men.[80] On Saturday, May 12, he had to leave as a prisoner of the Allies in the evening. He used to be chauffeur driven in an elegant car when he left his office and was on view. This time he was near the harbour, but he had to walk to it, alone.

VIPs Visit

In the middle of May, the Home Secretary, Herbert Morrison, visited the islands.

He had been the person in the Privy Council most concerned about the welfare of the islanders. He wanted to visit the island to see the Germans rounded up. He wanted to express the sympathy of the government and the British people, for the difficult times the islanders had experienced. He was allowed to visit both islands on May 14 and 15.

He had explained to the States in both bailiwicks how it had been necessary…to withdraw British troops in 1940, and why the islands had not been taken by force after D-Day. He was able to assure the House (of Commons) that 'it was clear that these courses were both understood and approved.'[81]

The King and Queen paid a visit on June 7. There was an official meeting outdoors during which the Bailiff read a Loyal Address. The King replied, saying that he had felt deeply for the islanders during the occupation. He felt joy knowing that they were now free.

---

80 About 800 German troops were classified as suffering from malnutrition on May 9th when Huffmeier sent an officer to sign the surrender of Guernsey, Alderney and Sark.

81 Cruickshank, p 258.

35: Summer 1945: Evacuees Prepare to Return

Sharing the news—July election—News from Arthur—A surprise at Victoria Terrace—Long Delays—Keeping in touch—Journey home

Sharing the news in Burnley and Bolton

It was a strange summer. By the end of May, the British Post Office was handling mail between Guernsey and England, and evacuees sent letters to addresses which they hoped were still good, and replies started to trickle back. Those replies gave them treasured information and were carefully shared.

One day someone passed around a newspaper cutting from the *Hartlepool Northern Daily Mail*. It was a report describing how two small groups of courageous islanders had circulated summaries of BBC news after the Germans had confiscated all the wirelesses. Some had been sent to Germany after an informer betrayed them, but one group continued, at one time using the battery from a German lorry every night to make their radio set work.

"I think we're only just beginning to know some of the hardships they went through," Frances said to Gladys. "I can't imagine how I would have got through the war without a wireless and the BBC. It helped to keep me going when things were difficult."

Gladys looked worried. "It makes me wonder how our husbands will ever catch up, not having had any news, or very little news."

"They'll be catching up already; but I don't think we know very much about what's happened to them. Someone said in a letter, how nice it was to have salt from a packet. They had to carry buckets of sea water home to get salt!"

"We'll all have to listen to each other and try to understand."

They knew that they wouldn't be able to return to the island for weeks. Islanders had to recover from their ordeal of slow starvation. Supplies of food and basic services had to be normalised. Permits to return would not be given unless suitable accommodation was shown to be ready, and food and medical services reliable.

After VE day, Frances couldn't wait to get to Bolton, and she wrote to Grampy to arrange a visit on the last weekend of May, but she had to be patient. *That's a bank holiday weekend*, her father wrote back. *You'll never get a seat on a bus. Come the week after.*

She arranged to go on Friday, June 1, and the girls each carried a bag with their toys and clothes in it, a practice for their return to Guernsey. They arrived on Gran's doorstep by early afternoon. Rose was at home, which was good news, and the three girls disappeared to play outside. Gran put the kettle on. Frances noticed two suitcases in the kitchen.

"I managed to get those two second-hand suitcases last year," her mother said. "I was just wiping them over. It's no good packing anything yet though. We could be here for another month or more."

"That's what we were told in Burnley," said Frances, and she set out the cups. "I've got one suitcase, and Annie found a tea chest for me. It's about two feet high and twenty inches wide and deep, so I can pack quite a lot into it. I want to take some sheets and I'll ship it just before we leave, as long as shipping something is possible."

Gran set the teapot on the table. "A tea chest? That's a good idea, but you need to know someone like Annie—someone who works in a grocery—to get one. Now, from some of the letters people have been getting, they say the RAF bombed German boats in the harbour and all the windows in the town were blown out. They said they were boarded up after, but you can't very well go back with young children and live with boarded-up windows. Clearing up all that mess will take time."

"I was told the Germans even built a railway! I can't imagine where they found space to put it."

They were startled by Grampy's voice: "Frances, are you here?"

Gran looked at the clock. "He's off work really early today," she said. "He knew you were coming."

"Yes, hello Dad." Frances called back. She got up, and they gave each other a hug, and that was unusual.

"It's over!" he said. "And we'll be back at home this year! And Frank and Fred and Lionel came through it all right…" His voice faded a little and he paused. "At work they were saying petrol's not rationed anymore from today, so you should have more buses to choose from in future. Now, have you had a letter from Arthur yet?"

"Yes, but I think they aren't in very good shape. He and Pa are with Emily in her house in Victoria Terrace. They were living in Victoria Road and didn't have a garden or anything to grow potatoes; and her house was taken over by the Germans the whole five years."

"And your house?"

"Now, sit down and here's your tea," Gran interrupted.

Grampy settled in his chair and sipped.

Frances returned to her chair. "It's still there. The Germans used the house as a sunbathing station. They've damaged the furniture and things have disappeared, like the clock that had three different sets of chimes."

"I remember your friend Maud gave that to you for your wedding. Now, did Arthur continue to work at Leale's?"

Frances told them about Arthur's working problems.

"We were told that the banks on the island have been re-stocked with sterling," Grampy continued, "and they've exchanged all the German money at a good rate. The black marketeers must be happy. I just hope we'll be back in time to prepare for next year's tomato crop. They were saying that the crops on the islands are almost free from pests! I want to order seed and get started. Now, I hear that there's going to be a national election here, so I suppose we'll have to put up with that before we go home."

"Have you heard from Elsie? "

"Yes. She said it'll take a lot of work from everybody to get things set up properly. They are all at their house where we left them. She was happy that everyone had been given extra clothing coupons, sixty instead of our usual twenty-four. She wanted to buy stockings. Hers were full of holes and there was no mending thread."

"How is she?"

"Not too well, I think," Gran said quietly. "She didn't write much."

"I'm glad we have Bill and Geoff with us still," said Grampy. "I'll need some good strong men when we start up again."

"You'll be lucky if they stay with you for long, the way you work them," Gran retorted. "They'll want their evenings off and money to go to the cinema and take out a girl."

"They grow up too fast now. This damned war's changed a lot of things," Grampy muttered, and Frances smiled at her mother.

July election

It seemed to Frances that a lot of people were interested in the election. During the war there had been a coalition government, the Labour Party working with Churchill's Conservatives. However, at a Party meeting on May 21, Labour delegates voted to end their support, and an election was called for July 5. Churchill had been an inspirational wartime leader, and now Labour's Clement Attlee was running against him. The result would be announced on July 26 after the servicemen's votes had been counted.

It was summer, there were strawberries to pick, and everyone was busy. Frances continued her cleaning jobs at the Rileys and Mrs Fletcher to keep the structure of her week intact and build a small reserve of cash to go home. She cleaned out the tea chest and lined it with an old sheet, ready to start packing.

One day they all went to Manchester. Frances was looking for sheets and towels to pack in her tea chest and Annie knew her way around. They found a large furnishings shop which was like a huge Aladdin's Cave to the girls. They were now ten and seven years old and while Frances was looking around, they were free to go up and down wide staircases, and wonder at the variety of fabrics and furnishings they saw. There wasn't much choice yet, but Frances found what she needed.

The result of the election was announced at the end of July, and Frances had a shock: the Labour Party won almost twice as many seats as Churchill's Conservatives.

"What happened to Churchill?" she asked Annie, who had just come in from work. "Everyone thought he was so wonderful. What happened?"

Annie laughed. "We've been talking about it all afternoon in the shop. It's just that, people have given up so much in this war. Men are wounded and can't work and thousands have lost their houses. We've been promised better housing for years and nothing ever happened from the Conservatives. Attlee's promised full employment. We all need jobs, and better paid jobs than we used to have."

"Didn't Churchill promise that?"

"He talked about lower taxes for richer people, and more spending on defence; but there won't be any war for a bit. And Attlee's promised a free health service."

"Yes, I heard them talk about that on the wireless. They were saying it's based on the Beveridge Report—about affordable housing and free health care and so on. When Louise was here, she was telling me that women want jobs like men now, and better pay."

"Yes, it's about all of that. I brought home the newspaper. There's a lot about the election results in it."

The house was quiet after tea while they both read the papers and swapped it with a neighbour's and discussed it outside. The children wondered what had happened to make people not like Churchill, who had been everybody's hero.

Annie's new plans

Annie was organising her life with Leam now. It was unbearable to think of living at Cotton Row without Frances and the children. She planned to get married as soon as Frances and the children left, but not a minute before. She would move into Leam's house in Rawtenstall and they would both continue with their jobs. Later they would open a business together, somewhere in Lancashire, or even in Guernsey.

Early in August, Gran and Grampy came to say goodbye, and to wish her and Leam a very happy marriage. Annie was pleased. "Ee, I am glad you've come," she welcomed them. "I would have come to Bolton to say goodbye to you both, if you hadn't come to Cotton Row."

"Well, we've not had any news about returning to Guernsey yet," said Grampy, "and the buses are running more frequently—"

"And we like coming here," Gran interrupted.

"—So, you might see us here again."

Annie laughed and turned to Gran. "Are you sleeping better now with no more bombs or rockets flying over Bolton?"

"We're sleeping very well. Frances said you had one or two of those V1 rockets around here as well."

"Yes, we did. You know, we don't know how lucky we are to have escaped all that."

"And now those atomic bombs have been dropped in Japan. I hope that's the end of it all," said Grampy. "We don't want Truman to drop any more of those things. I wonder if Roosevelt would have agreed to it."

"Whatever's happened in Guernsey, at least it wasn't an atom bomb," said Gran, "and they did have a visit from the King and Queen in June.

Now, let's talk about something else."

A bag of onions was handed over and then they sat outside, they walked, they met Leam when he joined them at dinner time, and the chicken stew was delicious as always. Frances had made a cake, and the girls helped to lay the table. Grampy smoked a cigar afterwards and remembered not to start singing. The Bolton visitors left with fresh eggs in their basket and cake for the other four at home in Bolton.

News from Arthur

Arthur exchanged his Reichsmarks for sterling after Liberation Day. The British government had arranged a favourable rate of exchange with national banks. Guernsey currency had always been the equivalent of British, and a new issue had been secretly designed and printed by the Guernsey Press Company before the war ended. Almost all German currency was handed in.

Once he knew that he could rely on the postal service, Arthur sent Frances a five-pound note in a letter. It should cover fares and any expenses they might meet on the way back to Guernsey. It surprised Frances. She hadn't held a note of this value in her hands for years. Annie cashed it into smaller denominations for her and she kept it hidden, ready for the journey home.

In his letter he said it was good to see some buses in service again, and Emily had taken Pa for a ride on a bus to Cobo to talk with some of Ma's cousins. Now all vehicles were driving on the left-hand side of the road, and *The Press* was printed wholly in English. A few 1939 and 1940 model cars had emerged from under their wartime haystacks and were being updated.

Like many other men without work, Arthur had been offered employment by the States of Guernsey, clearing barbed wire from the cliffs. They were paid £1 (20 shillings) per week. As they worked, they saw how their strength had diminished, having to rest frequently. Sometimes they had a view of the minesweepers clearing some of the 54,000 mines that the German forces had laid around the island, and occasional explosions punctuated the day.

Sometimes they passed a group of German POWs clearing up mines, ammunition and equipment that had been dumped, and Arthur remembered the thin faces of the OT workers and the one who had caught the bread he had tossed out of his lorry's window. That man was one of many who most likely hadn't survived, and he stayed in Arthur's memory. He wasn't sure what survival meant any more. He still had a long way to go.

A Surprise at Victoria Terrace

In August, Frances received two letters from Nellie. The first told her that Otto had permission to return home on his own boat, sailing from Dartmouth to Guernsey with Bert, who was now sixteen. They would be out of sight of land for most of the twelve-hour journey, and planned to make the trip while daylight hours were long enough. They would have a two-hour trip before dawn, from Totnes down the river to Dartmouth, before the sea journey began.

Nellie's next letter told her that Otto and Bert had made two attempts to leave and had returned because of rough seas; but on the third try they were successful. They had taken a few chickens in lobster pots, carefully supplied with water and food. One had laid an egg by the time they arrived at St Peter Port early in the evening! Emily had previously written to them, offering them accommodation at her house when they arrived.

It had taken some effort for Emily to make her house on Victoria Terrace feel like home again, and Arthur and Pa had helped as much as they could to clean it up. There had been no gas or electricity in May, and it took time for services to be restored. As was their custom on the islands, the Germans had stripped anything of value from the house, and shipped it home to Germany or moved it to another house where they were living. The States had tried to help, making depots of furniture on the island, and previous owners had to go looking for items which might have belonged to them.

Victoria Terrace connected to Victoria Road, where they had just spent the last few months, and after tea Pa sometimes took a short walk over there to have a chat with Patourel. One evening in August he was preparing to leave when there was a knock at the door.

Emily opened it and he heard a yell: "Oh my! Otto! And Bert!"

Arthur and Pa hurried to join in the frenzy of welcoming two weary and wind-blown men. Otto had been able to leave the chickens with a friend who had some space at the harbour, and the two had been offered a lift in a van with an assortment of bags and boxes. Emily took great care of an egg that Bert presented to her.

In a while Pa put the kettle on. He stared across at Otto, and at his grandson, who was now a young man and a seafarer. He had thought about their journey like he thought about Noyon sailing away last November. It sounded as though Bert, like his father, was fully at home in a boat on the open sea. He felt tears on his cheeks again and wiped them away.

Otto was both weary and jubilant, but on seeing the thinness and lack of stamina of the three who came to the door, he quietened his voice and instinctively talked, suggested, and enquired in a gentler tone than was normal for him. He wanted to talk to his father about Ma and *Le Pré*, to talk to Arthur about seeing Frances and the girls in Bolton, and whether his house in the Charroterie was in good shape; to Emily about seeing Louise in England; but tonight they would focus on little more than the day's adventures, food and beds, and find out where they must register for rations.

Delays for evacuees

In the meantime, Frances and Annie kept to their usual routine. Annie had two good assistants at the Co-op, and she was learning a lot about the retail trade. In August, Frances still had not received permission to return home, and she sighed as she realised that they would miss Arthur's birthday again. However, both girls made birthday cards and they were sent off successfully. Cards made in previous years were already packed in the tea chest.

In Scott Park, the evacuees shared the latest news. The railway that the Germans had built in Guernsey had been torn up. The ramshackle huts of the OT workers had been burned. Jerry prisoners had been working to take mines off the beaches, the roller bombs off cliffs, and the explosive devices from fields where British parachutists might have landed. Electricity, gas and water services were being renewed. A lot of furniture and valued objects had disappeared.

> **Long delays**
> In August, the Home Secretary, Mr Ede, was asked why there were long delays for evacuees wishing to return to the islands. Some had been issued with travel warrants in June. He replied that priority had been given to those whose houses were fit to accommodate them. A delay had occurred because one of the two steamers which was in use had broken down and needed several weeks of repair work. He also stated that Islanders would need Red Cross parcels for months.[82]

Early in September, Frances received permission to return to Guernsey. Official travel warrants for the train and boat journey arrived in the post. The island schools were preparing to open later that month. She said goodbye to the Rileys and Mrs Fletcher, having a farewell tea at each house. The Riley girls said they would visit Guernsey in the future when things were back to normal.

Now she must complete the packing of the tea chest. Annie had not been able to obtain a second one, and there wasn't room for everything they wanted to take.

Annie tried to help in any way she could. This from Lynette's account:

The treasured Enid Blyton books and my drawing book were allowed space, but there wasn't room for a book which contained the story and picture of Snowball, a white cat, who pulled the fairy Queen's coach. It was my current favourite, and I cried at the thought of leaving Snowball behind. Annie had given me the book, and she tore out the picture and placed it in my drawing book. Mum thought that was a bit rash, spoiling a new book which another child would have liked, but Annie couldn't bear to see me leave in any way upset.

"Frances, what about the bikes?" Annie asked, as they completed the labels. "You're going to ship them as well, aren't you? They children ride them a lot now and you won't be able to find any on the island."

Frances shook her head. "No, Annie. It's been lovely for them to learn how to ride, but they'll have to wait for bikes. It's expensive to ship them

---

82   HC Deb 23 August 1945 vol 413 cc788-9

and I want to keep what money I've saved to buy what we need. Arthur's only getting about twenty shillings a week."

Annie kept her mouth shut. Twenty shillings wasn't enough to look after a family of four. The girls were listening and were obviously disappointed, but also kept quiet.

Keeping in touch

Two days before they left, Annie was in a panic about how to keep in touch with her wartime family. Only wealthy people had a telephone.

"We'll write letters to each other, Annie," Frances said. "As soon as we're back in Guernsey, I'll write to you."

"I've never written a letter, Frances. What do I write?"

"Just write the way you talk, Annie. I'll know exactly what you want to say."

"I never learned how to write a letter."

"Just write the words the way you speak them. You've seen me write to Dad, just like I speak."

"Please. Don't forget me. I'll come and see you when I can. Write to tell me you've arrived, and your address if it's any different. Just let me know how you're getting on." She gave Frances some envelopes with her own new address in Rawtenstall.

The tea chest was shipped to Guernsey, and a few days later, Frances and the girls boarded a train in Burnley with other evacuees, for a long but interesting train ride. In London, they found themselves in a huge railway station, and had to look for another one called Waterloo. Here they would find the Boat Train. There seemed to be a lot of evacuees wanting to board this train, but they all managed to squeeze in.

They were hungry when it arrived at Weymouth around midnight. The only food available was fish and chips, bought on the dockside. It was a greasy meal, but a welcome one. They squeezed on a bench on the deck of the SS *Hantonia* with other mothers and children, and ate, dozed, or were sick as the boat ferried them seventy miles south through choppy seas.

Journey home

On board the SS *Hantonia*, soon after dawn, someone walked past their bench and whispered that they could see the island, but not a soul moved.

Frances nodded to the whisperer and closed her eyes again. It was calmer now. Following a few difficult hours of choppy seas and seasickness, everyone was asleep.

All of a sudden, they were outside the harbour, and the mothers started to tidy up around them as children moved around the deck. A few people had managed to buy a cup of tea somewhere at an exorbitant price. The *Hantonia* nosed into the harbour and was soon in her berth at the White Rock.

Disembarking was slow but steady. There were a few cries of recognition, and many quiet, searching looks. Frances had heard of one or two women who had decided not to return; many were hesitant to wave before they were sure they recognised a family member waiting on the quayside. They had returned, in the spirit of 1945 Britain, to an island still working its way out of a bad dream.

Frances had a bag and a suitcase. Each of the girls had a bag, and they disembarked. The girls waited with the suitcase while Frances walked around the diminishing crowd, front and back. Was Arthur here somewhere? He was often quiet amongst strangers, preferring to observe until he knew the lie of the land; but people had been leaving and she could see that he wasn't here.

She left the suitcase in the care of an office worker who was watching over a pile of luggage. With the children, she walked down the White Rock towards the clock tower on the esplanade. The girls walked ahead and looked at boats in the harbour. They were tired, but they knew how to be patient. Behind them Lynette heard Frances talking to someone, a man who they had just walked past. She looked back. Frances was holding the man's hands and staring at him.

"Is that our father?"

Janice nodded. "I think so."

They had just passed the man but had been chattering. They turned and he smiled, and it was their father. Unshaven, he didn't look too inviting. They exchanged a kiss, and he seemed as shy as they were. Now Frances was talking about transportation to Woodlands and they all went back and someone called a taxi for them. It arrived, black and shiny. It would cost eight shillings!

"Oh no! " Frances said. "I'm not paying eight shillings. Is there some other way to get home? A bus?" But she had to agree, because there was no other way to get home from there.

In the taxi she closed her eyes. For a second, after they had met, she had almost wished she could go back on board and return to Cotton Row. Now she remembered those black days in Burnley, and knew how she had grown. She would cope with things here as she had done there. If he was weak, she was strong. She would manage their lives until he was whole again.

Later she would ask herself, why hadn't he arranged for someone with a van to drive them home. Did he think she might not return? But she had written. Was he unsure of how she and the girls would receive him, or whether he could cope with meeting them? Had he stayed with Emily for the night and walked to the harbour? No shaving kit at Emily's? He surely knew someone at work with a van...although he didn't work at Leale's anymore, did he? He couldn't get a job there because returning service-men got the jobs that were available, not the men who had stayed on the island.

They were at the brown gate that said Woodlands; they went down the steps, Arthur taking the suitcase. She followed him with the girls. He was so thin, so lost with his strange family; so blank without that spark of energy and humour; and perhaps so alone without his wartime family.

However, this property was now theirs, and he had achieved that. There was her beautiful piece of blue-green water. At the bottom of the steps she gazed at the bay and heard the waves splash down on the pebbles. A blackbird was singing. Suddenly, she had come home.

Afterword

Later, as soon as Annie had received a letter from Frances, she shipped the two bikes to Guernsey. It was a wonderful surprise for the girls and would save precious money on bus fares to St. Martin's School each day.

Pa had to wait until late in 1940 for the first boat taking passengers to Alderney. The Germans had made efforts to hide their secret concentration camps on that island. Pa was determined to bring back *The Dream*. However, she had disappeared and he was never able to trace her. He was very disappointed.

Pa lived with Emily for a while, then with his other children, and eventually lived in Saumarez Manor, after it was converted into seniors' housing. Emily moved to Edelweiss Lodge with Louise. She continued working with the church, living quietly.

Louise returned to Guernsey and continued to teach at Amherst, helping children with special needs. She retired early to take care of her mother. She was a member of Mensa.

The Riley girls did visit Guernsey and called on Frances while they were there.

Annie married Leam in September 1945. She tried to help Frances when help was badly needed and even tried to settle in Guernsey. She found her niche in the fish and chip business in Lancashire. She and Leam moved to Morecambe, where they started a mobile fish and chip service. When they finally retired, they enjoyed a cruise around the world.

In the meantime Annie's door was always open to Frances and her two evacuee daughters. She sometimes helped and sometimes created problems; but that's another story.

Poem: Mum

I saw her once
As Mum, from another generation,
Doing her best, still struggling ,
Proud of the few things she had accomplished.

The bonding of the war years
Never left us, gave me strength
When, isolated and lonely,
It was my turn to cry.

Our letters ping-ponged across an ocean,
Keeping the threads of family alive and nurtured.
She read mine to her mother, and didn't miss a detail.
I read hers fast, and tucked it aside for future nurturing.

I see her now as my sister,
Being now her age.
I re-read the lines of her letters
And find much between them,

Still strong.
****

Lynette.

Poem: Meeting.

You didn't know us, me and Jan: two tired kids
Walking along the harbour edge,
Ten and seven years old,
Just arrived with returning evacuees.
Did you guess it was us?
We passed by you, chattering about the boats moored nearby.
I didn't know we'd passed you.

Mum was behind us and then was talking… to whom?
We turned around.
"Is this our father? I asked Jan.
"Yes, I think so."
Yes, it was you.

Late that first afternoon, we went to the beach,
down the cliff path, to a stone-paved gap
between high fortress walls,
built by the OT slaves.

Beyond it, the white, rounded pebbles and the splashy waves.
The tide was going out and, barefoot,
we lifted winkles off the rocks,
a lot of them, as we stumbled around.

You boil them and then pull the winkle out with a pin,
nudging off its little door,
which is perfectly round.
Did we have butter, or was it just bread…

We never left a light on.
We kept the gas turned down while cooking something.
We ate all that was on our plate.
We were good at licking out a pot from semolina pudding.

We both walked to town with Mum on Saturday morning.
That saved eightpence,
almost enough for four ounces of ham;
The bus took us home with our heavy shopping bags,
And we ate boiled potatoes and flakey, fried bream.

We were told not to talk about the war,
not to ask questions.
So what's our common ground?
We live without shared history, hesitating,
Unwilling to hurt the person we need to know.

Lynette.

Acknowledgements

I would like to thank my family and friends, in and around Sutton, who gave me me a great deal of encouragement during Covid and after, while I wrote this book; some were my first readers.

Special thanks are owed to the WHWN teachers who directed my writing efforts as Covid took over. A special thanks to Rebecca Welton for her encouragement, steady support and guidance through the process of editing and the whole indie publishing experience. Thanks to Christine Choquet for her patient explanations, accessibility and good humour while she coped with the formatting. Thanks to my son Peter Vanha for help with maps and photos.

Many thanks to my sister Janice, whose memory and collection of family data have been invaluable. Our almost- daily discussions, thanks to FaceTime, have added to the balance of facts and memories. Thanks to Bert, Suzanne, and David, in Guernsey, who have contributed their help in many ways.

Questions for discussion.

1. Why did Annie worry that Frances might move to Bolton in the spring of 1941? What were some of her strategies to keep Frances at Cotton Row?
2. What did Frances experience that influenced her to stay at Cotton Row?
3. At one point Frances says that she knows five people who are working in the armed forces. Who were those people? Say something about each one.
4. Explain why the news and weather forecasts on the BBC were sometimes vague.
5. Why did the Allies not free the Channel Islands when they embarked on D-Day?
6. Using an atlas, look up the routes used by ships to deliver armaments from the USA to Russia. What route would be easier in peacetime?
7. Why did Churchill lose the 1945 election in Britain?
8. What social changes were affecting women during the war? How did it affect two of the characters in the book?

More Reading or Research:

9. How did bomber planes become more efficient between 1940 and 1945?
10. What was the Enigma Code, and how did it help the Allies after they deciphered it?
11. What is the story of tthe island of Malta, 1940-45?
12. When did WWII finally come to an end, and what action did President Truman take to end it? What happened to Japan after?
13. Why are two of the following battles remembered?
    El Alamein, Dieppe, Stalingrad, Kharkov.
14. The relationship between Churchill and Roosevelt was friendly, supportive, and co-operative. Why did this feeling not exist between them and Stalin?

Favourite Pages